Writing Like Writers

Writing Like Writers

Guiding Elementary Children
Through a Writer's Workshop

Kathryn L. Johnson & Pamela V. Westkott

University of Rhode Island
Kingston, RI

Narragansett Elementary School
Narragansett, RI

Prufrock Press, Inc. • Waco, Texas

PRUFROCK PRESS, INC.
P.O. Box 8813
Waco, TX 76714-8813
Phone: (800) 998-2208
Fax: (800) 240-0333
www.prufrock.com

Contents

Acknowledgments

Often our first teacher is our own heart.
—Hyemeyohsts

The children, who enthusiastically joined in this journey of writing and led me along the blue highways. The many authors of children's literature whose books have filled years of joyous reading and inspired my teaching. My Kentucky writing colleagues Marcia, Jerrie, Paul Brett, and George Ella, who taught me to think like a writer. Pam, my favorite teacher. Mama and Papa, whose lives have given me many stories to write. My sons, Jacob and Cliff, who write like writers. And always, Paul, my muse.

—KLJ

My family: Mick, my truest friend, and John, Mark, and Neal; administrators Janice DeFrances and Susan Naysnerski; technology specialist, Carol Batchelder; my colleagues at NES, especially, Carol Prest and Cheryl Blumenbaum; student teachers Faith Downey and Meghan Gordon; Kay's family for being patient while I took her away; and, above all, Kay, for nurturing me along, giggling with me, being patient, and sharing this journey of change. *Writing Like Writers* is the product of a process: collaboration among a group of people who teach and learn together. In that way, this book is like the writing that comes from Writer's Workshop. My heartfelt thanks to all my students, those who have shared this journey with me and those who are yet to come.

—PVW

Introduction

Write for the joy of discovery!
—George Ella Lyon

I (Kay) turn the calendar page to September and turn my thoughts to the Language Arts Methods class I'm preparing to teach. Thinking of the preservice teachers who will make up that class, I ask, "How do I want these college seniors to be different at the end of the course?" It's not just about what they will learn, but how their thinking will change and develop. I always ponder this as I plan for them.

In the first class of the semester, we study the word *method* to understand more fully the focus of the course. The dictionary tells us that it comes from the Greek word *methodos* which is made up of two words—*meta* meaning "change" and *hodos* meaning "journey." Combined they mean "journey of change." Preservice teachers will learn writing methods, strategies and techniques to guide young writers on a journey of change.

I (Pam) ask similar questions about my own group of third graders; "How do I want my students to be different writers by the end of the year?" Every class is filled with students who have diverse learning styles, interests and abilities. Mine is no different. I have students who enter third grade writing well and those who are emerging readers and writers. "So, how will I meet everyone's needs?"

Writing is a great differentiator. During Writer's Workshop, each student is engaged in meaningful ways. Individually, they respond to the teaching and take what they need. The workshop permits differentiation throughout its stages. We all have a lifetime of stories within us waiting to be written. It is my role to differentiate the instruction, encourage and guide students to find their own stories, and try what we share with them. I am always searching for methods I can use to become a better teacher of writers.

Why We Wrote This Book

The questions we asked and sought to answer led to the development of this book. The two of us (Pam and Kay) have worked together for 8 years. This book began as an exploration. We noticed how students wrote and asked lots of questions. We studied the writing process in dozens of books by gifted theorists and practitioners. Then we applied the ideas directly in the classroom. We journaled and reflected. We became writers ourselves along with our students.

We came away with clearer ideas and a deeper understanding. One of those beliefs is clear: Students become better writers as we become better teachers. The intent of this book is to share the findings we learned in our journey.

Using Writing Like Writers in Your Classroom

There are several features that can help you navigate easily through this book. We sectioned some chapters into a consistent format for easier access as you teach. Chapters, 3, 4, 5, and 6, Writing Process, Writing Strategies, Story Elements, and Writing Craft, respectively, all use the following format:

Key Elements—We begin with Key Elements that focus thinking on the essence of each topic. Every time we prepared to teach a mini-lesson, we had to research a considerable amount of information to find a few fundamentals about each topic. These are a resource for you to use with your students.

Connections to National Standards—Standards provide a framework for teachers, students, and parents as accepted measures of comparison. We have used New Standards, which show us clear performance targets of what it means to be a competent writer by the end of a specific grade level. Standards guide our teaching of specific writing skills.

About … (topic)—This section provides a brief rationale and background information for teaching each topic.

Examples From Literature—Some of the best teaching aids can be found in the children's books we read. We look to the writers we love to provide models for us (e.g., the manner in which they introduce characters, the approach to developing suspense).

One of the strongest pieces of advice we can give teachers of writing is to know the literature; read as many children's books as you can, varied genres and authors. Our teaching is strengthened when we can refer to the way a strategy or craft is used in specific books and guide our students to read, study, and emulate.

How Do We Teach … (topic)?—We listed many ideas because it is important to teach and re-teach strategies and writing craft in various ways throughout the year. You may select from a wide array of activities to teach based on your students' needs. It is not likely that you'll use all of the exercises, nor would you want to. They are there as a resource to support, not kill, the learning.

What I Know About … (topic)—These Think Sheets and others are a resource and guide for students to complete as you introduce a topic. They can be kept in their Writing Notebooks for quick reference.

1: Beginnings

The journey of a thousand miles begins with a single step.
—Lao-tsu (c. 604–c 531 B.C.)

Prepare Materials for a Writing Classroom

When those school bells ring, and usually long before, we know it's time to roll up our sleeves and get down to some hard work. Preparing the writing classroom takes time, planning, and some tough decision making. But, the time spent is well worth it. We want the classroom to rock with writing! We want anyone who passes through the door to have no doubt that this classroom is filled with writers.

This chapter gives a glimpse into a writing classroom and some ways to organize materials. As the year progresses, you might see wall charts of synonyms for *big*, Word Walls loaded with compound words, student writing dangling from the ceiling, expectations for fine writing posted on a bulletin board, personal wordbooks on children's desks, and children's published books lined up along the bookshelves. This is the stuff of writers. You can tell that writers live here.

Here are some ways we have built our writing classroom with the help of many people.

Writing Center is an area that houses important books and supplies that are readily accessible to students and teachers.
* Writing notebooks for students
* Resource books such as thesauruses and dictionaries
* Supplies (keep extra supplies labeled in clear, plastic boxes under the table):

clipboards	colored pens,	sticky notes	wallpaper books
yellow-lined paper	markers, and	hole reinforce-	envelopes (all sizes
(for drafts)	highlighters	ments	and colors)
white-lined, plain	pencils/colored	yarn and twine	paper cutter
paper	pencils	large-eyed needles	(rotary kind for
staplers	gel pens, crayons,	heavy-duty hole	safety)
tape	pencil sharpener	punch (1 and 3)	metal rings (for
glue sticks	scissors	oak tag board	bindings)

"**Today's Writing Stages**" is a daily organizational chart that shows where students are working. Write student names on cards, laminate, and put double-stick tape on the back. Every day the students stick their name cards onto the laminated chart to indicate where they are in the writing process.

Today's Writing Stages

Planning	Researching	Drafting	Rereading	Conferring	Revising	Editing	Publishing

Writing Notebooks for Students keep all ideas, resources, and writing organized and accessible for students. If possible, purchase good quality 3-ring binders, one for each student. You can use these same binders year after year. Only the contents go home with students at the end of the year. We subdivide the notebook into the following sections:

- **Section 1: Ideas for Writing**—Lists ideas for developing stories

- **Section 2: Resources**—Accessible information for reference while writing
  - Editor's marks chart
  - Most commonly misspelled words
  - Personal dictionary
  - Class-generated lists (e.g., list of synonyms for "went")
  - Rhyming words
  - Writing craft handouts, "What I Know About …"
  - Writing craft practice (writing to a mini-lesson)

- **Section 3: The Piece I'm Working On**—Current piece being developed
  - Student record sheet, "Where is My Writing Today?" (at the end of this section), which briefly tells what they plan to work on.

- **Section 4: Holding Tank**—All unfinished pieces
  - Stories student wrote, but did not complete.
  - Rough drafts and planning of published pieces.
  - Students may choose to return to these pieces at a later date to finish and publish.
  - It provides a way to look at the student's writing growth over time

- **Section 5: Publishing Ideas**—Handouts, notes, and sketches
  - Book structures they like
  - Publishing formats they are interested in, such as newsletters, magazines, etc.

Technology. Plan how you might incorporate technology into your writing classroom. Here are a few ways:

- **Research**—Find information about topics you are studying and bookmark the sites you want students to access.

- **Create a Web Page**—Consider building a class Web page that links to topics of study, such as authors' Web sites or nonfiction information sites.

- **Word Processing**—Students have the option of writing final copy by hand or by word processing. We have parent volunteers to assist. Create a newsletter or three-fold brochure, usually found in your word processing program.

- **Illustrating**—Children may illustrate their books with programs such as KidPix or copy and paste pictures from approved Web sites.

- **Webbing**—In the computer program Kidspiration, children can organize information and create a web.

- **PowerPoint Presentations**—Students develop PowerPoint slides to showcase the information they have learned about a specific topic. They may work together in teams and help each other. It's an opportunity for them to experience new ways to present what they have learned during a unit of study.

- **Digital Camera Photographs**—Students add digital pictures to their Web pages, brochures, and their books. They can take a digital photograph of themselves for the "All About the Author" page for their book publications

Connecting Writing Instruction to Writing Standards

Have you ever wondered, "What are the appropriate writing skills to focus on with your students? What are other children in this grade around the country learning about writing?" Standards are a set of performance targets that provide a guide for teachers and students as accepted measures of comparison.

The following list of standards that guides our teaching is adapted from the *New Standards: Reading and Writing Grade by Grade* (1999). Students are expected to have mastered these skills by the end of the year. It is a clear, solid guide for the process of writing that is appropriate for the middle to upper grades of elementary school. Become familiar with the standards your school has adopted. If you don't have standards for your class, you may use the ones listed in this book or find examples on the Web.

We have also rephrased some of these standards into "child language" to make them user friendly. Students have selected standards to make into bold, colorful cards to post around the room as reminders of what they are learning and applying in writing.

Throughout the book, we have connected the teaching of specific writing skills to the following standards:

1. **Habits and Processes.** Students should:
   - write daily;
   - generate their own topics and spend time refining their writing;
   - extend and rework some pieces of writing;
   - routinely revise, edit, and proofread their work;
   - polish about one piece a month for an audience in and beyond the classroom;
   - write for specific personal purposes (e.g., thank you letters, birthday cards, etc.);
   - study and emulate a particular author's craft as they revise their own work; and
   - use criteria to self-evaluate their writing.

2. **Writing Purposes and Resulting Genres**
   a. **Narrative Writing: Sharing Events, Telling Stories.** Students should:
      - orient the reader by establishing the time, and location and introducing the characters or lead into the story in an interesting way;
      - use precise words and detail;
      - write a sequence of events that are logical and natural;
      - develop a character by providing reasons for action and solving a problem;
      - develop a plot or tell about an event by describing actions and emotions of characters and using story elements of dialogue, how a character feels, descriptive details, and others;
      - add reflective comments when appropriate (autobiographical narrative); and
      - wrap it up with a conclusion.

   b. **Informative Writing: Report or Informational Writing.** Students should:
      - introduce the topic and provide a context;
      - use an organizational structure that helps the reader;
      - communicate big ideas or insights that have been elaborated on or illustrated by facts, details, and other information;
      - use diagrams, charts, and illustrations appropriate to the text;
      - write a conclusion that ties it all together; and
      - use a straightforward tone of voice.

   c. **Functional and Procedural Writing.** Students should:
      - engage the reader by establishing a context for the writing;
      - identify the topic;
      - provide a guide to action;
      - show the steps in enough detail to follow easily;
      - include relevant information;
      - use language that is straightforward and clear; and
      - Use illustrations to give detail to the steps.

d. **Producing Literature.** Students should:
- write stories, songs, memoirs, poetry, and plays that conform to the appropriate expectations for each form;
- after studying a genre, produce a piece that incorporates elements appropriate to the genre; and
- build on a story idea by extending or changing the storyline.

e. **Responding to Literature.** Students should:
- support an interpretation by referring to specific examples in the text;
- provide enough detail from the text so the reader can understand the interpretation;
- go beyond retelling the story;
- compare two works by an author;
- discuss several works that have a common idea or theme;
- make text-to-self connections as they relate the story to their own lives; and
- make text-to-text connections as they notice and discuss where they have seen the writing craft or ideas in other literature.

3. **Language Use and Conventions**
a. **Style and Syntax.** Students should:
- use their own language in writing;
  - use a variety of syntactic patterns to show relationships of ideas (compound sentences and complex sentences);
  - incorporate transitional words and phrases to show the reader a sense of time and place;
  - embed phrases and modifiers that make their writing lively and graphic.
- take on the language of authors;
  - vary sentence patterns and lengths to create rhythm, slow down or speed up a piece and create a mood;
  - embed literary language where appropriate; and
  - emulate sentence structures from various genres.

b. **Vocabulary and Word Choice.** Students should:
- use words from their speaking vocabulary and from reading and class discussions;
- use precise and vivid words; and
- take on the language of authors by using specialized words related to a topic.

c. **Spelling.** Students should:
- notice when words do not look correct and use strategies to correct the spelling;
- correctly spell familiar high-frequency words and wall words;
- correctly spell words with short vowels and common endings;
- correctly spell most inflectional endings, including plurals and verb tenses;
- use correct spelling patterns and rules, such as silent *e*, changing *y* to *i*, consonant doubling; and
- correctly spell most derivational words (e.g., adding word affixes, such as *–tion, -ment, -ing*).

d. **Punctuation, Capitalization and Other Conventions.** Students should:
  - use capital letters at the beginning of sentences;
  - use periods, question marks, and other end punctuation most all the time;
  - begin to use quotation marks;
  - use capital and lowercase letters properly; and
  - use contractions.

The Home/School Partnership

Informed parents are involved parents.
—PTO Parent

Parents are our students' first teachers and important influences in their children's learning and in their lives. We are sensitive to that relationship, nurture it, and build upon it. We want parents to work collaboratively with us in our classroom to better support their child's learning.

Knowing what busy lives families lead, we provide a variety of times and events to connect with parents and accommodate their demanding schedules: before school, during school, and after school events. This is a compilation of experiences from many years of teaching.

Informing Parents

Information Packets. We developed a packet for parents in response to their questions about what their children are expected to do and learn in this grade. We distribute these packets, which include:

- **Benchmark Sentences**—As a whole class, children brainstorm ideas and then write a benchmark statement that answers the questions: who, what, when, where, how. This is to demonstrate the kind of sentences we expect third graders to write at the beginning of the year.
- **Writing Rubric**—Shows one way we evaluate the evidence of traits in writing.
- **Writing Standards**—Skills students are expected to have mastered by the end of the year.
- **Narrative**—Piece from a third-grade child who meets the standard. Shows the rationale of why it met the standard.
- **FAQ and Answers**—For example: How do writers get started? How can I help my child spell a word?
- **Editor's Marks**—Shows students how and where they need to change their writing to communicate better.

Looking at Student Work With Parents. We offer evening sessions once each grading period to practice a collaborative process of looking at a piece of student writing for a specific reason. We work alongside parents while reviewing and discussing what we notice in the work. Parents provide a different view of writing. Their insights often provide clarity as we examine our own teaching practice.

Conferring With Parents. This is an opportunity to have a conversation—to listen and to talk about what they love most: their child.

- Early in the year *before* I have individual conferences, I like to place a phone call to the parents just to tell them how much I enjoy having their child in class. It helps to have established a positive relationship with the parents if I have to discuss a problem later on.
- I begin a conference with some positive story about their son or daughter. I want them to know that I like and appreciate their child as a person and as a learner.
- My favorite book to recommend to parents is *How to Talk So Kids Will Listen and Listen So Kids Will Talk* by Mazlich and Faber. I keep several copies in my classroom library and let parents check them out.

Newsletter. Have students write monthly updates of what they are learning and send it home to parents.

- Use some periodicals such as *Time for Kids* as models to get ideas for monthly topics.
- Include some poetry or original stories by students. Each month different children can contribute.
- Do group research on a topic of interest and list some interesting facts.
- Allow writing articles for the newsletter to be a part of Writer's Workshop.
- Add a character web that students have created on the computer.
- Include a parenting section with tips.
- List specific Web sites that are useful.
- Appleworks Brochure Software makes newsletter formatting easy!

Writing Night. Parents are invited to visit the classroom to learn about how students think, learn, and write throughout the year.

- We showcase what students have written as parents look through their Writing Notebooks, class books, and individual publications.
- We review traits of writing, writing standards, benchmarks, and rubrics. Parents go through the process of evaluating sample pieces of writing while using a rubric.
- We demonstrate how Writer's Workshop is structured and cover its components and stages. We show a videotape of a student writing conference.

Events to Showcase Student Writing

Author's Night. This evening showcases student writing. Students sit in the Author's Chair and read one of their original stories, books, or other published pieces.

- It follows the same format of Writer's Workshop. It models our practice!
- The student gives a personal anecdote about the piece of writing.
- After the reading, the child entertains questions from the audience.
- There are three comments taken from the audience about something they liked.

Classroom Museum Visits. Our classroom (or hallway) transforms into a museum as children display their work to showcase what they have studied and learned. Invitations and free tickets are sent home. Students become docents and give tours to parents. Here are some examples:

- Walls are covered with charts students have generated, such as "Synonyms for Little" or "Visual Imagery We Love" or "Advice from Authors."
- Display boards feature an author study or genre study with pictures, facts. and reflections.
- 3-D writings dangle from the ceiling.
- Shoeboxes are transformed into dioramas to illustrate various habitats.
- Poetry and illustrations fill a bulletin board.
- Students' original books line the bookshelves.
- A videotape runs to highlight a day in Writer's Workshop.
- Notebooks at their desks show the complete writing process. from their seed ideas through their final copies.
- Author Web sites, literature ladders. or cyberguides are facilitated by individual students who have used them for a technology project.
- A slide show created on PowerPoint showcases a small group's research project.

Involving Parents

Guest Readers/Teachers. Invite parents to participate in the class.

- Have a parent read a book or poem.
- Tap into the culture and special interests of parents (e.g., entomology, photography, musical instruments, etc.).
- Ask parents to coteach a unit on a special interest in which they are experts.

Know Parents and Their Skills. Provide a checklist of options parents can sign up to do, such as:

- word process student writing;
- bind books;
- assist with researching information on the Internet or in the library;
- listen to someone read a piece he or she has written and provide positive feedback;
- read with a small group;
- do creative drama with a small group;
- organize the writing center; or
- create class charts and mobiles.

Where Is
My Writing Today?

Writer's Name: _____

Story Title or Topic: _____

Date	Stage	Planning for Tomorrow

Date Published: _____ Teacher's Initials: _____

2: Living the Writer's Workshop

Nothing great was ever achieved without enthusiasm.
—Ralph Waldo Emerson

© Pamela Westkott

Have you ever noticed a child who is totally immersed in writing? Peep into our Writer's Workshop and watch Devin for a moment:

Devin sits at her desk with head down as she peruses her writing from yesterday. Her sparkly hazel eyes are focused, mouth set. She chews on a twisted strand of auburn hair. One leg is folded under her body, the other swings to a silent meter as she highlights a spot in her writing. She resumes reading, then stops and revisits that highlighted place. It is important enough to warrant a clean sheet of yellow draft paper. Squiggling into a comfortable position, number 2 Ticonderoga in hand, Devin begins. Nothing around her matters. She is a writer.

Devin is thriving in the learning environment we call Writer's Workshop. It is a structured time for all students to work toward improving their writing.

Our students can become proficient writers if we:
- *honor* their voices and their writing;
- *write* daily within a predictable structure;
- *study* the literature and notice authors' writing craft;
- *scaffold* their thinking and writing in sequential steps;
- *model* for them what they need to learn;
- *encourage* them to take risks and apply what they have learned;
- *assess* what they do well and still need to learn; and
- *celebrate* their accomplishments.

The Structure of Writer's Workshop

Writer's Workshop begins the very first day of school and continues throughout the year. A key component of Writer's Workshop is the predictability it provides for both students and teachers. We come to expect and value the structure that frames the time for writing. A regular writing period of about 45 to 60 minutes per session is established. This time block is broken into suggested segments:

5 minutes	Check-In: • Pass out materials, such as Writing Notebooks. • Students move their name card on the class chart, "Today's Writing Stages," to indicate at what stage they are working. • Record information onto "Where is My Writing Today?" sheet. • Have quick check-in conferences before work begins.
10–15 minutes	Teach a writer's craft mini-lesson.
30 minutes	Students work at their respective stage of the writing process.
5 minutes	Students share from the Author's Chair (a weekly schedule guarantees all writer will have a turn during a week's time).
5 minutes	Check-Out: • Plan what to do the next day in Writer's Workshop. • Organize paper in notebooks.

Scaffolding Writing

Scaffolding is the support that teachers give students as they learn new skills and strategies. We model, engage, teach, and guide, gradually moving students toward independent writing.

After all the formal structures of the Writer's Workshop are in place, we can shift our teaching toward the writers and their writing. We begin teaching mini-lessons, using thinking strategies. The six strategies listed below are strands that continue across, around, and through all our writing experiences.

1. *Read the literature.* The teacher begins by sharing a text with the class for the purpose of enjoying and understanding the literature. We frequently use picture books for several reasons. Picture books are about the same length as the stories middle elementary students write. Many have rich, descriptive language, illustrations, and a concise plot. They provide exemplary models for students to emulate.

2. *Study the writing.* We use the strategy Read Like a Writer (RLAW). As we read together, we pause to appreciate the writing and analyze how and why the author wrote in this way. RLAW is an essential component of the work we do during every Writer's Workshop.

3. *Model the process.* Step by step, the teacher demonstrates how to use a skill, craft, or strategy in our own writing, such as how to replace an overused verb with a more precise one. Sometimes, confusion arises when educators use the word *model*. There is a huge difference between the view of a model as something we see as an example and the current teaching practice of a model as how to demonstrate a concept.

Model (the noun)	*Model* (the verb)
- a particular version or example of something - tell students to do it like the example	- the step-by-step process you follow when you show them how to do something - talk about what you are thinking as you demonstrate each step - show how to make a choice

4. *Engage the writers.* Include students' ideas as you model a process. They may share the chalk as they add their writing to yours on the board.

5. *Guide the writers.* The teacher instructs how to use a skill, craft, or strategy. Students practice while the teacher supports, encourages, and guides their thinking. Notice who has used the strategy or skill correctly and have them share their writing with the class.

6. *Apply new learning.* Students return to their writing so they can determine if what they've learned will benefit the piece they are developing. They practice writing independently with authentic content.

Teaching and Learning Strategies Used in Writer's Workshop

"We" is stronger than "I." This is the case as teachers and students work together. This happens every day in Writer's Workshop—the exchange of ideas, the questions we ask each other, and the ways we explain our thinking. Then, writers can return to their work with clearer thoughts, ready to write independently. Some of the strategies use cooperative learning, in which students work together to achieve a common goal.

Think Aloud. This strategy gives students a peek into your mind as you walk them through a part of the writing process telling out loud what you're thinking and wondering. This demonstrates how they can begin to ask themselves questions, thinking about their writing. The following Think Aloud example is a revising mini-lesson.

Revise a small section of writing in front of the students using a transparency. We suggest that you type out the story "New Red Sled" in large font, triple spaced. Think aloud as you decide what needs to be changed or added. Cross out and write your revisions in the spaces between lines. Example:

Original story, "New Red Sled": "Ben, wake up!" shouted his brother. "It snowed last night—no school." Ben went downstairs to eat. Then, he went outside. Ben was excited to try out his new sled. The whole neighborhood would be at the big hill in back of the school. He was on his way.

Text of "New Red Sled"	What I Was Thinking About
"Ben, wake up!" shouted his brother. "It snowed last night—no school."	*Good lead. Dialogue brings the reader right into the action. Boy, I hope we get a snow day soon. I love the fun I have in the snow.*
Ben went downstairs to eat. Then he went outside.	*No ... this needs to <u>show</u> how excited Ben is. Hmm ... I'll change this to ...*
Throwing off the blankets, Ben raced to the kitchen for a quick breakfast before he jumped into his snowsuit.	*That's better. More action and details.*
Ben was excited to try out his new sled.	*Oops. This <u>tells,</u> not <u>shows</u> me he's excited. Let's shift to ...*
He grabbed his sled, his brand-new red sled, from the basement. It had been waiting for this snow for two months!	*Okay. I like that.*
The whole neighborhood would be at the big hill in back of the school. He was on his way.	*That works for me. Now, I'll go back and reread this part of the piece and see how it sounds.*

<u>Revised story:</u> "Ben, wake up!" shouted his brother. "It snowed last night—no school." Throwing off the blankets, Ben raced to the kitchen for a quick breakfast before he jumped into his snowsuit. He grabbed his sled, his brand-new red sled, from the basement. It had been waiting for this snow for two months! The whole neighborhood would be at the big hill in back of the school. He was on his way.

How Writing Partners Work Together. We are all writing partners in a writing classroom. At the heart of working together is listening. Writing partners learn how to listen to each other and listen well. After all of your teaching and positive modeling, students will learn how to respond to someone's writing. There are guidelines for the writer and the responder. Go over a few tips and post a chart. Include:

> **How Writing Partners Work Together**
>
> **The Writer:**
> * Tell the partner what you need.
> * Read one part of your writing aloud.
> * Listen to comments offered.
> * Thank the partner for helping.
> * Reread and decide what to do next.
> * Revise your writing.
>
> **How Writing Partners Work Together**
>
> **The Responder:**
> * Ask what your partner needs.
> * Listen to the partner read.
> * Tell something specific you like.
> * Suggest an improvement.
> * Thank the writer for sharing.

This is a rich process that we first model with another student, working through each step in the charts "How Partners Work Together." This scaffolds their thinking as they observe, confer with a teacher, then use it with a partner.

These are some comments I've heard my students say to each other:

* "I like how you …"
* "I wonder why you …"
* "How did the character get from here to there? You might have a hole at that point. It would help me if you add more details there."
* "I heard how lots of your sentences begin the same way. Can you think of some other ways to start them?

© Heather Ferraro

- "The way you said, 'Gazing into the depths of the lake' paints a better picture than saying looking into the water."
- "Thanks for sharing. You've given me an idea about my own story."

We all need instant feedback. Even if it's not what we're anticipating, it provokes new thinking or solidifies decisions we make. We may even choose to disregard the comments that have been offered by our peers. That is one of many choices writers make.

Fish in a Fishbowl. The fishbowl strategy uses role play and observation to teach a skill. Elicit from students what it is like to watch fish swimming in a transparent bowl. Introduce how they will observe you and a fellow student in a similar way.

This is what it looks like. Two people sit in the middle of the "fishbowl" and the rest of the students sit in chairs around them in a circle. Clarify what their role will be as observers. They will notice how the "fish" work together. Announce the purpose for the fishbowl observation, role play the scene, and afterward discuss the process, sharing the observations made about the fishbowl experience.

A Script From One of Our Fishbowl Revising Conferences:

Mrs. W: (to the whole class) Today, Vicky and I are the fish in a fishbowl you will watch. Our focus for this lesson is how to be a helpful revising partner. All of you sitting in this circle are observers of our revising conference. Your task is to notice how I listen and respond to Vicky and how Vicky talks with me about her writing. When we finish, all of us will discuss how Vicky and I communicated with each other. Questions? Let's begin.

Mrs. W to Vicky: Tell me what's going well in your story, Vicky.

Vicky: I like the idea of my story. My opening grabber is good. I used dialogue and there's action, too. When I reread it today, I decided I wanted to talk to you about something.

Mrs. W: What's on your mind?

Vicky: There are two main characters, two girls. Um ... I think they're talking a lot.

Mrs. W. Isn't that what good friends do?

Vicky: Yeah, but I noticed there's lots of chit-chat. It's a little boring.

Mrs. W: What if you underline with a crayon everything that's not dialogue? Those sentences would be your action. Then you can see if you have a balance, since you don't want "all talk and no action." Does that sound like a first step?

Vicky: Okay. I'll get a crayon. (Vicky starts marking her paper while she rereads. In an actual conference, Vicky would return to her desk and begin revising.)

As a whole group, we debriefed what had just happened. I asked them to share what they saw and heard.

> *Christopher*: Vicky does a lot of talking.
> *Gina*: I like how you said good friends talk and listen to each other.
> *Alisa*: First, you asked her about the things she likes about her story.
> *Cam*: You gave her a suggestion. She decided to try it.
> *Kelsey*: I want to know if using that crayon really helped.

> *Epilogue*: Vicky returned the next day to discuss if using the crayon helped. We thought of some ways she could revise the section to give it more action and less talk.

Think-Pair-Share. This strategy is really a peer conference that often helps to organize the writer's thinking and provide clarity for story development. It can take place at any stage of the writing process.

> *Think:* Children think about what they want to discuss about the piece.
> *Pair:* Get with a partner, exchange writing pieces, and read them silently.
> *Share:* The reader talks about the story just read, offering comments and questions. The writer asks questions if something is unclear and may take additional notes about the suggestions the partner offered. They take turns with this process, then return to their desks to revise.

Chalk Talk. This strategy is a whole-class activity in which children take turns posting their ideas on a chalkboard without speaking.

Have students consider the character from a book you are reading aloud in class. After the first couple of chapters, pause to think about this character. On the board or on large chart paper, begin a web by putting the character's name at the center. Then, write a question you have about this character. Taking turns, students come up and write their own questions on the board. Observe how their ideas may be original or how they may piggyback off of what someone else has written. The entire activity is done in silence.

This photograph is an example of our "chalk talk" of *Passager* by Yolen. (Or, as Christopher wondered, "Why do you call it a 'chalk talk?' Isn't it a 'marker talk?'")

After students wrote their questions about the character, we went back to categorize and color-code them by the character attributes of Looks, Speaks, Acts, and Feels. These four combine to make fully developed characters.

Make a list of questions into a chart to post as a resource. As they begin to write a new story, guide them to use this question bank to develop their character more fully.

- What does the character look like?
- How does the character speak (e.g., expressions, sounds, dialect, etc.)?
- What is happening to the character? What do you think will happen?
- Why is the character acting this way?
- What is the character feeling? What words tell me?

Accountability in Writer's Workshop

Student Accountability

- Write daily and participate in all aspects of Writer's Workshop.
- Keep work from all stages of the writing process.
- Organize all papers in their Writing Notebooks.
- Update the class chart every day, placing name cards on the chart to indicate at what writing stage they are working.
- Plan and write what they will work on tomorrow.

Teacher Accountability

- Prepare all materials needed during Writer's Workshop.
- Read lots of literature and collect examples of various writing craft.
- *Always* ask student's permission before using their writing in any way.
- Keep a writing journal and share it with students.
- Maintain formal and informal records about students' writing.
- Use assessment information to guide teaching.
- Encourage independence. Get out of their way and let them write!
- Have students share their writing regularly. Set up a weekly schedule ensuring all students an opportunity for sharing. Respect those who don't choose to share.
- Notice, acknowledge, and celebrate their achievements and small successes.
- Involve parents: Inform them through writing and conferences, demonstrate how children learn to write, and showcase students' writing.
- Show humanness. Take risks, make mistakes, try again, laugh, and persevere. And do it with enthusiasm.

3: Exploring the Writing Process

Genius is one percent inspiration
and ninety-nine percent perspiration.
—Thomas Edison

The Writing Process is the way students develop a piece of text. There are six stages—prewriting, drafting, conferring, revising, editing, and publishing—that follow a logical sequence as students move from conceiving their ideas to writing the final copy. We deal with each stage as a separate entity for the purposes of teaching, but in reality they often blend together. As writers become more proficient, the stages overlap and are not so clearly defined.

Prewriting

Key Elements of Prewriting:

- Word Study: *prewrite*
  pre = before
  writ = express ideas with words
- Choose a topic.
- Organize thoughts.
- Generate ideas.
- Identify the purpose and audience.
- Select a format for the writing.

Writing Standards:

1. Habits and Processes
   - Write daily.
   - Generate their own topics and spend time refining their writing.
2. Writing Purposes and Resulting Genres
   - Producing Literature
     - Write stories, songs, memoirs, poetry, and plays that conform to the appropriate expectations for each form.
     - After studying a genre, produce a piece that incorporates elements appropriate to the genre.
   - Responding to literature

– Make text-to-self connections as they relate the story to their own lives.
– Make text-to-text connections as they notice and discuss where they have seen the writing craft or ideas in other literature.

About Prewriting ...

"The Thinking Stage"—that's what children's author Marcia Thornton Jones (*Bailey School Kids* series) calls the Prewriting stage. And it is. Before children begin to write, they must think about what they want to write. This is an important time for teachers to help children develop and organize their ideas so they can write stories with personal meaning. Donald Murray supports this idea and calls Prewriting the "Discovery Stage." He compares it to a warm-up exercise for athletes. Limbering up their muscles to get ready for the main event is like writers stretching their thoughts as they prepare for composing an original piece.

You may have experienced, as we have, children sitting at a desk staring at that blank white page. They may become even more paralyzed as students all around begin to fill up their pages with black letters. How can you help these children? How can you help make the initial writing a pleasant experience, even one that they are eager to begin?

I remember the morning when Anthony came to me with a predicament of not having a topic for a new story. His frustration was apparent as he watched all the other students hover over their papers, pencils scratching the surfaces. He ran through the litany of strategies he had learned about how to think of a topic. After he finished the list, Anthony still wasn't sure how to proceed. I listened, nodded, and said, "Hmmm. I see that you're thinking hard. I'm confident that one of those strategies will work for you." He thanked me for listening and returned to his seat. I observed him for a few moments, noticing how his eyes slowly scanned the classroom. Then, his eyes paused on the large wall clock. He whisper-shouted a "Yes!," and eventually a delightful personal story about a clock poured out onto his paper.

This is an example of how the act of simply listening allowed a student to work through his own questions. It was tempting to tell him what to do, to suggest one of the strategies he had named. But, I refrained. He already knew a variety of strategies. He just needed to select *one*—*he*, not *me*. Students have taught us how powerful the art of listening can be and that it isn't always essential for us to answer them—just support and trust their thinking.

The purpose of this chapter is to teach many different strategies about how to begin a story. Through our teaching, we can offer students a pocketfull of strategies, as Anthony had. Children will not use all of these ideas when they write. We show them many ways and let them explore and find the ones that work best. This is what good writers do.

Authors' Thoughts About Prewriting

Jane Yolen from *Letter From Phoenix Farm:*

> People always ask, "Where do you get your ideas?" The answer is—from everywhere. From pictures and books and songs and other stories and from

listening quietly to conversations. (p. 26)

Cynthia Rylant from *Best Wishes:*

> I roamed around a lot when I was growing up. No one expected my roaming to turn me into a writer. But it helped. I saw what was happening inside houses. I heard what people were saying outside stores. All these things I remembered when I became a writer, and I put them into books. (pp. 8–11)

Jack Prelutsky from his Web site:

> Read! Read! Read! and Write! Write! Write! Keep a notebook and write down things you see, hear, and think about. Ideas disappear quickly unless you jot them down. When you have an idea for a poem or story, write down anything you can think of that has to do with that idea. Study your list and you'll start to see connections among certain items.

How Do We Teach Prewriting?

Word Study: Prewriting

Ask students if they know what the prefix *pre* means. Many will know already that it means "before." The important connection here is for them to think about several words beginning with *pre* that they already know.

Write a few of these on the board, such as *prefix*, *predict*, and *preschool*, and talk about the meanings. Based on that knowledge, let them tell you the meanings of words they may not have thought about before, such as, *prepay*, *preheat*, and *preteen*. Now, what do they think the word, *prewriting* might mean (the things you do <u>before</u> you begin writing a piece)?

Show Your Own Personal Journals. If you don't already keep a journal, this is a good time to begin. It's important to think, write, and share along with students throughout the year. Show how you add thoughts from books and conversations, words you like, and other interesting artifacts you put in this book that will help you as a writer. Encourage students to keep their own journals as they become writers.

I bring in my own writing journal as a way to show how I keep my thoughts and ideas in a book. Children wonder what lives in my book and laugh as I pull out a four-leaf clover, pictures of my boys, ticket stubs, feathers. It gives them a glimpse into who I am and what is important to me.

Rainstorming and Brainstorming. To emphasize this metaphor, you might walk in with an open umbrella and write "rainstorm" on the board. Ask students what a rainstorm is and what happens during a rainstorm (rain peppers down, wind blows, thunder, lightning, clouds gather, etc.). Then, put a "B" in front of "rainstorm" to make the word "brainstorm." Now, discuss what a brainstorm could be. They may have done brainstorming in previous grades, but the visual connection is memorable. Talk about ideas being like a rainstorm: ideas pepper down like rain from our brain, ideas blow around like wind in our minds, ideas flash like lightning in our thoughts, words gather like clouds, and so on to continue the metaphor.

Create an Idea Journal. Ask any writers how they get ideas, and the response will be "everywhere!" They will also tell you that they must write down ideas immediately or they disappear. Students designate the first section in their Writing Notebook as "Ideas for Writing."

Model for students how to develop an idea list. Think of a topic and write it on the board, such as "Pets." Underneath, bullet a few seed ideas—small beginnings that could grow into a complete story. Your seed ideas will be your own personal stories that go with that topic. Point out how you did *not* write the complete story, but only listed ideas that would jog your memory when you're ready to write the story. Example:

> **Pets**
> • Hamster in the couch
> • Chameleon on my shoulder
> • Ducks in the toilet

Tell students the whole story about one of your seed ideas. (My students always want to hear "Ducks in the toilet!") A technique that writers use is going back to their seed ideas and selecting one they want to develop fully.

Now, guide students to set up their own "Ideas for Writing" in their Writing Notebook. At the top of one page, have them write a topic you selected. Here are a few topics we have used:

- My earliest memories
- Something unique about a parent or grandparent
- The pet I wish I had
- A brother, a sister (or the ups and downs of being an only child)
- Something you did for the first time
- Scars on my body
- A time I was proud of myself

Give them time to write silently and constantly for a few minutes. Remind them to bullet idea phrases, like you demonstrated, that relate to that topic. Leave a whole page for each topic so they can come back to this page later and add new ideas as they think of them. After a few minutes of writing, announce another topic that they will put at the top of a new page. Continue this process for a few topics. Another day, add some more.

Planting Seeds. Set up a regular practice for expecting students to add new ideas to their journals. I begin Writer's Workshop with this exercise about once a month. Try a number of ways:

- You give them topics to bullet lots of thoughts.
- Let them choose a topic from a box and write their brainstormed ideas.
- Allow time for them to peruse children's magazines and make personal connections.

It is well worth the time to keep them thinking and exploring. Because of this practice, I rarely have a child complain, "I don't know what to write about."

Mini-Journal. Sometimes, students might like to have a small journal they can carry with them rather than their Writing Notebook. Cut wallpaper into 8½ x 11 pieces. Fold it in half and add as many folded white letter size sheets as you want. Use a long arm stapler to secure the pages. We find that students love the small, intimate journals they have created themselves. Give students an option of making a mini-journal so they can have it with them when an idea sprouts.

Use Books as a Stimulus. Books are full of writing ideas. Although we get ideas for our own writing from every book, there are a few books that specifically hone in on memories. These books can provide a rich source for adding to student idea journals. Occasionally, read one of these books with children ready to write down their ideas as they connect with one of the author's. Here are a few:

- *Wilfrid Gordon MacDonald Partridge.* Mem Fox focuses on the significant concept of "memory" in her beautiful picture book. Before reading this story, ask students, "What is a memory?" Get a variety of responses. This question is explored in the book. Read it aloud (it comes in big book format). How were students' ideas of memory similar to or different from the various definitions of memory in the book? This is a segue into writing their ideas about early memories.

- *Higher on the Door.* This whimsical autobiography by J. Stevenson provides a model of story seed ideas based on the author's experiences, such as:
  – a special birthday;
  – neighbors;
  – things you can't do that you want to do;
  – what you like to play with friends; and
  – more ideas on every page!

- *To Sail a Ship of Treasures.* Lisa Weil's book is another rich source for writing ideas.

Prompts with Meaning. Lucy Calkins suggests that, if you give students prompts for their writing subjects, make sure that they are open-ended and relevant to children's lives. Avoid giving silly, disconnected prompts that have no personal meaning ("Pretend you are a shoe and describe your trip from home to school" is an example of a disconnected prompt). There are too many important ideas for children to explore without wasting time on irrelevant topics.

Explore Various Text Structures. This playful activity moves from Read Like a Writer to Write (or Publish) Like a Writer. We put this in Prewriting rather than in Publication because students often need to plan the structure of the piece before it is written, not as an afterthought. It showcases a wide range of possibilities for writing text. Refer to the Publication section for more ideas.

Throughout the year, we constantly notice and discuss different types of structures in books. It's energizing when students approach me with a book in hand, telling me that they want to write a book similar to this one. For example, Jacob said he wanted to write a book that ended like Paul Brett Johnson's *The Cow Who Wouldn't Come Down* by having a surprise illustration on the last page and no words. The picture gives a clue to the reader that something else is going to happen—and leads into a sequel! Jacob proceeded to do this by writing a train book that ended with an airplane picture—that led to the sequel. He used a common text structure based on what he had observed in published literature.

Have students "borrow" a book structure idea they would like to use. Guide them to write in a similar format. The choices are endless, but here are a few text structures that middle elementary students enjoy emulating.

- *Narrative Poems*. These are stories told in poetic form, such as *Out of the Dust* by K. Hesse, *Bringing the Rain to Kapiti Plain* by V. Aardema, and *Carver: A Life in Poems* by M. Nelson.

- *Alphabet Books*. There are hundreds of formats for this genre. Look at what can be done with alliteration, as in *Animalia* by G. Base, where each letter has an alliterative phrase, (e.g., A = An Armoured Armadillo Avoiding An Angry Alligator).

- *Diary*. The main character writes thoughts, feelings, and events in a diary or journal format, such as *Tales From the House of Bunnicula* by J. Howe, *Catherine Called Birdy* by K. Cushman, the *Dear America* series by Scholastic, and *A Gathering of Days* by Bois.

- *Letters*. Friendly letters abound in literature: *Dear Mr. Henshaw* by B. Cleary, *Dear Mr. Blueberry* by S. James, *Letters From Rifka* by K. Hesse, *The Jolly Postman* by J. Ahlberg, *The Gardner* by S. Stewart, and others.

- *Factual Fiction*. Some books successfully combine fictional narrative with loads of factual information, such as these series: *The Bailey School Kids* by D. Dadey and M. T. Jones, *The Magic Tree House* by M. P. Osborne, and *Magic School Bus* by J. Cole.

- *Timeline*. Many biographies include a timeline to put a famous person's life in perspective. An especially engaging format is Mohammed Ali's biography, *Float Like a Butterfly*, which presents 18 small pictures representing 18 important events in his life. A timeline could even be a framework for organizing the report.

Web Your Ideas. Webbing is a technique for helping students to structure their thinking. Have students put one topic or central idea in the middle of the page. Then, add related ideas about the topic all around it. It looks similar to a spider's web, which is the metaphor of connected thoughts. Students seem to like this process, and it helps to make their ideas visual and concrete.

Grocery List. We all make lists to help us remember. This simple technique can be used in writing also. Have students brainstorm many thoughts—the order doesn't matter. Some ideas will be good, others not so good, and that's fine. It allows them to quickly shake loose a lot of ideas. They can then select one that may lead into a story.

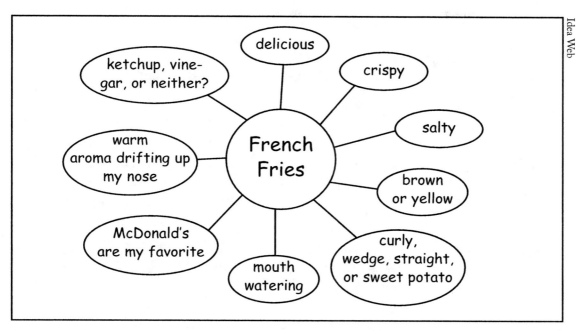

Planning With a Story Map. Another way to help students plan their stories is to have them routinely fill in story maps during the prewriting stage of Writer's Workshop.

Model how you fill in a story map while planning your story. This organizer is a tool to help students get started. It is a guide for writing that can be changed as the story develops. Therefore, we don't require every box to be completed, as we acknowledge that some of our stories unfold as we write. Distribute the Think Sheet "Story Map" (at the end of this section) for students to begin planning.

Look Around You. Most published writers discuss how they are aware of everything around them— fuzz on a peach, a unique expression, a belly laugh. Direct students to observe what is around them to see if they can find a seed idea in simple, ordinary things. For example: Notice the clock on the wall in your classroom and ask yourself some questions:

- Does it shake loose any thoughts about a clock, watch, or timepiece?
- Does it help you think about watching the clock and waiting for a special event?
- Does it snag your interest about something that might have happened at an exact moment in time?

- Does it make a connection to another story about time?

Study a Photograph. Bring in a stack of photographs, some old, some black and white, and see if those pictures can rattle free an idea or two. Ask students to think, "Who are these people in the picture? What might they be thinking or doing? What if ...?" Perhaps a photo can lead to an interesting story.

A Picture's Worth 1,000 Words. Chris Van Allsburg is a master at utilizing his drawing as a stimulus for a story. He tells how he often draws a picture with nothing particular in mind. Then, he studies it and lets his imagination take over as a story unfolds. Only then does he begin to put words onto paper. Guide your students to experiment with this technique: 1) draw a picture, 2) study it, and 3) write a story about it.

What if ...? Anne Bernays and Pamela Painter wrote an entire book of writing exercises entitled, *What If?* They say, "To be a good writer you must know how to do two very different things—write like a writer and think like one" (p. xv). But, it's the thinking that is the harder part.

Ask students to think of "What if" questions, then answer them. This activity can help to set their thinking in motion and look at something in a new way. For example:

- What if my story were set in the desert instead of on a farm?
- What if the main character had a twin brother?
- What if the character had a pet iguana instead of a cat?

Interview Your Family. Parents and grandparents have stories to tell, lots of stories! Plan with the students some open-ended interview questions, such as:

- Tell me a funny story about when I was little.
- What was one of the most memorable family events?
- What was the most regrettable thing you ever did?

Let them interview a family member and jot down some notes in their journal. This is also a good home-school connection, as parents become more involved in the story's development.

And the Author Said ... Read to students about the ways authors conceptualize stories based on real experiences from their own lives. This helps to establish the reading-writing connection. In her autobiography, *Best Wishes*, Cynthia Rylant talks about the *Henry and Mudge* stories coming from events that happened with her son. Have students focus a story on a real experience from their own lives, but let it happen to a character in their story.

Current Events. Pulitzer Prize-winning author Isabelle Allende (*House of the Spirits*) credits some of her most memorable scenes in her books to newspaper stories she collected. When she finds an interesting or bizarre story, article, or photograph, she clips it out and stores it in an Idea File for later use in her own writing. Likewise, Jane Yolen tells that her *Commander Toad* books developed from a newspaper story about a jumping frog contest (p. 26).

Encourage students to collect interesting or funny story articles from the newspaper or from children's magazines such as *Time for Kids, Sports Illustrated for Kids, National Geographic for Kids, Odyssey Adventures in Science, Cricket, Creative Kids,* or *Ranger Rick.* Model how you can take an idea from a magazine and let it become the seed for a story.

Talk it Over. This is a strategy that works well with individuals who may be struggling with how to get started. Have students get with a partner to talk about one of the story ideas they want to write. Sometimes, talking about the idea helps to develop it. I tell students, "If you can tell it, you can write it." This should be a brief consult with one partner only. Then, it's time to begin writing.

Afterward, process with students the effectiveness of discussing the story. However, not all writers agree with this strategy. The caveat is this: Sometimes, you can talk away the excitement.

Focus on Research

Researching Fiction. Richard Peck said, "All fiction is based on research. If I were limited to writing what I know, I'd have produced in all these years one unpublishable haiku." Writers conduct research, whether they are writing fiction, nonfiction, or poetry. In my class, John began a creative story about a boy who found a salamander under a rock. He didn't know much about salamanders, so he researched the subject. Using this information, he wove it into his story (p. 113).

As you read students' writing, help them identify the places where a bit of research about a topic could enrich their stories.

Focusing a Topic. When my son, Neal, came home from school and announced that he was going to research Abraham Lincoln, I gulped, knowing what a huge topic this was. I pictured him buried under at least 500 books on the subject. After he read through the first book, I suggested that he list several ideas about Lincoln's life that were interesting. Neal was drawn toward the information about the Civil War—until he saw that 400 of the books were on that topic! He decided to narrow his focus on the time Lincoln was a young lawyer in Illinois and had a deep look into the man, the orator, his humor. He was able to do this because the topic was concentrated, his research more focused.

When students have a topic they want to learn more about, help them narrow it to make it a manageable study. Here are a few questions to help students focus:

- What part is the most interesting to me?
- What could I study deeply in the amount of time I have?
- On what part of the topic could I become an expert?
- What could I study best with the resources I have?

Collecting Information. Review with students the various resources available to gather information:

- Read books and periodicals about a topic.
- Search the Internet.

- Write interview questions and conduct an interview in person or by phone, e-mail, or letter.
- Visit a museum or place connected to the story.
- Find photographs or drawings about the person, place, or thing.

Beginning With Questions. Having students raise questions about what they want to know is an essential way for them to set a purpose for learning. Model how you consider a topic, writing what you wonder. Example: Before I read "On Top of the World" from *Time for Kids*, I wondered:

- How did someone figure out how high Mt. Everest is?
- How do people prepare for a climbing expedition?
- Where do the climbers get their confidence to do such a dangerous and daring climb?
- Is it worth the risk?

Demonstrate how asking questions can help us focus our research. Write a question on one side of an index card. Record all notes that answer the question on the reverse side. Use one card for each question.

(Front) **Question:** How do people prepare for a climbing expedition?	(Back) **Notes:** • oxygen tanks • high-tech thermal clothing • satellite phones • physical training and experience • Sherpa guides

Taking Notes. While taking notes about each question on the reverse side of the card, direct the children to write only key words and phrases (see example of Question and Note cards in "Beginning With Questions" activity). This process encourages students to find the most important information and it develops genuine writing about a topic in their own words. Explain that we only use a sentence if we need to quote an author directly. This is a good opportunity to talk about plagiarism and the importance of crediting our sources.

When my third graders work this way, their reports sing with voice, *their* voice, not a regurgitation of someone else's words.

Closing the Book. Another approach to gleaning information if you don't use the question and notes format is to literally "close the book." After reading one section of information in a nonfiction text, guide children to close the book and write down what they can remember in their own words. Then, go on to the next section and repeat the process.

Variation. Guide them to pause after reading each section and write one sentence to summarize. This organizes their thinking and focuses their note taking, section by section.

Culling Through the Notes. Culling is an important step all writers must do to keep the writing focused. It means to sort through, keep the best, and eliminate the rest. Young writers need guidance to learn how to work through the culling process. It's hard to let go of some words we've spent time writing.

Direct students to return to their question cards: "Read through your questions to see if they directly relate to what you want to learn." Have them continue this process with each card to make sure the written notes match the questions/purposes of the research: "Check to make sure your notes help you answer only this question. If you find some that don't, eliminate those notes."

Poetically Speaking

We get our ideas for poetry in many places. If you are doing prewriting specifically for writing poetry, here are a few suggestions:

- Collect and have available many poetry books for them to reference.
- Read, notice, and analyze a variety of poems with the same structure.
- Read a lot about a topic they will write about.
- Brainstorm ideas and images. Especially images. This is one element that makes poetry poetry.
- Use the five senses and notice, really notice, all the details about your topic.
- Play with descriptive language.
- Have them choose one published poem they like, share it with the class, and tell the reason they chose it (e.g., pattern, visual imagery, invented words, humor, rhythm, alliteration, title, etc.).

Name _____ Date _____

Story Map

Title: _____

Setting: _____

Characters (1 or 2): _____
_____

Opening Grabber (Lead): _____
_____
_____
_____

Beginning Situation: _____
_____
_____
_____

Expand an Important Part! _____
_____
_____
_____
_____
_____
_____

Problem or Adventure: _____
_____
_____
_____

Solution or Conclusion: _____
_____
_____

Ending: _____
_____

Drafting

All writing is experimental.
We don't know what works until we try it.
—Donald Murray

Key Elements of Drafting:

- Word Study: *draft* (v.)
  to compose a first written version of a text
- Review plans from Prewriting
- Take time to compose
- Focus on content, rather than mechanics

Writing Standards:

1. Habits and Processes
2. Writing Purposes and Resulting Genres
3. Language Use and Conventions

See Chapter 1, *Beginnings*, "Connect Writing Instruction to Writing Standards," for reference to specific writing standards as needed.

About Drafting ...

Drafting is the stage in which children review their idea and compose. In a classroom where writing is valued, drafting is usually an enjoyable time. All pieces that students begin will not be completed or published. It is not necessary, or even desirable, to approach every writing piece as a publishable story.

When teachers model writing a story, we demonstrate an important aspect of drafting for young writers. Students need to see how someone begins to put the ideas into a more structured form. They observe this process as we write in front of them and as we think aloud. The mini-lessons taught during Writer's Workshop directly connect to their writing. Our scaffolding models how to draft, engages their participation, then encourages independent writing. We hope that students will stretch themselves and boldly attempt some new techniques with each story. That's the way writers grow.

Authors' Thoughts About Drafting:

Anne Lamott from *Bird by Bird: Some Instructions on Writing and Life:*

> This is how it works for me: I sit down in the morning and reread the work I did the day before. And then I wool-gather, staring at the blank page or off into space. I imagine my characters, and let myself daydream about them. A

movie begins to play in my head, with emotion pulsing underneath it, and I stare at it in a trancelike state, until words bounce around together and form a sentence. (p. 56)

James Howe from his autobiography, *Playing With Words*:

I don't start writing right away. First I need to open my mind to my work. I read for a while. Sometimes I draw. Sometimes I just sit quietly and jot down ideas and thoughts. Or I go back and forth doing all these things. When I'm ready to write, I reread what I wrote the day before. Then I edit or rewrite it. This gets me thinking about what to do next with my story, and I don't have to face a blank page. (p. 12–14)

How Do I Teach Drafting?

Word Study: *Compose*.

Look up and discuss with the class the word *compose*.

- Latin origin, *componere*
- *com-* means "together"; *ponere* means "to put"
- to put things together to form a whole
- to arrange things in order to achieve an effect

As students compose, we see that they put together not just words and sentences, but also life experiences, thoughts, and dreams.

Class Chart: Guidelines for Drafting. Decide what you believe is important about drafting and make a class chart of the guidelines. Students can refer to the chart at the beginning of the year, and eventually it becomes second nature to them. Our guideline chart looks like this:

Guidelines for Drafting

- Think, plan, compose
- Use yellow, lined paper
- Put name, date, and page numbers on every page
- Write on one side only
- Keep 1-inch margins on right and left sides
- Skip lines—mark x's on every other line

<u>Yellow paper</u> clearly distinguishes the draft from the white, final copy paper.

The <u>date</u> indicates when pieces were written, marking the point in time for possible comparison between earlier and later writing.

Writing on <u>one side only</u> allows the entire story to be spread out on the floor and perused all at once. We can reread and revise without having to flip pages and lose our place. If needed, we can cut and move sections without destroying any writing on the reverse side.

<u>Margins</u> allow generous space for revising and comments. For some reason, it seems to be the nature of elementary students to cram in as much writing on a page as physically possible, with no regard to top, bottom, or side margins. It takes a lot of guidance for children to be liberal with blank space. But, they learn early how important the questions and feedback are from both the teacher and peers. Ample space honors, welcomes, and encourages comments.

<u>Skipping lines</u>, like margins, provides sufficient space to revise and add comments. Students put x's on every other line as reminders of where to write and where *not* to write.

Model Some Strategies. Our mantra is model, model, model. Student teachers always report to me how much easier it is for them to learn a new method if they <u>see</u> it in practice. This holds true for all learners. So, we model how we think, plan, and compose using various strategies to <u>show,</u> rather than tell.

Children will benefit when you show how to take a prewriting seed idea and begin to write a story. On a lined, overhead transparency demonstrate how you draft ideas. Think aloud as you write so they can see how the writing evolves. Let them hear you wonder, then write those words down on paper, just like they will do. Keep going even when you make a change—just strike out words (don't stop and erase) and write on. One of the goals of drafting is to become fluent in writing. Older and more skilled writers may draft, edit, and revise at the same time, but emerging writers should learn to keep writing their ideas without interruptions.

Go Solo—Mostly. We agree with Nancie Atwell's suggestion of having students write their stories independently, not in pairs. It's okay to allow paired writing occasionally since many children enjoy collaborating. However, most of their writing should be individual. We, as teachers, can evaluate and help writers grow only if we know who is doing the thinking and the writing.

Let the Music Play On. Our ideal goal is to create a peaceful writing atmosphere in which students can think and draft. Many students find soft, classical music to be a background conducive to writing. Others, however, may prefer silence. Experiment with using various types of music or background sounds, such as ocean or rain. They may come to associate the music with the writing time and it can more clearly define the Writer's Workshop segment of day.

Five-Minute Writing. Natalie Goldberg, in her classic book *Writing Down the Bones*, suggests that writers "keep their hand moving" without pausing to edit. Have students keep writing for a brief period without thinking or judging—keep the graphite scratching the paper. This is a great exercise, particularly for reluctant or hesitant writers. Sometimes, our uncensored ideas have energy and merit.

Write Their Words. We all have had students who had difficulty writing many words on paper. Sometimes, we need to help them develop independence in writing. This has worked for us: Have the children talk through the story as you record their ideas. Sometimes, the initial writing assistance gives them confidence to proceed on their own by elaborating on the notes you wrote. Occasionally, you may have a child who benefits best from your scripting the exact words. Then, encourage the individual to continue the story independently.

Follow Examples of Book Formats. In all stages of the writing process, we Read Like Writers to notice and study distinctive formats found in books. As you share these with children, nudge their thinking about how they can use these special formats in their own writing. Here are some examples of styles that we especially love, but the choices are abundant:

- *Snowflake Bentley* by J. B. Martin—(Borders with information) This story is anything but cold as it tells of the life of scientist William Bentley. The main story reads like fiction, but it is biography written in an interesting and engaging way. Notice the borders: They are filled with facts that focus on Bentley's development of microphotography.

- *The Magic School Bus* series by J. Cole—(Combining fact and fiction) Three strands lend a little magic to this award-winning series: 1) the fictional storyline with interesting characters is the main text, 2) humorous dialogue is written in cartoon-like speech bubbles, and 3) handwritten research notes line the sides and provide scads of facts and information about the book topic.

- *Everything on a Waffle* by P. Horvath—(Recipes) This delicious chapter book is unique in that there is a recipe at the end of every chapter that connects to some food mentioned earlier. Each recipe is peppered with voice and humor, told by the protagonist, Primrose Squarp. Could students follow the example of using recipes in a new way—for friendship, for peace, to chase away sadness? Perhaps a teaspoon of kindness …

- *A Bookworm Who Hatched*—by V. Aardema—(Family tree) Notice how Ms. Aardema begins her autobiography with a family tree. What an inspiration and model for our own budding writers. A family tree of their own family or a family tree of a fictional character? Hmmm …

- *Knots in My Yo-Yo String* by J. Spinelli—(Maps) A map of J. Spinelli's neighborhood begins this autobiography and puts his young life in geographical perspective. Throughout the book, I found myself thumbing back to that map to see where everything was that he described. Many writers use this mapping technique. It helps students develop a clearer setting when they can picture it in their own minds and draw it for their readers.

- *The True Story of the Three Little Pigs by A. Wolf* by J. Scieszka—(Old story, new perspective) This version is from the viewpoint of the wolf. Any story can change and become original when written from another character's point of view.

- *Doodle Dandies: Poems That Take Shape* by J. Patrick Lewis—(Concrete poetry) The poems are shaped like their subject, such as Giraffe, Weeping Willow, Umbrella, Skyscraper, and so on. Students could create a class book of concrete poems modeled after this or any concrete poetry book.

Create Memory Boxes. Many teachers have students create memory boxes in response to a book. They collect a variety of objects that represent something significant about a character's life. We like to use the same idea, but with a different slant.

Guide students to gather interesting items from around their house and bring them to school in a shoebox. As they develop a story, have the children sort through their box, select one, and study it. Imagine how that artifact could add to the story. It might apply to a setting or a character. For example, the millions-year-old rock from Mammoth Cave might prompt creating the character as a spelunker or a setting in a cave or a long-ago time period. This helps young writers realize that we can get ideas when we observe objects from our lives.

Nonfiction

Structure of Nonfiction. Collect an assortment of nonfiction books. Compare the structures of fiction and nonfiction and discuss how and why they are different. List the components that make up nonfiction literature, such as:

- table of contents;
- introduction;
- headings and subheadings;
- text;
- questions and answers;
- illustrations or photographs with captions;
- diagrams with labels;
- text boxes for additional information;
- tables and graphs;
- timelines;
- summary;
- glossaries; and
- indexes.

Topic Sentence, Supporting Details, and Concluding Statement. We start with the questions students are interested in learning about a topic. (For more information, see "Focus on Research" activity in Prewriting section.)

Model for students how you begin drafting a nonfiction paragraph using one of the questions that you researched about a topic. Have students help you reframe the question into a statement that best summarizes what you have learned. Next, demonstrate how you review and expand the notes into several sentences telling information about the topic. In the last sentence, show how you bring the subject to a close. You might restate the main idea in different words to summarize what you have written.

The example uses Julia's focus question, "What is our Sun made of?" We restated her question into a topic sentence and used her notes to write detail sentences, then concluded with a wrap-up sentence. This process scaffolds their thinking as we model for them, elicit their ideas and words, and compose the paragraph together. Now, students are better able to write paragraphs on their own.

What is Our Sun Made of?

Our Sun is made up of gases, mostly hydrogen. At the center is its core that is like a nuclear furnace. On the Sun's surface it may be 100 million degrees! The gasses explode and send solar flares out into space. Flares can go out a million miles. Our Sun is one big hot gassy ball!

> **What is our Sun made of?**
> - sphere of gases
> - mostly hydrogen
> - core - a nuclear furnace
> - explodes + sends solar flares a million miles out into space
> - surface - 100 million degrees

Then, have students select one of their questions and follow this process with their own nonfiction writing. With more experienced writers, use this model for developing sections of paragraphs under subheadings.

The Important Thing About … Many teachers use, *The Important Book* by M. Brown as a fine example of topic sentence, supporting details, and summary sentence. Read a few pages of this book, discussing how she constructed the paragraphs. Have students use this format to write a paragraph about a nonfiction topic they are studying. This connects well to other content areas. The example is from a space unit from science.

> **The Important Thing about Neptune**
>
> The important thing about Neptune is that it is blue with blue storm clouds. Methane gas in its atmosphere is what makes Neptune look blue. If you strike a match, stare at the flame. The methane gas, It's the same blue gas Neptune has in its atmosphere. Neptune is very far from the Sun. If you visited there, You'd freeze, But the important thing about Neptune is that it is blue.

Conferring

Children develop language through interaction, not action.
They learn to talk by talking to someone who responds.
They must therefore learn to write by writing to someone who responds.
—Mem Fox

Key Elements of Conferring:

- Word study: *Confer* (v.)
    con = together
    fer = to bring
- Bring ideas together in conversation
- Have a specific reason for a conference
- Discuss how the student is progressing
- Identify how the writer can improve

Writing Standard:

1. Habits and Processes. Students should:
   – extend and rework some pieces of writing;
   – routinely revise, edit, and proofread their work;
   – use criteria to self-evaluate their writing.

About Conferring ...

Writing conferences are a special time together for teachers and students as we work collaboratively to study a piece of writing. We talk *with* students—we converse. When we view conferring as a conversation, it shifts the focus of the conference session. It moves from the teacher telling students what they did wrong and how they should correct it, to a dialogue about what is working well, what needs changing, and what could make the writing better.

Doris Lessing said, "That is what learning is. You suddenly understand something you've understood all your life, but in a new way." One of the values of students conferring with a teacher is that we have years of life experience and knowledge of literature that we can use to help children see their writing in a new light.

One of the best pieces of advice we can give teachers is to become familiar with authors and many pieces of fine literature. The better we know the literature, the better we can help emerging writers notice during conferences how authors use particular strategies. Because I know Paulsen's style, I guided Jadra to look at how Paulsen used one-word sentences and repeated phrases in *Hatchet* and how that might be an effective strategy for her to use. During Jon's conference, we noted how Curtis used hyperbole in *The Watson's Go to Birmingham—1963*. What an interesting technique to use with one of his characters. We learn from the masters; we appreciate how fine writers write.

We view the conferring time of Writer's Workshop as an enjoyable and personal time with every child. It is a time that we assess each writer's growth and give individual instruction to raise the level of each student's writing. We cherish these special moments of listening, sharing, and learning.

Example of Conferring With a Young Author:

Transcription from a Revising Conference between Pam and Haley:

Mrs. W.: Tell me about your writing, Haley.

Haley: Well … I'm not sure how I want to end my story about the frozen watch.

Mrs. W.: I remember the beginning of this story, Haley. Your descriptive language is rich. One scene that stands out in my mind is when you show how silent it was outside in the snow. I can connect to that. I like, too, how you have suspense building up toward your ending.

What if we read the conclusion you've written so far? Does that sound like a plan?

Haley: Okay. (Haley begins reading several paragraphs before the place where she had stopped writing the day before. I notice the inflection in her voice.)

Mrs. W.: (After Haley has finished reading…) The way you read with expression tells me how much this story means to you. Let's get back to why you wanted this conference. What are you thinking you might do to end the story?

Haley: I guess my real problem is I have four different ways I could end this story, and I can't decide which one I like best.

Mrs. W.: This is a good problem to have! Tell me what endings you're considering.

Haley: There's one for *feelings, memory, decision,* and *a wish.* (Haley tells about each ending.) See, I like them all!

Mrs. W.: Ooh, what a hard decision this is going to be. All these endings work. I'm wondering if you've tried reading the whole story each time with one of your endings. (Haley shakes her head *no.*) What if you do that and listen to how your story sounds with each ending?

Haley: So, I go back and read the story first with the *feelings* ending, then read again with another ending? Okay, I'll try it. Thanks. (She collects her papers, settles down with a pillow in a corner of the room, and begins reading softly.)

How Do J Confer With Students?

A Conference is a Conversation. Carl Anderson likes to view conferences as conversations between writers. Talk with students about what good conversations entail—sharing a story, asking and giving advice, encouraging someone, talking about a common interest, thinking about something together, and so on. Establish the idea that all writing conferences are personal and constructive conversations.

Different Kinds of Writing Conferences. We can confer with young writers at any point during the writing process. What we say and do depends entirely on where students are in their writing and what they need. Before coming to a conference (except for Quick Check-ins), students should come prepared with a completed "Writing Conference Plan" (found at the end of this section). A "Publication Plan" should be completed for a Publishing Conference (found at the end of the Publishing section). Here are a few ideas for each stage:

- *Quick Check-in Conference*. If students have small detail questions, allow opportunities to answer them so they don't have to wait. You can do this at various times: before individual conferences, during a conference while a child is making notes or thinking through an idea, between conferences, and after conference time.

- *Prewriting Conference*. Help students find ideas or resources. Guide them to consider brainstorming, searching through their idea journal, perusing books, thinking quietly, noticing objects around the room, talking with a partner.

- *Drafting Conference*. Support children in getting their ideas down onto paper: talk about what they want to say, discuss the story elements, plan which writing crafts to apply.

- *Revising Conference*. Guide individuals to review their drafts to make them even better: identify areas to work on, decide if it all makes sense, add or expand something, take something out, divide it into sections or chapters, change a part or genre or point of view, use the senses to give clearer images, brainstorm more precise language and zoom in on an important part, and so forth.

- *Editing Conference*. Review the entire piece during this final conference before they write their final copy. Assist writers in learning how to edit their work: use editing strategies and checklists; notice how writers have used conventions in published works; review spelling, punctuation, capitalization and other conventions; guide them to organize their piece and use paragraphing.

- *Publishing Conference*. Have students present their "Publication Plan." Guide them to decide what publication ideas work best with their writing piece. If needed, direct students to return to their desks, and think through these ideas to revise their plan.

The Writing Conference Plan. The purpose of using a plan is to focus students' thinking on a specific area in the story that they want to talk about with you. The Think Sheet "Writing Conference Plan" (at the end of this section) is a concrete way to have students consider their writing and prepare for the conference. It places the responsibility on the student and helps keep the conference brief.

Model for students how to use the "Writing Conference Plan." Put a piece of writing on the overhead and read the page, thinking aloud to <u>show</u> how we select a particular part of the writing to take to a conference. Using the "Writing Conference Plan," demonstrate how we would write in a question we have. After completing the rest of the form, they're ready to meet with the teacher.

Students should come prepared to read aloud only the part of the story the conference is about, not the entire story. You may need to quickly peruse it to put the one section into context. Work together on one portion so that the conference is manageable and productive. Even though there may be a lot of parts that need attention, it is still important to concentrate on one section at a time.

However, sometimes the best laid plans … You may find that something else emerges that is more important to deal with than what they identified.

Simple Record Keeping. All teachers develop their own management system over time. I have tried several different ways of keeping track of students' progress, and I finally settled on this simple, but efficient tool suggested by Carl Anderson. The record sheet "Writing Conferences" is a grid with each student's name listed in a box. At the end of each conference, I date and list notes (in my own coded shorthand) about skills and crafts students are working on. It gives a clear overview of who has conferred and who needs to meet with me. At the end of the week, I analyze the pattern of needs that could lead me to work with an ad hoc group or reteach a craft skill to the whole class. It's simple and visual.

Writing Conferences	Mrs. Westkott	Week of 5/12 → 5/16	
Alex 5/13 - Check-in re: beginning Pub. plan. I'll take home 1 page story to get ready for conference.	**Alisa** 5/13 - updating + revising her "About the Author" piece for her book.	**Alison** 5/16 - Planting Seeds re: ideas for new story.	**Angelica** 5/12 Q✓in re: getting idea for next story. 5/13 → 16: webbing drafting.
Gina 5/14 - ✓notes re: Ppt 5/16 - worked on condensing info into bullets from sentences	**Cameron** 5/15: ✓in Clarification re: section of story he revised.	**Christopher** 5/14 - worked on developing plot 5/16 - follow-up: revising conf.	**Daniel** Absent 5/16 - planning for new story
Haley 5/12 - revising conference re: paragraphing Focus- transitions	**Jaclyn** 5/12 - J. sought help to imbed her characters' descriptions into story.	**Jadra** 5/14 - reviewed notes for Ppt 5/15 - began drafting piece for brochure	**James** 5/12 - James + Jos needed help finding website for research. 5/14 - Told to "get started" on draft
Jonathan 5/14 - final edit of Aurora Ppt. 5/15 + 5/16 - Practicing Ppt presentation	**Kelsey** 5/13 - poem "The Cat's Hat" final edit 5/14 Q✓in - Pub. ideas for poetry bk.	**Marc** ☺ Off to Disney World!	**Mariah** 5/13 - Brainstormed title ideas for her book.
Nanase 5/15 ✓in re: illustrations	**Nathan** 5/15 - found some new web-sites for research ✓in for approval to access + to bookmark them.	**Vicky** 5/13 - ✓in re: research for a new story. 5/14 - Story map + began drafting	**Joshua** 5/12 w/James researching Atlantic Ocean Needs to begin

Roles During Conference Time. Teachers and students have specific roles in a writing conference. Before the conference time begins, check the "Today's Writing Stages" chart to see who needs a conference.

What is My Role During Conference Time?	
Everyone's Role • Respect the student and teacher who are conferring • Use the "Ask 3 Before Me" Rule* • Expect a brief, 5–10-minute conference	
Teacher's Role in Conference	**Student's Role in Conference**
• Review student's "Writing Conference Plan" • Listen to the focus passage • Think about how to help the writer, not just the writing • Offer positive comments/connections • Ask questions and converse about the piece to help the child think more deeply • Provide a few (only a few!) instructional comments • Suggest a strategy or craft you've already taught. • Encourage the student to try something you suggested • Make notes and update records	• Come with completed "Writing Conference Plan" • Read the focus passage aloud • Share what you like about it • Identify what you want to work on together, if anything • Listen to the teacher's comments and suggestions • Think, plan, and return to your piece • Attempt to do something you learned in the conference

*Ask 3 Before Me Rule: Students follow the guideline of asking three other people or check resources before interrupting a writing conference.

Ask Open-Ended Questions. We all know that the way we question helps students to think more clearly. Keep the questions open-ended so that students have an opportunity to articulate their thoughts, rather than answer "yes" or "no." We model asking open-ended questions and find that children emulate them as they question their peers. Here are a few:

- What questions do you have about your writing?
- What's on your "Writing Conference Plan" that you want to talk about?
- Tell me about where you are in your writing.
- How do you feel it's going?
- What do you like about …?
- I like how you …
- Let's look at it another way.
- Which strategy could you use here?
- Explain what you have decided to do next.
- We can figure this out together.

- Thanks for permitting me to Read Like a Writer.

Specific Conference Strategies. There are many strategies that we utilize based on students' needs. While conferring, remind them, to use a strategy you have taught. Here are a few examples:

- *Getting Unstuck.* If children are stuck about what to write next, say, "Tell me about this part in your own words." Listen, then guide them to write those words onto paper. For some writers, you may need to script for them or list their ideas to get them unstuck.

- *Focus on One Technique.* Guide students to try one technique they have learned about the writing craft you have taught in a mini-lesson. Refer them to a particular book that illustrates how a writer used that technique. For example, "Remember how Jane Yolen wrote the sound of the owl in *Owl Moon*? '*Whoo-whoo-who-who-who-who-whooooooo.*' Let's look back in the book at exactly <u>how</u> she wrote that sound. See how she stretched out the sound with the added *o*'s? We can almost hear that owl call. Where could you add a sound word to let your readers feel like they are right there in the story? Write it in and decide how you want to spell it to <u>show</u> the sound to the reader."

- *Walk a Mile in Your Character's Shoes.* If we are able to put ourselves in someone else's shoes, we can understand them better. For students who have an underdeveloped character in their story, guide them to write what the character is feeling, thinking, and saying. Then, imagine what they would feel and think if they were that character. Consider the character as a friend and ask questions, then answer them. Refer them back to the Think Sheet "In My Character's Shoes" (at the end of the character section in this book) as a way for students to plan how a character looks, acts, thinks, and speaks.

- *Name That Strategy.* As you confer with students, call a strategy they are using by its name. This helps children make the connection between the mini-lessons you teach and the writing strategies they use.

- *Circle the Transitions.* Direct the student to circle the transitional words to indicate where changes are taking place in the story. Review how these words can mark where paragraphs begin: change of time, change of place, change of idea and change of speaker. If there are no or few transition words, some may need to be added to make smoother transitions. If there are transitions without new paragraphs, this can help guide them where to begin paragraphs.

- *Zoom in on One Spot.* Ask children to identify the important place that calls for the reader to slow down and read carefully. Imagine looking at that one spot in the writing through the lens of a camera and zoom in until it is very large and detailed. Next, write down every detail of what is happening in that one scene so that the reader can picture it through a mental camera lens.

- *Focus on the Five Senses*. Have students close their eyes and get a clear image of the setting or character or developing action. Listen to what was seen, heard, touched, tasted, and smelled. Some senses will be more prominent than others. Now, direct them to jot down some of these sensory ideas and incorporate them into the writing piece.

- *Show, Don't Tell*. One of the most important ways to help improve writing is to teach children to <u>show</u> the reader, rather than <u>tell</u>. Give a reminder about this strategy and listen to the student shift the word choice to give the reader a clearer depiction of the event. You might say, "You have said, 'The boy played with the dog,' but I can't quite see what they're doing together. Tell me in words so that you <u>show</u> me, not <u>tell</u> me. Then, I can see what you (the writer) have in your mind." With time, guidance, and practice, this may become their best revision strategy.

- *Brainstorm Together*. Brainstorm together some more precise language, especially those strong action verbs. Encourage them to use some of these words when writing.

- *Snap a Photograph*. If their stories ramble, ask students to point out the most exciting part. Have them close their eyes and take a mental photograph of that moment in the story and then describe that photograph to you. Ask, "Who is in the photo? Where does it take place? Look around you—what do you see? What is happening?" Now have them write it.

Have a Peer Conference—With Yourself. Nancie Atwell suggests this: Have students pretend that they are reading their own piece of writing for the first time. Their job is to approach it as if they were a peer editor. This fosters independence and helps them to be their own objective critics. Here's how they might proceed:

© Heather Ferraro

- Comment on something you like.
- Ask a question about something you don't understand or want to know more about.
- Ask yourself what you plan to do next. Then, do it.

Sticky Wonders. Direct individuals to switch papers with a partner. They can write a few questions about the story onto sticky notes. Then, have the writer elaborate on it.

Name _____ Date _____

Writing Conference Plan

Story: _____

Circle type of conference: Prewriting
                               Drafting
                               Revising
                               Final Editing

I'm prepared for a conference because I've:

_____ reread more than once

_____ identified a place in the writing that needs help

_____ self-edited

_____ numbered pages and put them in order

During the conference, I want to focus on: _____

_____

_____

_____

_____

_____

Teacher's Initials: _____

Revising

The secret of good writing is rewriting.
— Mem Fox

Key Elements of Revising:

- Word study: *Revise* (v.)
    re = again
    vis = to see
- Look at the text again and see it with new eyes.
- Honor a good piece. Change it and improve it.
- Explore new strategies.
- Participate in constructive discussions.

Writing Standards:

1. Habits and Processes. Students should:
    – generate their own topics and spend time refining their writing;
    – extend and rework some pieces of writing;
    – routinely revise, edit, and proofread their work; and
    – use criteria to self-evaluate their writing.

3. Language Use and Conventions:
    a. Style and Syntax
    - use their own language in writing
        – use a variety of syntactic patterns to show relationships of ideas (compound and complex sentences)
        – incorporate transitional words and phrases to show the reader a sense of time and place.
        – embed phrases and modifiers that make their writing lively and graphic
    - take on the language of authors
        – vary sentence patterns and lengths to create rhythm, slow down or speed up a piece, and create a mood
        – embed literary language where appropriate
        – emulate sentence structures from various genres
    b. Vocabulary and Word Choice. Students should:
    - use words from their speaking vocabulary and from reading and class discussions;
    - use precise and vivid words; and
    - take on the language of authors by using specialized words related to a topic.

About Revising ...

We agree with Ralph Fletcher's description: "Revision is more than just a way to fix a broken piece of writing. It's also a way to honor a good piece and make it even better" (http://www.ralphfletcher.com). But, it's hard work. And it's often not fun. But, the end result of a better piece is worth our hard work. Revising is self-evaluation in action. With a positive attitude and a willingness to model, we strive to <u>develop the writer, not just one piece of writing</u>. We nudge their thinking with comments and questions so they will reach for their own answers. This is the stage where we listen; listen hard to their stories, their concerns, their questions.

Last year, I took one of my short stories into Pam's class to model a revising conference. Using the "Writing Conference Plan," I identified the section of the piece to work on. I read the story aloud and pointed out my concern that the high point didn't show the readers a clear picture. They listened, thought about it, and Alex suggested that we dramatize the scene so we could "see" it. We did, and then we brainstormed how I might develop this part more fully by zooming in on this moment.

I thanked them for their help and started to sit down. Julia said, "Ms. Johnson, I hope you're not planning to send that story for publication yet. No one will take it with that sad ending. Everyone wants to read a happy ending." Every head in the room nodded in agreement. The group made several suggestions of how to change the ending. Prompted by their astute comments, I went straight over to my laptop and spent the next 30 minutes of Writer's Workshop revising my story while they revised theirs. At the end of class, I reread my story aloud with many of their ideas embedded, and they cheered. This story was done (including a happy ending!)—with the approval of 20 third graders. It was hard work. But, the story was improved and, more important, I grew as a writer.

I learn each day the importance of living what we teach and being willing listen, to try new ideas, and explore a different way of looking at a story. Isn't this just what we want our students to do? We allow a lot of time to play with the story through the revision stage, give students much feedback and encouragement, and enjoy making a good piece better.

An Author's Thoughts About Revising:

Marcia Thornton Jones of *The Bailey School Kids* series from a personal interview:

> Real writing happens during the revision stage. That's when words, sentences, ideas, style, and voice are carefully crafted together into a cohesive and expressive whole.

> I don't necessarily wait until a draft is finished to start revising. I find that the honing, chiseling, and molding of revision occurs quite naturally throughout all stages of the writing process. For example, when Debbie Dadey and I coauthor a book for one of the several series we write, we take turns writing chapters. We call it "hot-potato" writing. Once a few chapters are drafted, I e-mail them to Debbie. Debbie reads what I've written before writing the next few chapters. As she reads my chapters she invariably finds something I've written that she wants to change. The same happens when I read the chapters she writes. I start from the beginning of the story and read it through. Sure enough, I find areas that need work. Maybe something she's

written sparks my muse and I elaborate upon what she's written. Sometimes she cuts wordy passages of mine. Then there are times we try to make a passage more humorous or suspenseful through dialogue, action, or sentence structure. Back and forth the story is sent. With each chapter written, more revising happens. By the time we "hot-potato" that story back and forth, it has been revised anywhere between six and ten times.

A more daunting job of revision comes after the story has been sent to an editor. When an editor responds with a request for revisions it sometimes seems like an impossible job. To make the revisions more accessible, I organize the editor's major suggestions on a revision chart. I start by listing the positives. After all, I want to build on what I've done well. Next, I list the areas for improvement and suggestions made by the editors. Once I've made sense of their suggestions, I brainstorm possible ideas for implementing the revision.

I have learned that good revising makes my stories and my writing much better.

How Do I Teach *Revising*?

Word Study: *Revise*

Check out the dictionary to fully understand the word *revise*.

- *re* means "again" and *vis* means "see"
- to look again
- to come to different conclusions about something after thinking again
- to amend a text in order to correct it, update it, or improve it

Discuss with students that revising is what writers do. Look at the piece of writing again and see what we like about it and if there are changes we can make to improve it.

Revising vs. Editing. It's important to distinguish between these two stages of writing. We place importance first on the <u>way</u> students communicate their ideas through the Revising Stage. In this stage, they apply what they learn through all the mini-lessons you teach on strategy and writing craft. In this stage, they develop, not just compose. In contrast, the Editing stage focuses on correcting errors of conventions in our language. Good writers work through both stages, often many times.

Revising	Editing
• reread the writing	• reread the writing
• look again at the content and improve how you say something	• correct errors in capitalization, punctuation, spelling, grammar, and paragraphing to make the writing clearer

Sticky Notes Revising. We wish we had bought stock in this company based on the number of sticky note pads we use throughout a school year—all colors and sizes. There are various ways to use sticky notes, and you may devise the system that works best in your classroom. Here are a few ways we have found successful:

- Teachers always use the same color and size (different from what students use). That way, it's always clear which note is from us.
- Teachers or peer editors mark the places with questions and comments that children need to revisit. They always include something positive!
- Students stick questions on their own writing for a revising conference.

My third-grade writers use sticky notes when they exchange papers with a partner. Both read and notice what and how the writing is communicating. Kelsey began with a positive on Angelica's first page, "Great grabber!!!" Student writers are getting regular feedback from very special critics—their peers.

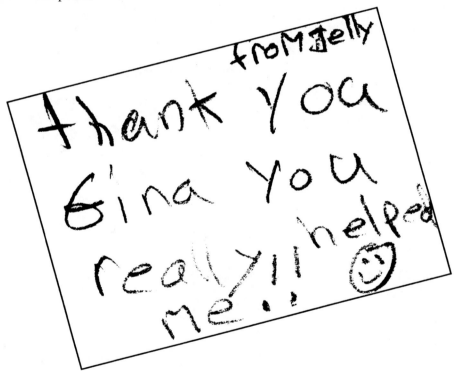

Wait Awhile to Reread Their Own Writing. Our goal is for children to become objective and independent readers of their own writing. They will eventually learn to revise by themselves and not rely on the teacher or a partner to "tell them what to do."

Advise students to let some time pass between the end of the writing and when they pick it up again to reread. The temporal distance can provide objectivity and the ability to read with renewed interest. Have students pretend that they are reading it for the first time.

Author's Chair Revising. One of the reasons student writers come to the Author's Chair is to seek help revising a piece of their writing. This is a rich segment of our writing program.

I find that children astute-ly notice holes in the writ-ing and gently offer a suggestion to help a friend reconsider something. They see my modeling and try it themselves. Student writers value what their friends have to say. They also know that any comment may be rejected since the final decision will be their own. Everyone's writing is hon-ored when we take our turn in the Author's Chair. This is the sharing process we follow:

Writer	Audience
• Plan to be ready. Tell what the writing piece is about and what they need help on. Read that part aloud.	• Look at and listen to the writer.
• Listen to comments and make notes, if needed.	• Tell first what they like, then offer a comment or suggestion that may help.
• Thank everyone for listening and helping.	• Applaud at the end.
• Decide which suggestions may work and revise it to make the story stronger	

Show Some Revision Strategies. Here are a few ways to focus students' revising and build up a repertoire of strategies as they become independent writers.

- *Color Code*. Have students use a single color to underline one particular element to see the balance throughout the piece. For example, underline the action. It shows visually where the action is—and is not! Sometimes, children have nothing under-lined and it tells them they need to add something.

- *Add an Asterisk*. Show children how to use an asterisk to add a section to the writ-ing. Put an asterisk in the piece to mark where additional writing needs to go. They can write elsewhere (in a margin, on another page, etc.) what they will add and signal it with an asterisk. For several additions, students may use color or other symbols to match where each addition goes.

- *Cut and Tape*. Slice up a part of the text and tape it to change the order of events or to add in more writing.

- *Grow Spider Legs*. Have student writers cut out words or sentences and tape them onto the main story at the place where they would be added. They may dangle over the edge of the page and look like its description—the legs of a spider. Some students will get carried away with this process and enjoy the playfulness of it. But, meanwhile, the text changes and develops. However, one problem with spider legs is that sometimes the "legs" fall off.

Is It Finished Yet? How do we know if the writing piece is completed? Do the words "The End" make it done? Distribute the Think Sheet "Revising Checklist" (at the end of this section) for students to use as a final review.

Simple Math: Add, Subtract, Divide, and Change. At his Web site, Ralph Fletcher presents a clever system of thinking about revision. We've adapted and added to it. Ask students to consider these options:

Add:
- something to make the writing clearer
- a description to help readers get a picture in their minds
- more information to explain a nonfiction piece better
- another character to balance the story
- transitional phrases to move from one setting or time to another

Subtract:
- a part that doesn't move the story
- a secondary character who doesn't add anything to the piece
- extraneous transitions

Divide:
- large sections into chapters
- nonfiction into subheadings
- a large paragraph into two

Change:
- *Lead*—Have students explore a different way of beginning the piece. They may ask themselves which lead works best and then use it.
- *Endings*—Consider the other types of endings, such as surprise, circular, conclusion/summary, personal reflection, final wonder, and others.
- *Verb Tense*—If it's written in past tense, consider changing it to present. Or present to past.
- *POV*—If it's written in first person point of view, think about changing it to third person. Or third person to first person.
- *Genre*—Use a different form to write a piece: poetry, letter, diary, factual fiction (combination of fact and fiction), picture book, alphabet book, newsletter, and others.

were pretty very pretty ~~Amy~~ out the
in her pocket. Later they got tired. The
Jennifer
Amy remembered that
their moms packed them sandwiches to Jen
Jennifer's When
her nick name, and Amy came by a rode
picnic
pick nick table they eat down
and feed their horses and aet their san
wichs. Tony and Amy rode on. They car
in a tall tree. and Ten was right

pebbles. then
and Hungry and
rode

Name _____ Date _____

Revising Checklist

_____ I wrote a catchy beginning.

_____ I started the sentences in different ways.

_____ I varied the sentence structure.

_____ I developed 1 or 2 strong characters.

_____ I zoomed in on a main event.

_____ I used precise words to *show* what I wanted to say.

_____ I wrote an extended ending.

Editing

Be lavish and abundant with your words.
Let yourself go in first drafts and learn to come back
to your writing with a calmer, more careful editing eye.
—Naomi Nye

Key Elements of Editing:

- Word study: *Editing*
  - to prepare for publication by correcting errors
  - to ensure clarity
- Proofread their own writing
  - first, read to listen to the sound of it
  - second, reread to identify and correct errors
  - third, read a final time with the changes

Writing Standards:

1. Habits and Processes. Students should:
   – routinely revise, edit, and proofread their work; and
   – use criteria to self-evaluate their writing
3. Language Use and Conventions:
   c. Spelling. Students Should:
   - notice when words do not look correct and use strategies to correct the spelling,
   - correctly spell familiar high-frequency words and wall words,
   - correctly spell words with short vowels and common endings,
   - correctly spell most inflectional endings, including plurals and verb tenses,
   - use correct spelling patterns and rules (e.g., silent *e*, changing *y* to *i*, consonant doubling), and
   - correctly spell most derivational words (e.g., adding word affixes, such as *–tion, -ment, -ing*).
   d. Punctuation, Capitalization, and Other Conventions. Students should:
   - use capital letters at the beginning of sentences,
   - use periods, question marks, and other end punctuation most all the time,
   - begin to use quotation marks,
   - use capital and lowercase letters properly,
   - use contractions.

About Editing ...

Writing and editing their own work is really the way children learn, not in isolation doing worksheets. After modeling how to edit and then practicing together, we expect children to edit independently. By the end of the year, we see that it has become a natural process: Many children are editing while they draft and revise. Eventually, there are fewer edits during the editing phase. Students are required to come to the final editing conference with their pieces edited by themselves and by a peer. Some are embarrassed when they notice errors they have overlooked and say, "I can't believe I missed that period." We see how proud they are of their editing skills and of the way their final writing looks, reads, and communicates. They are writers!

When we reach the end of a piece, we want it to look its best if it is to be published. We do lots of modeling on the overhead to show how writers use special editing strategies and editor's marks. These special marks can guide us to see where changes are needed for capitalization, punctuation, spelling, grammar, and paragraphing. Students learn what drafts look like when they are filled with editor's marks and how these final changes can improve the clarity of the writing for the reader.

Before I send a book to Libby, my Prufrock editor, I have tried to edit it the best I can by myself. But, when the book is published, I want it to be as perfect as possible, and I welcome any final judgments from Libby. I don't want any errors in the final publication. So, I tell students that I will become their final editor <u>after</u> they have made their best efforts at editing. Together, the student writer and I will correct any errors before the formal publication. This is how it works in the real publishing world.

However, not all of their publications need this careful editing. It depends on our purpose and where students are in their writing development. Sometimes, particularly in the primary grades, it's fine to informally publish their stories with their wonderful invented spelling included. We can celebrate their writing as it is at that point in time, and it becomes a record of their growth and development as a writer throughout the year. Some teachers, however, may feel differently about this issue and want to ensure that all conventions are correct. Decide what is important to you and define these expectations for your students. The writing will grow increasingly sophisticated throughout the year as they develop as editors.

An Author's Thoughts About Editing:

From a personal interview with writer Jerrie Oughton:

> Editing—that last fateful step in the process before you turn *in* your story to a teacher or turn *over* your story to an editor. Last chance.

> Actually, editing can be layered. It may consist of several "fateful steps." To edit, I have to take a break, however small, away from the manuscript. When I re-enter the world of story for this last phase, I want to do so as a reader. In becoming the reader, I can spot where the story sags, is stagnant, is full of unnecessary side-trips.

> If at all possible, I also get someone I trust to read the manuscript. All comments by this person, this "objective reader," are not necessarily on target. But, I listen hard to each one and use what I deem worthy. What fits my vision of the story.

Finally, the last step in editing, the closing of the door, is hard. It's a farewell. I'm no good at goodbyes. I stand on the porch and wave and blow kisses. When I put my book in the mail, I stand outside the post office and wish it well. "Goodbye, little book. Go, do, and be and become," I say. I dream about it. I gradually separate from that piece of myself I sent out into the world and turn to my next story … which I don't fall in love with right away. That comes in time.

How Do J Teach Editing?

> ### Word Study: *Edit*
>
> Webster defines *edit as:*
>
> - to prepare for publication or presentation by correcting errors, ensuring clarity, and ensuring accuracy;
> - to cut and arrange, deciding on a final order; and
> - to remove material because it is lengthy.
>
> And, the thesaurus says:
>
> - prepare for publication;
> - correct, tidy up, check over; and
> - change, alter.
>
> Discuss the meanings with students in the framework of this final editing stage—the proofreading and correcting stage—before the writing is published.

Review Five Conventions. The editing stage focuses on the standardized conventions of our language. Have students focus their final proofreading on:

- *Capitalizing.* Titles, proper nouns
- *Punctuating.* Sentences, phrases, dialogue, possession, for emphasis
- *Spelling.* Check word wall words and personal dictionaries
- *Grammar.* Use correct and varied sentence structure.
- *Paragraphing.* Change of speaker, time, place, or topic.

Have the "Editing Checklist" (at the end of this section) available to guide students through the editing process.

For emerging writers, review and practice editing one or two conventions at a time so they don't get overwhelmed and confused. Notice when your experienced writers start to merge the stages as they are drafting. This indicates their level of advanced achievement.

Edit for Spelling. We don't expect all words to be spelled correctly on every writing piece. We hope to see growth over time. Because spelling is a major component of editing, we have certain strategies that students find helpful. Scaffold their writing development so they will become better spellers for life, not simply memorize lists of words. Guide students to:

- use what they already know, such as word families and plurals;
- chunk out sounds by breaking words into manageable parts;
- check high frequency Word Wall words;
- add words that they may use often to their personal dictionary;
- practice spelling words they use frequently so that words can become automatic;
- use what they know about prefixes, suffixes, and root words;
- circle words in their writing they think look wrong;
- check with a neighbor about the correct spelling;
- use dictionaries with a group of classmates to divide a lengthy task; and
- be patient with themselves and know they will improve little by little each week.

Read it Backward. Although this is a slow process, reading a section of writing from end to beginning, word by word, can allow students to concentrate on correct spelling. Our eyes are not reading what we think it should say in context because we are focused only on separate words. Consider having students proofread their writing or peer writing backwards for a specific section.

Use Editor's Marks. Editor's marks are shortcuts that make the editing process easier and faster. They show exactly where the errors are and indicate what needs to be corrected. Distribute the Think Sheet "Editor's Marks" (at the end of this section). Put on a transparency a piece of writing that needs some editing. Explain how you read through a piece and use these marks to indicate where change is needed.

Give students a piece of writing to edit using editor's marks. Have them practice editing, then check it together. They will begin to use these marks on their own pieces and as they edit.

Punctuation Marks Chart. Post a class chart of "Punctuation Marks" as a reminder of punctuation that writers use. Point to particular errors students have made, then reference the chart to guide them nonverbally.

Punctuation Marks	
period	.
comma	,
question mark	?
exclamation point	!
hyphen	–
parentheses	( )
quotation marks	" "
colon	:
apostrophe	'
underline	____

Three-Color Coding. Select three colors of markers for editors to use throughout the year. Assign one color to the student authors for use in self-editing. Give a second color to peer editors and a third for teachers. Be consistent with these designated colors throughout the year so you can tell on every draft who made the editor's marks and corrections. We avoid using the "red" pen

© Heather Ferraro

because of long-entrenched negative connotations. (Egad! Remember those high school English papers that were riddled with red marks, glaring at us to show how badly we wrote?)

Last Chance: Editing 1-2-3. Have students read their piece the first time to listen to how it sounds. The second read should be slow and careful to identify and correct errors. The third and final read, their last chance, is to appreciate the clarity and accuracy they have achieved through their careful editing.

Editing Checklist

_____ I proofread my piece first, then reread to edit it.

_____ I began sentences with CAPITAL letters.

_____ I ended sentences with: . ! ? or ".

_____ I spelled Word Wall words correctly.

_____ I began the sentences in various ways.

_____ I indented new paragraphs to change speaker, time, place, or topic.

_____ I left spaces between my words.

_____ My final copy is neat.

Editor's Marks

Mark	Error it Shows	Example
≡	Capitalize	going to rhode island
/	Make lower case	big Dogs
˅ or /\	Insert punctuation	I like Lynne's apples, pears and peaches
^	Insert a letter or text	It was ruby red.
✗	Remove letters or text	the big barn door
⬭	Correct the spelling	Mt. Rushmore (Rushmoore)
¶	Begin new paragraph	¶The next day he rode the horse.
↶	Move where shown	She went home later
∽	Reverse letters or text	third
⌣	Close a space	book case

Publishing

Be dazzled by their writing.
——Lucy Calkins

Key Elements of Publishing:

- Word study: *publish*
  - to make public
  - to announce

Writing Standards:

1. Habits and Processes. Students should:
   - polish about one piece a month for an audience in and beyond the classroom; and
   - use criteria to self-evaluate their writing.

About Publishing ...

I still remember the day in sixth grade that my first poem was published. It appeared in the West Broadway School Newsletter. A teacher stopped me in the hall and said, "Kay, I read your lovely poem. I didn't know that you were so poetic." I had no idea what the word *poetic* meant, but I knew from her smile and tone that it was something good. I was elated and eager to write another poem. Enthusiasm, motivation, and pride are a few of the benefits that publishing student work can accomplish.

There are countless ways to publish text. Students can be actively involved in designing and creating ways to present their writing using all of their multiple intelligences. We view publishing as an integral part of the writing process, not just a compilation at the end.

When students become more aware of various publishing possibilities, they may plan *before* they begin writing because it may help them in the development of the book. As they notice the size, shape, and structure of books, they can emulate these to create their own masterpieces. The publishing process can be a motivating experience and may lead to richer writing, carefully planned books, and a real celebration of writing.

Not all writing that students do will be published. It's expected that they will begin many stories that will remain in rough draft. They will choose from their body of work a few pieces to carry through the entire publishing process.

Finished books are displayed in the classroom all year. Children frequently read each other's books during silent sustained reading time. At the end of the year, their books are placed in their portfolios and taken home. When I was teaching in primary grades, we created so many class books (with each student contributing one page of writing and illustration) that the last day of school, I let each student select and keep one. They not only had a sample of their own writing, but stories by their classmates. Some of these students tell me what it means to them when they read through that book years later. I can hear in their voices the sense of pride they still feel about their published writing.

An Author/Illustrator's Thoughts About Publishing:

From a personal interview with writer and illustrator Paul Brett Johnson:

> Have you ever anxiously waited for a notice to arrive in the mail, and when it finally does, you're afraid to open it? You're hoping for good news, but you're afraid it might be bad news? That's exactly how I feel when I get my first copy of a newly published picture book. By now, it will have been about a year since I put the last dab of paint on the final illustration for the book and sent it to my publisher. During that time, the publisher has gone about the slow business of printing the pages and otherwise putting the book together. Along the way they have sent me proof sheets, so I have an idea of how the words and images are going to work together. But, I am never quite prepared for the final transformation.
>
> The book is something less and something more than its parts. When I first hold that new book in my hands and open it and pour over each spread, I feel somehow let down. The pictures aren't quite as vivid as I remembered them, or I'm not quite sure of the pacing. Should I have done this or that differently? But, then I tell myself to quit fretting. It's only a book.
>
> Even so, I can't help carrying the book around with me. For the next few days, I eat breakfast with it. I keep it beside me on my desk. I even place it on my nightstand, taking yet another look before I turn out the light.
>
> Without knowing exactly when or how, I become in awe of my new book. I realize that these mere pictures and words have been brought together in a way that has yielded something entirely new—something with a life of its own. It may now be held and read by thousands of other people. It may even make a difference to some of them, this book. My book.

How Do I Teach Publishing?

Word Study: *Publish*

The dictionary tell us that *publish* means:

- to announce something publicly

This definition applies to our process in various ways. Talk about how we share our work with other people (the public). We bind our stories into individual or class books, create class newsletters, develop PowerPoint presentations, and read our work aloud.

Set up a Publishing Center. Establish a designated area that houses everything needed for publishing. Include:

- Wallpaper books (discontinued ones are free from many paint shops)
- Colorful fabric pieces, felt, lace, leather scraps
- Paper—white and colored, card stock, wrapping paper, construction paper
- Pencils, crayons, colored pencils, pastels, paints, markers, paint brushes
- Tape, clear and colored
- Glue, paste, and brushes for pasting
- Tag board and mat board (free pieces from many frame shops)
- Long-arm stapler and regular staplers, colored staples
- Paper cutter (we prefer a rotary trim kind for safety)
- Rulers
- Scissors
- Hole punch (three-hole and single)
- Muffin tins (old) or Styrofoam meat trays for paint
- Yarn, string, ribbon, and twine
- Metal ring fastener and brads
- Magazines (for cutting out collage pictures)
- Coloring books with large, simple pictures to use as templates for shape books
- Envelopes, all sizes (free from many drug stores after special holidays)
- Book-binding machine and plastic bindings (if you're lucky, your school will have one, but it's not necessary)

About the Author. Every book has a section that tells about the author and illustrator. When our students publish their texts, they, too, will write an autobiographical sketch. First go to the literature and notice the "About the Author" passage on book flaps. Discuss what interesting information is included.

Have students emulate writing an "All About the Author" blurb for their own books. We have the children type it on the computer and add a digital picture of themselves for their first publication. Students print out a copy for their book and always have it on file for each additional publication throughout the year, updating it as needed.

The same procedure can be used for publishing class books. Designate students to compose the blurb about their class as a whole. Include a group photograph.

Make a Publication Plan. Help students think through the process about how to

Alison was born on January 3rd, 1994. She was born in Rhode Island. Alison lives with her mom, her dad and a sister named Kristin. Alison is eight and her sister is thirteen years old. She has fifteen pets. Alison likes cats and bunnies, because she thinks they're cute. She loves ANIMALS, any kind of animal except spiders. Alison hates spiders because they are really gross!! One day there was a HUGE spider in her room. She might even write that spider story some day. Alison loves to write stories about friends, animals and her trip to Ireland.

© Heather Ferraro

publish their text. Model how to use the "Publication Plan" (at end of this section). This form states expectations and provides choices for students to consider. It informs them if they need to revise or commence publishing. Demonstrate your ideas on a transparency as you walk them through the process of completing the plan.

What Do Published Books Look Like? It's easy to assume that, since students have read so many books, they know what to include in their publications. But, they may not. Guide students to observe how published books look and what they can include in their finished manuscripts, such as:

- Cover
- About the Author (on the flap)
- Book Summary (on the flap or back cover)
- Title Page, Publishing Company and City (Make one up! Get creative!)
- Copyright Page
- Dedications
- Illustrations
- Table of Contents
- Other features students notice and want to include

The Elements of Illustration. Have you ever been disappointed with the illustrations your students created for their stories? We certainly have. Even though students basically know how to draw, they still need guidance to raise the level of their illustrating. Go to the literature and select the finest examples of illustrated books. You could use books that received the Caldecott Awards, which are given each year to the artists for the most distinguished American picture books.

When we study the effectiveness of these illustrations, we bring in lots of examples and have students notice the following elements:

- *Match*—Does the picture go with the words? Does it enhance what the text says?

- *Color*—Is it bold? Pastel? Primary colors? Black and white? Dark? Light? What mood does the color create?

- *Medium*—What materials did the author use to convey a message? (watercolor, oil, collage, pencil, pen and ink, photographs, etc.)

- *Detail*—Does it show a lot of specific information or just give a hint or suggestion? Both can be desirable, depending on the book.

- *Size*—How large or small are the illustrations?

- *Placement*—Where on the page is the illustration located? Where do the words go? Is there a border?

- *Style*—What distinguishes this artist's pictures from other illustrators? (e.g., Jan Brett is famous for her intricate borders that often give a glimpse into what will happen on the next page.)

Illustrating Original Books. Most of us are not artists but we can help children to "Illustrate Like an Illustrator." We can help students become aware of the elements of illustration and how artists use them in their books. Set high expectations and scaffold their development.

Informally evaluate how your students illustrate. Notice what they do well. Determine what needs improving. For example: Do you still have students who put a little strip of blue sky, a straight line of brown ground with a few rudimentary figures and the rest of the page is white? Take them outside to observe what they see—a horizon line. It looks like the sky touches the ground or the trees. There is no white separating the blue sky from the ground (unless there is cloud cover). Have them apply their observations to their illustrations.

Send students on a hunt to find one book with illustrations they like. In a class discussion have students share their books and explain what appeals to them about the illustrations. Does this overview help them think about possibilities for their own books?

Encourage your students to use some various styles of illustrating throughout the year, emulating illustrators they like. Guide them to notice if their pictures match their words and revise the text to fit their illustrations. Post a class chart as a reminder.

How Do I Illustrate My Book?

- Consider illustration elements:
  - color   – size
  - medium   – placement
  - detail   – style
- Explore, experiment, and play with design
- Match the illustrations to the words
- Present in a professional way

Model After Published Books. Many of our ideas for creating class books come directly from the literature. Published books trigger our thinking. Have students notice specific formats, such as shape books, pop-up books, alphabet books, and so forth. Have students decide on a model and tailor it to showcase their content. Alphabet books can be used for any grade to research at least 26 subtopics about a subject. The following example is from Mrs. Cushman's fourth-grade class during a study of Land and Water. Each letter included an illustration and descriptive paragraph, such as C - canyon, I - iceberg, S - stream.

Emulate an Author. My son, Cliff, read every *Redwall* book and began to write a similar series called *Hawk Island*. He created original characters, but used some elements that Jacques did. A classmate added small square pencil illustrations at the beginning of each chapter, just like in the original books. Emulating Brian Jacques was a wonderful writing experience and raised his level of writing.

Direct students who are interested in a particular author, book or series to note some of the features they like, such as characters, maps, dialect, time period, location, and so forth. Then, guide them to use some of those features in writing an original story.

Across the Curriculum. Expand children's writing beyond language arts. There are wonderful books to be written on science, social studies and math. Here are some examples:

Science

- Poetry book about life cycles of the Monarch butterflies
- How-to book on (individual topics)
- Box book on the desert biome
- Advice column in a newsletter, "Protecting Our Earth From Pollution"
- Sphere book, *On Planet XXX*, that include research on planets
- Poetry book, *Space Songs*
- Class book on original inventions with labeled diagrams
- PowerPoint research project on a space topic

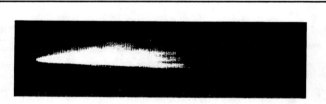

PowerPoint Slide

Social Studies

- Journal of Columbus' voyage from the first-person perspective of a crew member, such as *Gomez's Log, 1492*
- Question and answer book on (individual topics)
- Timeline biographies of famous people
- Pop-up book of jobs during the American Revolution (e.g., candle maker, cooper, tailor)
- Dictionary of Narragansett Indian words
- Book of *Letters to Ruby Bridges* (copies, since the originals were sent to Ms. Bridges)
- Class book of *Our Recipes for Peace*
- History book of our town, *Narragansett Yesterday and Today*
- Tri-fold marketing brochure, *Welcome to Narragansett*
- A Web page about our town
- Bio poems of historical figures
- Book jacket of a biographical subject

Math

- Story problem book of questions and answers based on the book *Math Curse*
- Dictionary of geometry terms
- Alphabet book of mathematical terms
- Retelling of *The Doorbell Rang* with a focus on fractions
- Class story problem book on space, *Multiplication Is Out of This World*

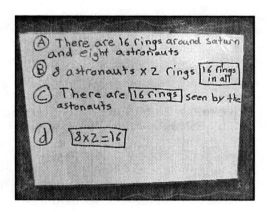

Newsletter Lunch Sessions. Do you feel pressed for time when producing a newsletter with your class? Robin Phillips and Cindy Kneller solved this problem by having a "working lunch" with the reporters for each newsletter. Select a few students to write specific articles, such as what they are studying, special events and assemblies, and so forth. Others can take digital photographs and collect samples of student writing. Work together for one or two lunch periods to write, share, and support each other as your "Literary Staff" create a newsletter together.

Book II: The Sequel. Sequels and prequels are ready-made story ideas. Discuss with students how an author continues characters and plot in subsequent stories. Linda Rezendes' second graders became interested in the Dr. De Soto books through an author study of William Steig. They asked (actually, begged) to spend the next few weeks writing Dr. De Soto sequels. The children maintained the integrity of the original characters, the mouse dentist and his wife, but devised clever plot twists (such as having a jack-o-lantern come to Dr. De Soto with a cavity on Halloween evening). William Steig would have been proud! We certainly were. Guide students who are interested in this idea to select a book they want to continue and create a sequel. Have them jot down the traits of the character they plan to use in their book. They could add a new character, change the setting (or keep it), and, of course, develop a new plot.

A Few Kinds of Publication Structures and Bindings

- *Shape Books*—Endless possibilities here! The entire book can be a shape, including the pages, or just the front and back cover can be a shape.

- *Books With Graduated Pages*—Many marketing brochures use this model because the reader can locate information easily. They have overlapping pages that show the tabs to label the sections, similar to thumb-indexed address books. Paper can be cut or folded to create these simple, but effective books.

- *Magazines and Newsletters*—Both are excellent venues for including all students' writing to cover multiple genres and strengthen the home/school connection.

- *Mobile Book Summaries*—Books dangling from the ceiling! Pages hang in a vertical line with text on one side and illustrations on the other. We usually have a circle-shaped page for each story element—character, plot, etc.

- *Pop-Up Books*—Pop-ups are simple to create and they look sophisticated as a character jumps to life, surprising the reader as each page is turned. Understandably, these are favorites for children to make.

Electronic Publication of Research Project. We use Microsoft's PowerPoint program for students to create slides for a presentation. Children use technology to showcase their learning in contrast to a written research report. Scaffolding is essential to guide students through the research process and develop the presentations. Host a PowerPoint family night for students to showcase their remarkable electronic publications. See the template "PowerPoint Plan" (at the end of this section) to show how we organize the Space Research Project.

Reader Responses. What could be more gratifying for children than publishing a book? Having their peers tell them what they like about it! Develop a Reader

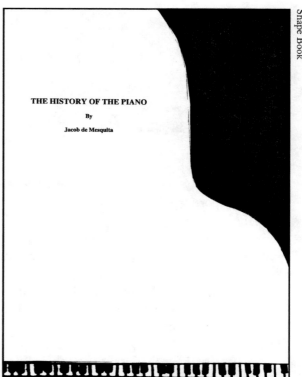

Shape Book

THE HISTORY OF THE PIANO

By

Jacob de Mesquita

Comment Form to put in the back of each student's original book. Everyone who reads it has the opportunity to give a positive comment to the author. Include Title, Author, Reader's Name, and Comment section. This will be cherished and read for years to come.

Pop-up Book

VIP Book. Throughout the year, we celebrate each individual in the class as a part of building citizenship and community. A favorite event is the Very Important Person Week, which focuses on one class member. The randomly selected VIP for the week fills a bulletin board and table with pictures and memorabilia he wants to share with the class. We videotape the presentation so the family has a permanent record. Afterward, each student writes a letter with an illustration to the VIP. These letters are bound into a class book.

Model how to write a friendly letter to someone. Tell a few special things you like about that person or share a story about something you did together that has special meaning. Have students follow this process when they write to each person in the class. This will be a prized possession.

End-of-the-Year Class Books. My boys still read the Class Books they wrote in first grade. And they love reading their friends' stories, as well as their own. It is such a treasure for them to have samples of writing from all class members who worked collaboratively throughout the year in a writing community.

Let students choose one sample of their writing to include in an End-of-the-Year Class Book. Create a Table of Contents with the title and author of each story. Make copies of the entire book to give to each student as a memento of their writing journey in your classroom. It will always be remembered and so will you!

Dear Dan, I love your cats Vaca and Michae. I liked the pickcher that you took of Vaca where Vaca wa sitting in a basket looking at something that was very cute. You

Name _____   Date _____

Publication Plan

Author: _____   Date: _____

Title: _____
TEXT
handwritten: _____   word processed: _____
BINDING
spiral _____   sewn _____   rings _____   other _____
SHAPE
rectangle _____   3-D _____   other _____
Plan completed before teacher conference _____
Revisions needed   _____
Teacher's approval   _____

Front Cover Design: Draw a thumbnail sketch	Include:
	Title Author Illustrator Illustration "About the Author" page printed and inserted ___ Book summary written for back cover _____

Title Page Design	Include:
	Title
	Author
	Illustrator
	Illustration
	Copyright Date
	Publisher
	City

Design of One Page in Book	Include:
	Sketch of Text Placement and Illustration

PowerPoint Plan

Power Point
Space Research Project

Directions:

1. Name new file & save in your folder.
2. Name & save pictures as jpg. files.
3. Write all text on slides before customizing (pictures, sound, animation, transitions)
4. Follow the guidelines to help you develop each slide

Slide 1 - Title

Title of Space Topic

Strategies for Titles:

alliteration - *Sensational Saturn*,
announce it - *The Last Planet*,
play on words - *The Hothouse Venus*), etc.

Image _____.jpg

Your Name
Date

Slide 2 - Opening

Opening grabber: _____
Location of planet: _____
Compare to Earth:
  Year? Revolution (trip around Sun)
  Day? Rotation (one spin on its axis)
Who discovered it?
Have we "visited" it? If yes, tell how.
Insert image saved as _____.jpg.

Slide 3 - Focus Question

Write your focus question.

What is it (topic) like? Describe it.
  Size (compare to what we know: Earth or other planets):
  Diameter
  Surface
  Atmosphere
  Gravity. How much would you weigh there?
  Moons? How many?
Image: Draw it on 4 X 6 paper & scan it. Insert here.

Slide 4 - Special Facts

Best known for . . .

_____
_____
_____

Insert picture saved as _____.jpg.

Slide 5 - Image Collage

Insert several images saved as

_____.jpg.
_____.jpg.
_____.jpg.
_____.jpg.

Share your feelings about the topic while
presenting the pictures in this slide.

Slide 6 - Grand Finale!

Choose how you want to end the presentation.
You could:
  • summarize what you learned
  • end with a question you still wonder about
Write what you decided: _____
_____
Insert picture saved as _____.jpg.
"Thank You" to the audience.

4: Teaching Effective Writing Strategies

*Writing is about learning to pay attention
and to communicate what is going on.*
—Anne Lamott from *Bird by Bird*

Writing Strategies are the carefully devised plans of action writers use to write and communicate clearly. We present four overarching strategies that weave through our teaching that have specific and distinctive characteristics.

Read Like a Writer

*I spend at least an hour a day reading.
Reading gets me thinking about my own writing,
and makes me eager to get back to work.*
—James Howe

Key Elements of Read Like a Writer:

- <u>Notice</u> the author's writing craft and style.
- <u>Name</u> the craft(s) the writer uses.
- <u>Discuss</u> why you think the writer used this craft.
- <u>Make connections</u> to the text.
  - text-to-self: to a personal experience
  - text-to-text: to another story
  - text-to-world: to knowledge about the world
- Think about how to <u>apply</u> this craft in your own writing.

Writing Standards:

1. Habits and Processes. Students should
   - Study and emulate a particular author's craft as they revise their own work.
2. Writing Purposes and Resulting Genres
   d. Producing Literature
      - Write stories, songs, memoirs, poetry, and plays that conform to the appropriate expectations for each form.

– After studying a genre, produce a piece that incorporates elements appropriate to the genre.
– Build on a story idea by extending or changing the storyline.
    d. Responding to Literature
       – Support an interpretation by referring to specific examples in the text.
       – Provide enough detail from the text so the reader can understand the interpretation.
       – Go beyond retelling the story; compare two works by an author.
       – Discuss several works that have a common idea or theme.
       – Make text-to-self connections as they relate the story to their own lives.
       – Make text-to-text connections as they notice and discuss where they have seen the writing craft or ideas in other literature.
3. Use and Conventions
    b. Take on the language of authors.
       – Emulate sentence structures from various genres.

About Read Like a Writer …

Before we are writers, we are readers. Emerson said, "'Tis the good reader that makes the good book." As we Read Like a Writer, we pause to notice what good writers do. The word, *notice* comes from the root *noscere,* which means "to come to know," "to become aware of through the senses." Read Like a Writer is a strategy that beckons us to notice writing in complex ways.

As readers, we analyze how and why published authors write a certain way. Authors of the literature we love provide models for us to emulate. We store away what we learn and apply it in our own writing. The application of this knowledge allows us to Write Like Writers.

Example of Read Like a Writer:

Throughout the year, we observe how students' writing reflects what they've noticed other authors doing. After a study of visual imagery in *Winter Eyes*, Marc came to the Author's Chair proudly sharing his winter story. Students responded by commenting on the positive elements of Marc's writing, particularly the descriptive language.

Nate commented on a line, "Icicles hanging from the eaves outside his hospital room shimmered in the dazzling January sunlight." "That's visual imagery," Mariah said, "and a strong verb, too." Marc said he thought the sentence sounded better than writing, "It was a cold winter day." Marc's writing showed us all how he applied what he had read and noticed in other texts as he Wrote Like a Writer. Before we are writers, we are readers.

How Do We Teach Read Like a Writer?

Word Study: *Read*

The word *read* has some definitions that can clarify the meaning of Read Like a Writer:
   • to find something out by studying written material;

- to interpret information in text in a particular way; and
- to have an understanding of something by experience.

Discuss how these definitions apply directly to the strategy of Read Like a Writer.

Metacognition. Have you ever listened to that little voice inside your head while you are reading? (No, not your conscience or Jiminy Cricket.) The one we all have that thinks, connects, and asks questions when we read. But, do we allow ourselves to pause long enough to notice how this thinking helps our reading?

Being aware of how we think and learn is really metacognition. *Meta* means "change" and *cognition* is "the learning and knowledge we gain through perception, reasoning, and intuition." So, when we put it all together, *metacognition* is the way our learning changes as we think and reflect about the way we gain knowledge. Simply said, it's thinking about our own thinking processes. When we Read Like a Writer, we read with insight, raise questions, and appreciate the author's language. Ask students to notice how they think and learn as they become more aware of specific strategies we use as readers and writers.

We Notice (Writer's Craft) Chart. Decide which craft your writers need to learn or practice at this time. Name the writer's craft and list examples from various texts. Children can add to this chart from their independent reading. This becomes a class resource in two ways: (1) Refer to these charts in Writer's Workshop to analyze how and why authors used a particular technique. (2) Use these charts in conferences to guide students in how they might use a similar one in their own writing. Example of a class chart:

We Notice Visual Imagery	
So many sparks flew out of its tail (Halley's Comet) that, even though it was night, the entire countryside lit up and all the roosters set to crowin'!	n.p., from *Davy Crockett Saves the World* by Schanzer
(Hollis describing one of her foster homes) There was the green house where the door didn't quite close; the wind blew in and up the stairs, rattling the window panes.	p. 4 from *Pictures of Hollis Woods* by P. R. Giff
(Willa Jo describing the sunrise) A thin rim of orange-red so deep and strong my heart almost breaks with the fierceness of that color. Moment by moment, there is more of it to see. So hot and bright, I cannot look but at the edges. Even when I look away, look clear away to the waning edge of darkness, I can see that color in my mind's eye, feel it beating in my very blood. I breathe color.	pp. 2–3 from *Getting Near to Baby* by A. Couloumbis

Name the Writing Craft. As students talk about the techniques the author has used, help them to give it a name, such as "Visual Imagery" or "Precise Words." Expect students to use these names when they are discussing them. This gives them the *language of literacy*.

Becoming Craft Detectives. Get out the magnifying glasses! Engage your students in some detective work to search for rich language in every book. We shared J. K. Rowling's lead in the fifth Harry Potter book. She writes,

> The hottest day of the summer was drawing to a close and a drowsy silence lay over the large, square houses of Privet Drive. Cars that were usually gleaming stood dusty in their drives and lawns that were once emerald green lay parched and yellowing; the use of hosepipes had been banned due to drought. (p. 1 from *Harry Potter and the Order of the Phoenix*)

Some of the comments:

> Several kids exclaimed at once, "That's Harry's street!"
> Cam added, "Drowsy silence is a great way to say it's getting late."
> Jaclyn loved the "Cars that were usually gleaming stood dusty ..." What contrast!

> Reading like writers! And noticing and connecting like writers. They have grown to appreciate the fine, descriptive writing from beloved authors.

Making Connections. Strong readers relate authors' ideas in the text to something in their own experiences. Readers who reflect about the text notice and name these connections: text-to-self, text-to-text, or text-to-world. Writers also use these connections, borrowing ideas from personal events and other writers and reshaping them into their own stories.

Post these three categories of connections and model how to use them when we read. Have students make connections as they read literature and their own writing.

Connections	
Text-to-Self	An author's words that make us recall personal events or feelings.
Text-to-Text	Something we are reading or writing that reminds us of other writing.
Text-to-World	Text that links the writing to something we know about the world.

What We Notice About our Partner's Writing. Sticky notes are the means of marking text where we pause and think about what we notice. Copy and use the Think Sheet "What We Notice" (at the end of this section). My students developed a system of shorthand listed on this sheet.

Model how to use sticky notes using a piece of student writing. First, read aloud a brief passage. Next, find a place where you have a question or wonder about something. Using "What We Notice" as a guide, mark the abbreviation "?" on a sticky note and place it on the text. Show a few more examples.

Direct students to exchange a writing piece with a partner. Read and use sticky notes to mark observations about the partner's writing. When finished, return the papers and individually think about the notations. Then, each pair discusses what they noticed in the writing. Individually, the writers decide whether to make changes.

Questions and Wonders. The Think Sheet for this activity provides a record of students' thinking processes as they read a story. This is a concrete way to develop metacognition: They will stop and listen to that voice inside their heads while they read. When students begin to read stories in this way, they become actively engaged and their comprehension increases.

Distribute the Think Sheet "Questions and Wonders" (at the end of this section). Read a story aloud to the whole class. Stop at a certain point and have students write in the first box what they're wondering or asking themselves. Continue reading and pausing to allow time to record.

They may also use this strategy in their writing. Have students exchange papers with a writing partner. Direct them to read their partner's story, pausing at certain points to write their Questions and Wonders. They can stop at the end of a page, paragraph, or at points the writer has designated. Then, return the sheet and the story to the writer. The writer may use these ideas to revise.

Study One Book. Model for students how they can notice the various writer's craft used throughout one book. Taking a book I love, *Owl Moon*, by Jane Yolen, my students and I observe the richness of the language, beautiful visual imagery, and other craft. I nudge their thinking with questions such as these below, but encourage them to engage in a discussion with each other, not just answer my questions:

- Find one descriptive passage that touched your heart. Explain why you felt that way.
- Which phrases created pictures in your mind? How did Yolen do that?
- What strategy does the author use in her lead? Why is that lead effective?
- Think about the author's intent: Is the child a boy or a girl? Why do you think she doesn't reveal that to us?
- Identify other craft Yolen used.
- How might Yolen's strategies help you in your own writing?

Study One Writer. Many writers have some individual writing styles that students may enjoy emulating. We learn by trying new styles and eventually finding our own. Have students become familiar with one or two writers and study what they do with craft.

Writer's Craft Analysis. When I read children's literature, I'm always searching for craft so that I can take excerpts back to the classroom to share with students. I follow the same process as my students of using sticky notes to mark passages. A partial example of how I organize the findings on my computer is at the end of this section, "Writer's Craft Analysis" of *Getting Near to Baby*. Included is a "Writer's Craft Analysis Guideline." Although compiling the list is time consuming, it is a helpful resource for Writer's Workshop. I have extensive records on many books and can reference these when I'm looking for specific craft to teach. Have students find more examples, and the repertoire will grow. Devise your own system of locating and organizing writer's craft.

Nonfiction

Read Like Nonfiction Writers. When students are preparing to write nonfiction, have them notice the language and style of nonfiction authors. To understand the genre more clearly, compare and contrast nonfiction to fiction writing. Take the best of what they see in the nonfiction books to use when they engage their readers in their own nonfiction text. They are learning to Read Like Nonfiction Writers.

Poetically Speaking

Write Like a Poet. Read lots of poetry to the class. Poetry is loaded with elements to Read Like a Writer, such as visual imagery, line breaks, form, and so forth. Have students notice and study one of these elements, then Write Like a Poet.

The following is a script of a how we applied the strategy Read Like a Writer to poetry. The book *Mockingbird Morning*, by Joanne Ryder, is a collection of 15 poems that chronicle a young girl's early morning walk. I read aloud the poems in this book, pausing after each one so we could Read Like a Poet. Thinking about the writer's craft of Visual Imagery, we studied how the poet's careful word choice, along with our own personal experiences, gave us pictures inside our minds.

> Lying on the grass
> you watch
> a chase

in slow motion –
a shark chasing
a cat
chasing
a boat
chasing
a kangaroo
floating
beyond reach. (n.p.)

Alex: I've done that. I laid down in the grass and watched the clouds go by.

Josh: Me too. At the beach. You can see the whole sky.

Mrs. W: I'm wondering how you knew what the poet was describing. Let's look at her opening words: "Lying on the grass you watch a chase in slow motion." What else do the poet's words describe?

Jaclyn: I thought about "a chase in slow motion." They don't go together: A chase is usually very fast.

Mrs. W: Why do you think the poet chose those words?

Jaclyn: She wanted us to think about a chase in a different way?

Mrs. W: How do we know this?

Gina: She goes on and says how they keep changing into another animal. Clouds do that. They keep changing.

Mrs. W: Why does the poem keep repeating, "chasing a …"?

Dan: We're looking at the whole sky, so there's more than one cloud, and there's more than one animal chasing each other. It's like there's a whole line of them.

Mrs. W.: I'm still thinking about the ending of this poem, "floating beyond reach." What has the poet revealed here?

Cam: That's how she tells us they are clouds.

Mrs. W.: Well, why not just say they are clouds? (A chorus of groans, why I can't see the obvious!)

Christopher: Oh, Mrs. W., it's a poem. The writer wants us to <u>see</u> the visual imagery, not tell us.

Kelsey: She wrote with the best words.

Mrs. W.: So, how can we do this in our own writing?

Kelsey: I can think of ways to use words to describe what I see, not just come out and tell what I see.

Mrs. W.: It's a great day outside. Let's get our notebooks and pencils, go out, and write some more of our own free verse poems. As we know, in free verse we can focus on precise word choice and visual imagery without thinking about rhyme. Explore, find a spot, and write for about 10 minutes. You may find it easier to begin planning and drafting your ideas and then go back to write the visual imagery. How you work is up to you.

© Heather Ferraro

What I know about ...

Read Like a Writer

- What do I _____ about the author's writing?

- Which _____ does the writer use?

- Where have I seen this craft before?
  (text-to- _____)

- Does it remind me of a personal experience?
  (text-to- _____)

- Does it make me think of something in the _____?

Name _____ Date _____

What We Notice

Directions: Mark these abbreviations on sticky notes as you make observations about a piece of writing.

Connections:

T-S	Text-to-Self
T-T	Text-to-Text
T-W	Text-to-World

Questions:

?	"I wonder" questions
? C	"I'm confused about …"

Visualizations:

V	Words show a picture

Language:

L	Record words I like!
L ?	Record words I don't know.

Predictions:

P	I think I know what will happen next.

Writer's Craft:

WC	I notice a writing strategy.

Name _____   Date _____

Questions and Wonders

Title: _____

Directions: Stop at certain points in the story and write a question or something you were wondering.

| |
| |
| |

Writer's Craft Analysis

Excerpts from *Getting Near to Baby by* Audrey Couloumbis

Lead—What kind? Action Lead

Aunt Patty is fed up with me. She told me so last night. When I got into bed, there was a sick feeling in my stomach that stayed with me through my sleep. I came out here to breathe deep of the fresh air but that sick feeling has not yet gone away. (p. 1)

Main Characters and Descriptions—how characters look, act, think, speak

Willa Jo—an almost 13-year-old girl who has gone with her sister to live with Aunt Patty

(Aunt Patty had just said chocolate goes to her hips.) Which I had to agree was not a place where Aunt Patty needed another single thing to go. I didn't say so, of course. (p. 15)

"I'm going to tell my aunt Patty," I yelled. I was suddenly so angry with her tears spurted right out of my eyes, and my mouth was so full of spit I could hardly hold it in. Even Little Sister was taken aback. "I'm going straight to the drugstore to call her and you can't stop me." (p. 107)

Theme—how a family needs to stick together when dealing with loss

I know just how she feels. And Uncle Hob rests his hand on the back of her neck, like he knows too. But it is none of it Aunt Patty's fault and I am about to overflow with feeling for her. I scooch over to sit on Aunt Patty's other side. (p. 205–206)

Voice—(Couloumbis captures the sound voice of an angry, hurt, and emotional 12-year-old girl. Willa Jo is stubborn and at times sarcastic and tongue-in-cheek.)

(Aunt Patty just threw out all of Willa Jo's clothes and dressed her up in brand new ones.) "Thank you, Aunt Patty," I said, without so much as a smile. I knew I ought to try to work up some enthusiasm but I have never in my life wanted to be cute as a button. Besides, those sandals were already rubbing a blister on my little toe. (p. 11)

Show, Don't Tell

I know it doesn't really happen this way, but it always looks as if the sun creeps up to stand teetering on the edge of the earth. I waited. It stayed there for long moments until I wondered, *Is it stuck there.* Just when I thought it, the sun made a little jump, and then it floated free. (p. 132)

Five Sense—sight, sound, touch, taste, smell

<u>Touch</u>: I inch across the roof that feels like it has been sprinkled with coarse salt, liking the way the scratchy surface clutches at the fabric of my shorts, clings to my skin. (p. 4)

Precise Words—nouns, verbs, adjectives, adverbs

<u>Adverb</u>: Mrs. Teasley walks <u>smartly</u>, as if she'd meant to come see Mrs. Biddle all along. (p. 30)

Writer's Craft Analysis Guideline

Title of book _____ By _____

Genre

Lead—What kind? Quote first paragraph(s) of book

Main Characters
    Who They Are
    Character Descriptions (the way characters look, act, think, speak)

Theme(s)—Passages That Support the Theme

Point of View/Past or Present Tense

Setting Descriptions

Plot Summary

Show, Don't Tell

Five Senses: Sight, Sound, Touch, Taste, Smell

Zoom!

Precise Words: Nouns, Verbs, Adverbs, Adjectives

Repeated Words and Phrases

Sound Words

Transitional Words and Phrases

Visual Imagery

Voice

Other Interesting Features (e.g., use of italics or colons, one-word sentences, brand names, etc.)

Your Opinion:
    Rating from 1–5 Stars
    Connections: Text-to-Self, Text-to-Text, Text-to-World

Show, Don't Tell

Start with a scene the reader can see.
—Sol Stein

Key Elements of Show, Don't Tell:

- Word study: *show* and *tell*
  - *show* = to cause something to be seen
  - *tell* = to put something in words or writing
- Develop a picture in the reader's mind
- Use precise words
- Write with vivid images.

Writing Standards:

2. Writing Purposes and Resulting Genres
   a. Narrative Writing: Sharing Events, Telling Stories
      – Create a believable world and use precise words and detail.
      – Write a sequence of events that are logical and natural.
   b. Informative Writing: Report or Informational Writing
      – Use diagrams, charts and illustrations appropriate to the text.
   c. Functional and Procedural Writing
      – May use illustrations to give detail to the steps.
3. Language Use and Conventions
   a. Style and Syntax
      – Use their own language in writing—Embed phrases and modifiers that make their writing lively and graphic.
   b. Vocabulary and Word Choice
      – Use precise and vivid words.
      – Take on the language of authors by using specialized words related to a topic.

About Show, Don't Tell ...

Mark Twain said, "Don't say the old lady screamed. Bring her on and let her scream." This vivid image sums up the principle behind the writing strategy Show, Don't Tell. We've heard that a picture is worth a thousand words—and Show, Don't Tell is a way to create that picture in our readers' minds through our choice of words.

We tend to write like we talk, which is often telling people something. Show, Don't Tell is a strategy that helps us change "telling" into "showing." What we now call "movies" or "theaters" used to be called "picture shows." And they were called that for a reason. The screen "showed" the audience moving pictures of what was happening. We, as writers, strive to do the same— put a "picture show" in the readers' minds.

Example of Show, Don't Tell From Literature:

From *All the Way Home* by P. R. Giff:

> Loretta's kitchen was a mess, Brick thought, a great mess. Magazines were piled everywhere, one opened on the countertop. There were other things, too: flowers in jelly glasses, ivy in cups, and knitting needles stuck in a ball of wool the color of apples on Claude's trees.
>
> It was the strangest thing to sit there under those pictures, eating melted cheese sandwiches with thick slices of tomato for supper. His mother had never made them ... warm yellow cheese running onto the plate, buttery toast. They were as messy looking as the rest of the kitchen, but they were terrific even though the crusts were burned. (pp. 55–56)

How Do I Teach It?

Word Study: *Show* and *Tell*

Look at the difference between *show* and *tell*.

- *Show* means "to be visible or allow something to be seen easily."
- *Tell* means "to give an account of something in speech or writing."

Have students connect with their experiences of "show and tell."

Share a story with the students in two ways. First, tell them: Talk about something that you did. Then, contrast this. Show them: Reveal it through pictures or with a prop that explains it. Ask students, "Which one was easier to visualize?"

Help students understand that fine writers use their words to create images in readers' minds:

- In picture books, illustrators create pictures based on the images the author has written.
- In chapter books, there are few or no pictures, so writers create images with their words.
- In television shows and movies, the scenes are made based on a strong visual text: the screenplay.

"Show, Don't Tell" Chart. The literature is often our best teacher. Read some passages from your favorite books that exemplify the writing strategy Show, Don't Tell.

Create a class chart of examples. Have students post other excerpts as they find them in their reading.

Show, Don't Tell—Examples from Literature

from *Lily's Crossing* by P. R. Giff	Lily received three and a half presents for her birthday that Monday. Two were books, one was a secret, and the last was a half-eaten candy bar. Margaret Dillon gave her the candy, a Milky Way. The end of the wrapper was torn back, and teeth marks dented the chocolate. (p. 12)
from *The Wall* by E. Bunting	Flowers and other things have been laid against the wall. There are little flags, an old teddy bear, and letters, weighted with stones so they won't blow away. Someone has left a rose with a droopy head. (n.p.)

Talk about the passages in your Show, Don't Tell Chart. For example, you might ask questions like these about the excerpt from *Lily's Crossing*:

- What is the gist of this passage?
- Which words can you see clearly?
- What did the author, Giff, do that gave us these pictures in our minds? (The little details make the items clear. The way she wrote *Milky Way* instead of *candy bar* allows us to <u>see</u> the exact kind of candy. We all know what *teeth marks dented in chocolate* look like. Ooh—*a secret*. I wonder what it is. *Three and a half presents* creates more interest than just three.)
- Which do you prefer to read: something that tells or something that shows? Explain your preference.

Guide students to use the Show, Don't Tell strategy in their own writing. Here's an example of how a fifth grader showed how cold a "two-dog night" was by using descriptive language and comparisons. This was based on the book *A Five Dog Night*.

Show Your Feelings. How do we know what people are feeling? Sometimes, we can "see" their feelings through their actions. Role-play some actions that show a feeling, such as "angry." Slam the door, stomp into the classroom, sit down with arms folded, and glare at someone. Ask students what they think you are feeling and how you showed it through your actions. Explain that characters in our stories have feelings just like we do. Writers show these feelings through describing specific actions, not just telling how a character feels.

Distribute the Think Sheet "Show, Don't Tell Your Feelings" (at the end of this section) to groups of three or four. Decide to either provide feeling words for students to write in the Feeling Words column or have them select their own. Then, direct the groups to complete the sheet by writing action words to show each feeling.

Feeling Words	Actions That Show the Feeling
Angry	make fists, frown and wrinkle brows, stomp foot, slam door, yell at someone, take deep breaths, stomp around, fold arms across chest, mutter under your breath.
Surprised	
Frightened	

Discuss afterward:
- How did you decide which actions matched the feelings?
- What did your group do when you had different perceptions of what the feeling might look like?
- In what ways did some actions overlap several feelings?
- Describe what mixed feelings are. How could you Show, Don't Tell a character's mixed feelings when you write?

And the Oscar Goes to … This activity provides another opportunity for students to dramatize and write specific descriptive actions that show feelings. Select two girls who will read and act out a scene from *The School Story* by A. Clements. Direct "Natalie" to exaggerate the movements so that children can "see" her feelings. In this excerpt, Natalie has written a story and has given her manuscript to her best friend, Zoe, to read.

> Natalie couldn't take it. She peeked in the doorway of the school library, then turned, took six steps down the hall, turned, paced back, and stopped to look in at Zoe again. The suspense was torture.
>
> Zoe was still reading. The first two chapters only added up to twelve pages. Natalie leaned against the door frame and chewed on her thumbnail. She thought, *What's taking her so long?*
>
> Zoe could see Natalie out of the corner of her eye. She could feel all that nervous energy nudging at her, but Zoe wasn't about to be rushed. She always read slow, and she liked it that way, especially when it was a good story. And this one was good. (p. 1)

Discuss what Natalie was feeling and process how the actor <u>showed</u> the class those feelings through her actions.

Next, write some feeling words on separate cards. Let each pair of students pull one card from a basket. Have them act out the feeling and let the class guess what they are dramatizing. On a class chart, write each feeling word and what students did to Show, Don't Tell. These words and phrases can become resources for students to use in their own writing.

Change Show Into Tell. We have fun with finding that visually packed passage and then rewriting the text in an ordinary, mundane way. The contrast is striking as children realize how special an author's language can be. We find that students have had a rollicking time writing as boring as possible. Christopher even said, "It's getting hard to write bad!"

> I puffed my cheeks and blew as hard as I could. The saxophone only squeaked, squawked and groaned, then sounded like it was making up words like ahwronk and roozahga and baloopa.
> (p. 235 from *Bud, Not Buddy* by C.P. Curtis)
> Jake's rewrite — I blew on my sax, but it didn't sound good.

Select a Show, Don't Tell passage from a book and write it on a sentence strip. Underneath, demonstrate how to write what the author could have said, but in a humdrum way.

Direct students to choose a Show, Don't Tell phrase from a book and write it on a sentence strip. Beneath, write a phrase that just <u>tells</u> what the author was saying. Share, discuss, and hang examples in the room as reminders.

From Tell to Show. This exercise is a variation of the previous activity, "Change Show Into Tell." Make up a sentence that tells about something that happened, but doesn't give the reader a clear picture. Together, rewrite it to put images into the readers' minds.

Use the Think Sheet, "From Tell Into Show" (at the end of this section) for additional practice of this strategy. Here's one example:

Words That Tell	Words That Show
She walked into the room and told her dad that she had made 100% on her math test.	She danced into the kitchen, high-fived her dad, and shouted, "Yesss! I did it! I aced that math exam!"

Have students mark in the second column the words that were more descriptive. Then, complete the sheet. This hones in on the precise words that Show, Don't Tell.

The Mysterious Stone. Walk students through the process of creating a piece of writing to Show, Don't Tell. They should be familiar with how to use precise words and visual images to create pictures.

First, narrate a story that simply <u>tells,</u> rather than <u>shows</u> what happens. This example is entitled *The Mysterious Stone*:

Text that <u>tells</u>:
> One day, I picked up a stone and I suddenly turned into a cat. The end.

"The end?" they may ask. Discuss how that didn't give the reader a very clear picture about what actually happened between the time I picked up the stone and turned into a cat. Continue the modeling. Pull a stone out of your pocket and drop it on the floor. Begin telling the story again, but with this descriptive lead:

Text that <u>shows</u>:
> One day, I was walking home from school and saw something glistening in a rain puddle. *What an unusual rock*, I thought, as I reached down and grasped it. Hmmm. This was odd: The stone was warm and began to throb. What could this mean? I began to feel strange. I felt hot. I looked down and saw thick black fur popping up all over my legs. I started to shout, but what came out of my mouth was …

Guide students to complete the passage by giving their readers a picture of the transition of a person turning into a cat. Ask, "What do we know about cats? How do they look and act (eyes can see in low light, acute sense of smell, sharp claws, meow, fear of dogs, climb trees, body features, etc.)? Let them *show* the transition, not just tell that you changed.

Infer, Don't Tell. Sometimes, we need to draw inferences about a character's feelings if the author doesn't come right out and show us. This activity moves us to a deeper level of thinking, in which we identify the subtle ways that writers reveal feelings. This is really Infer, Don't Tell.

As you read books together, notice the subtleties writers use to show how one character feels. Find the clues in the text. Select a book and find some passages that exemplify inferred feelings. Type these and give students a list of feeling words to match with the excerpts. Debrief the process.

This example is from *Toad for Tuesday* by R. E. Erickson. Directions: In small groups, match one feeling word with each statement.

Feeling words:
Anxious, Hopeful, Proud, Desperate, Terrified, Accepting

Page	Toad said …	Which feeling word goes with each statement?
35	"Only four more days—I must do something soon."	
36	"Maybe if I tie some of the feathers to my arms, I could glide to the ground."	

37	"And of course, I won't be so warm, and I won't have my skis, but I'll be free."
42	"Unless … unless George changes his mind. Then I won't need the ladder at all. Why, he may not eat me at all."
45	"Of course, everything my brother makes is delicious."
47	"What would it be like?" Warton wondered with a shudder.

This is what happened in my classroom: Students began with confidence matching the feeling words as they went down the list. However, when they approached the bottom two, they realized that the remaining choices didn't fit. They decided to rethink all of their matches, carefully considering the fine distinctions among feelings. Here are some of their comments:

- "He has to be <u>desperate</u> if he's crazy enough to think he can make wings and fly," John pointed out. "<u>Anxious</u> isn't strong enough."
- Eric analyzed, "*But* is the signal word when Warton is deciding how he'll give up his warm sweaters and skis and says, *but I'll be free.* I think he's <u>accepting</u> his decision."
- They all knew what the author meant when he told how Warton *shuddered* after wondering what it would feel like to be eaten by George the Owl. They agreed they would be <u>terrified</u>, too, and commented that it was a text-to-self connection.

The process of discovery and the rich dialogue expressing their thoughts was far more important than a "right" answer. They were unlocking authors' language and learning how writers use words to Infer, Don't Tell. Challenge your students to notice the subtle ways of expressing feelings in books they read, then use it in their own writing.

Nonfiction

Nonfiction. Books of nonfiction Show, Don't Tell in various ways. Lay out some nonfiction literature and have students notice special features that put a picture in the reader's mind, such as: descriptions, illustrations, maps, photographs, and diagrams.

Give each student a separate nonfiction book that has an illustration or photograph (flagged by you earlier). Have them write about the flagged picture using descriptive language. Then, give them time to share their descriptive pieces with the class. After students read aloud what they wrote, ask them to hold up the illustration or photograph to determine if the written description matches the visual. Ask questions such as:

- Which words Show, Don't Tell?
- What do you see here (pointing to a part of the photograph)?
- Have you thought about …

Poetically Speaking

Free Verse Stories. There have been some lovely books written in the last few years that tell stories through free verse poetry. When we get involved in the story, we sometimes forget that it's really poetry because it reads like fiction. Read some excerpts from books, such as *Out of the Dust* by K. Hesse, which is filled with Show, Don't Tell. Guide students to listen, notice, and discuss the images. Encourage them to write one of their stories in free verse. Or, have each student select a famous person to study

and write poetic biographies to compile in a class book. This can develop a fuller appreciation of poetry and its various structures.

Other poems that Show, Don't Tell may come from books that explore a topic, such as *Listening to the Rain*, *Space Songs*, or *Winter Eyes*. Encourage students to develop a specific subject richly. They may need to research it, then write about it with words that present the topic visually.

What I know about ...

Show, Don't Tell

- Word Study:
    <u>Show</u>—to cause something to be _____
    <u>Tell</u>—to _____ something in words or writing

- Develop a _____ in the reader's mind.

- Use _____ words

- Create vivid _____

- Give an example from a book you are reading.

Name _____   Date _____

Show, Don't Tell Your Feelings

Directions: Write some descriptive actions that Show, Don't Tell the feeling words.

Feeling Words	Actions That Show the Feeling
Example Angry	make fists, frown and wrinkle brows, stomp foot, slam door, yell at someone, take deep breaths, stomp around, fold arms across chest, mutter under your breath.
1.	
2.	
3.	
4.	

From Tell to Show

Name _____ Date _____

Words That Tell	Rewrite the Paragraph to Show
Example: She walked into the room and told her dad that she made 100% on her math test.	She danced into the kitchen, high-fived her dad, and shouted, "Yessss! I did it! Aced that math exam!"
1. He was mad. He didn't want to go.	
2. Mark showed the book to his sister. He knew that would keep her quiet for awhile.	
3. Patrick kicked the soccer ball into the goal.	
4. Kristen knew the answer. She raised her hand.	

Use the Five Senses

I get my ideas from living my life wide-eyed and awake.
I sit on the edge of chairs. I pay attention to wherever I am.
—Drew Lamm

Key Elements of Use the Five Senses:

- Sight
- Sound
- Touch
- Taste
- Smell

Writing Standards:

2. Writing Purposes and Resulting Genres
   a. Narrative Writing: Sharing Events, Telling Stories
      – Use precise words and detail.
3. Language Use and Conventions
   a. Style and Syntax
      – Use their own language in writing.
      – Take on the language of authors.
   b. Vocabulary and Word Choice
      – Use precise and vivid words.
      – Take on the language of authors by using specialized words related to a topic.

About Five Senses ...

Oioink, oioink! Sixteen classmates looked with puzzled faces at the show-and-tell box I was carrying. These were not the usual sounds we heard in my first-grade class. They gathered around in anticipation as I opened the cardboard flaps. A pig! A baby pig! Mostly black with a white band circling his neck like a collar. Soft fine bristles sparsely covered his body. His pointy hooves made him look like he was standing on tippytoes. I had tied a blue silk ribbon around his neck for his visit to my school. I lifted him gently out of the box as a flurry of hands petted him. He tried to run, but the waxed tile floor was so slick that his legs slid out in four different directions as he splatted flat on his belly. We giggled and he squealed. *Oioink, oioink!* We helped him up, then chased him around the room. Everyone tried to catch him as he darted under desks and hid behind a table. In a few minutes, we got a whiff of a barnyard scent and knew what he was doing back there! Whew! We lured him out with a baby bottle of milk that he glugged and slurped like it was the best ice cream soda in the world.

This story comes back to me when I pick up a book about a pig, or drive through the country and get a whiff of "barnyard aroma," or hear that familiar *oioink* on television. All the senses were engaged the day I took the piglet to school, which made the experience multifold strong. And the sensory memory is still powerful today. That's how it is when we use our senses. And that's the way it is for readers when we incorporate all the senses into our writing. Good writers provide clear descriptions allowing us to relate, connect, and remember.

Examples of Five Senses From Literature:

Sight—something we see, envision or view

From *The Trolls* by P. Horvath:

> The ocean's different every morning. Sometimes it's pulled back, with hard flat sand to walk on and seagulls looking for mussels and clams to open by dropping them on rocks. Other times it's pulled up to shore like a bed that's just been made. Sometimes the sun sparkles on the water in a new-world way, and other times fog rolls in like a cozy fleece blanket over the beach. (p. 37)

Sound—a noise or a distinctive quality that identifies a particular movement

From *All the Way Home* by P. R. Giff:

> Ebbets Field! He'd heard the name a million times on the radio. He'd heard the sound of the bat smacking the ball, the yell of the umpire—"*Safe!*"—and the crowds of people, their screaming like the wind on the hilltop before a storm. (p. 34)

Touch—the texture, shape, and other qualities of objects through contact with a part of the body

From *What Jamie Saw* by C. Coman:

> He cried and cried and cried, huge air-gobbling sobs that he could feel in his back and that he couldn't stop. ...Then he drew in stuttery breaths and the pounding in his chest began to slow. He wiped his cheeks with the backs of his hands and they were so wet, so covered with tears, that he felt like he had washed his face. (pp. 124–125)

Taste—the perception of particular qualities of something, such as food, by means of the taste buds on the tongue

From *Guess Who My Favorite Person Is* by B. Baylor:

> Her favorite thing to taste is snow and honey mixed ... a little more honey than snow. (n.p.)

Smell—to detect an odor, aroma, scent, stink

From *The Great Frog Race* by K. O. George:

September
Sniff the air—
It smells
      Spicy. Sharp.
Like
      Freshly sharpened pencils. (p. 30)

How Do I Teach *Five Senses*?

Word Study: *Sense*

Discuss some definitions of *sense*:

- to become aware of through sight, sound, touch, taste, or smell
- an impression, awareness we get from a sensory experience

What I Know About Five Senses. As a class resource, make separate charts for the senses with a picture at the top as listed, such as eye, ear, hand, mouth, nose. Begin by posting on the charts a few of your favorite excerpts from the literature that go with each sense and encourage students to add to it. Some of these passages will overlap with other writers' craft. The same example could apply to Sense of Sight and Visual Imagery. But, that's okay. It's the process of having students notice and use the craft in their own writing that is important.

Sight: Artifact Description. The purpose of the nature walk is for students to use their sense of sight in an authentic way and write about their impressions. As you walk and explore, talk about what you see and notice. You and the students select and bring back one artifact each from the hike (leaf, rock, twig, feather, etc.).

When you return, have the children observe their artifact, focusing on size, color, shape, texture, and distinguishing features. If possible, have magnifying glasses available for closer scrutiny. Using the Think Sheet "Artifact Description: Using Your Sense of Sight" (at the end of this section), model how you observe, draw, list notes, and write a description of your artifact.

After students complete their descriptions, listen to them share what they wrote. Make the connection that we all took the same walk, but we wrote about different objects. It all depends on what we have in our sight. One of the beauties of writing.

© Heather Ferraro

Sound: The Sounds Around Us. The intent of this activity is to have students develop the descriptive language of sound. Prepare for this lesson by creating an audio tape of various recognizable sounds such as rubbing chalk on the board, slurping soda through a straw, turning pages of a book, and so forth. Model with an example, such as eating potato chips:

Sound	Connection and Description
Example	• in the lunchroom my friends <u>crunching on crispy chips</u>
	• seeing who can <u>munch the loudest</u>
eating potato chips	• my favorite snack food
	• huge bags of chips
	• like salt and vinegar flavored
	• greasy, salty fingers
	• sounds like <u>walking through dried leaves in the fall</u>

Copy and distribute the Think Sheet "Sounds Around Us: Using Your Sense of Sound" (at the end of this section). Have students close their eyes to screen out all visual input. Play the first sound on the tape recorder as an example and discuss to it together. Write all connections and descriptions they tell you, then go back and underline only those that connect to the sense of sound.

Continue playing the rest of the tape, but with students writing independently. Pause after each sound for them to write the identifications. At the end of the tape, direct students to go back and write the connections and descriptions. Volunteers can share what they wrote about the sounds.

Touch: Adding Texture to Writing. The purpose of this activity is to help students develop language to describe the feel of objects against their skin and the connections they make to them. Prepare paper bags that contain items for students to touch, but not see. Consider various attributes: shape, size, and texture, such as *bumpy, fluffy, smooth, sticky, rough, bendy, skinny, squeezy,* and so forth.

Model the process by feeling the object in the bag without looking. Talk through what your sense of touch is telling you. For example, if you have a paper clip in your bag, you might say, "It is smooth, oval-shaped, curves around several times, sort of coiled, thin, hard, a little bendy, about as long as the brush part of my toothbrush, has space in the middle." You could probably tell right away what the object was, but could your students identify it from your words?

Distribute one bag to each student. Tell them to reach in and explore the object without looking at or removing it. They may write their information on the Think Sheet "Adding Texture to Writing" (at the end of this section).

<u>Extension</u>: Make a comparison between an object and something else, such as, "When she went sledding, her frozen gray scarf was wrapped around her like a long skinny paper clip." This gives the reader a context to feel the cold, stiff scarf coiled around the sledder's neck.

Taste: Tasting Party. Salty, sweet, sour, peppery, hot, spicy, bitter, tangy—tastes abound. And they connect to so many of our memories—the sweet-sour of homemade lemonade, the gooey sweetness of an ice cream sundae. Through their writing, authors tap into our past connections to certain foods.

Read the following passage from *Everything on a Waffle*.

> [Miss Perfidy] was pouring herself a cup of raspberry tea and eating stale soft tea biscuits. Her cookies always tasted of mothballs. She pushed the cookies in my direction and I ate one to see if the flavor had changed since I had left but it hadn't and I looked around to see where I could spit it out without her noticing. (p. 60)

Discuss the excerpt. Make students aware of how the author constructed this passage with a balance of taste and reaction. Let them use this strategy in their own writing.

- What words did the author, Horvath, use to show us the sense of taste?
- What is the character's reaction to the taste of the cookie?
- How do we know she did or didn't like it?

Enjoy a tasting party with your students to trigger their sense of taste. On paper plates, put spoonfuls of assorted foods for students to sample. Number each food on the plate. On the Think Sheet "The Tasting Party" (at the end of this section), write the food names in the first column, copy, and distribute. Have students sample each item and record their descriptions, reactions, and memories beside the listed foods on the sheet. One of these descriptions could lead into a story.

Smell: Smelling More Than Roses. Write on the board the phrase "Stop and smell the roses." Asks students what they think this means. Challenge students to locate examples of smells in their books. Post these and discuss the ways authors write about them.

Help children to explore their own thoughts and memories about smells. Discuss some vivid smells they recall and what the circumstances were that contribute to those memories. Examples of distinct smells I recall:

- Lilac bush in the backyard of my grandmother's home. I cherish the time we spent in her flower garden, planting, weeding, picking, and talking.
- Campfire when we were in the Rockies. The smoky smell of our clothes and sleeping bags the next day were reminders of our late-night sing-alongs.

Have them write about their own memories on the Think Sheet "Smelling More Than Roses" (at the end of this section). Discuss how they might use some of the strong scent memories in their writing. Put one of your own memories on the board and model how you compose a paragraph incorporating something about the smell. Send them off to review their current stories to determine if there is a place where adding the sense of smell could enhance the piece.

Categorize the Senses. Read aloud a book that has many rich images, such as *Raising Yoder's*

Barn. Have students listen for examples of the five senses. As they hear them, write them on a class chart. Example:

Book: *Raising Yoder's Barn* by J. Yolen

Sight

... one Monday in July turned angry and dark. Black clouds scudded across the sky. Lightning, like a stooping hawk, shot straight down toward our barn. ...
The old timbers were still smoking, "Like an old man at his pipe," Papa said. ...
The barn grew like a giant flower in the field ... (and many others)

Sound

[cows] ran out the barn door and down the road, bawling all the way ...
... shouting instructions in a voice made harsh by the smoke.
... rang the bell long and hard to summon the neighbors.
... the sound of many hammers ringing ...

Touch

Soon the palms of my hands were covered with pearly blisters ...
Mama and Little Sister pumped until their own hands were raw ...
Mama was not amused, and attacked his face with a wet cloth till his cheeks were red as flames.

Taste

At noon, we ate on the trestle tables, a holiday meal served up by the women: soup with dumplings, ground meat sausages, pickled cabbage, potatoes and applesauce, apple butter slathered on fresh baked bread.

Smell

As you review the chart of sensory words from *Raising Yoder's Barn,* you will notice that there were no examples of the sense of smell. This is a good time to point out that not all books or chapters will include all senses. We never use a writing craft just for the sake of using it—we use it to enhance the story when it's appropriate.

Have the children follow the same model as they read their own books and complete the Think Sheet "Categorize the Senses" (at the end of this section). These are a few books we love that have a strong focus on the senses with many similes, metaphors, and descriptive language. You probably have your own favorites.

- *Guess Who My Favorite Person Is* by B. Baylor
- *Night Sounds, Morning Colors* by R. Wells
- *Emily* by M. Bedard
- *Owl Moon* by J. Yolen

- *Stellaluna* by J. Cannell
- *Thunder Cake* by P. Polacco
- *Because of Winn Dixie* by K. DiCamillo
- *Pictures of Hollis Woods* by P. R. Giff
- *Walk Two Moons* by S. Creech

Sensory Notebooks. Make notebooks for students to keep the sensory words they find, organized by sense. As they find words in their readings or in class discussions, they may add them to their notebooks. Each page could be titled "Sound (or Sight, Touch, Taste, Smell) Words I Like." Our students keep their pages in the Resource Section of their Writing Notebooks.

Poetically Speaking

Can You Haiku? When we are only allowed a few words, every one is important. Haiku is a lovely form of poetry that captures an essence of something, usually in nature, creating a mood and image. You may know that Haiku was originally from Japan and began as a 17-syllable one-line poem. Over time, it evolved into the three lines that we are familiar with today, broken into 5-7-5 syllables. This is one for a Texas unit, using the senses of sight and sound and touch:

> Walking in the breeze
> Bluebonnets whisper and dance
> On the silent trail

Read some Haiku poems for students to enjoy the sensory details. Discuss what comes into their minds. Play soft music in the background to enhance the mood. Put two Haiku poems on the overhead or board so they can see the verses. Let them tell what they notice about the way the two poems look and the common elements (three lines, the middle line is longer than the first and third, 5-7-5 syllable count, each creates a visual image). It's their turn to Haiku following these guidelines:

1. Select a topic.
2. Brainstorm words associated with the topic
3. Put the words into phrases counting out the syllables
4. Review the words to make sure they convey an image and have the correct syllable count for each line.

Extension: Encourage advanced writers to pen an entire book of Haiku poems on one topic. The example is excerpts from a book I wrote after a hiking trip in Colorado:

Homage to Long's Peak

> Gray Kentucky days
> Remembering a promise
> Good times in high places

> Rise before the sun
> Silent stars guide our steps

The summit awaits

A bitter wind blows
Flickering stars fade into light
A crisp morning breaks

A ray of sunshine
In the azure July sky
Shares its gentle warmth

A Cadbury bar
A welcomed sip of water
Nourish tired bodies

Onward toward the sky
Steady rhythm of our boots
Crunching granite soil

Blurring dreams recall
Scents of far away summers
To live them again

Gray Kentucky days
Thinking of summers to come
Eight boots over Long's Peak

What I know about ...

Five Senses

Write your favorite examples of each sense.

Sight

Sound

Touch

Taste

Smell

Name _____   Date _____

Artifact Description
Using Your Sense of Sight

Artifact: _____

Draw a Picture:

Notes about the size, color, shape, texture, and distinguishing features:

_____

_____

_____

_____

Write a description of your artifact.

_____

_____

_____

_____

_____

Name _____   Date _____

The Sounds Around Us
Using Your Sense of Sound

What Sound Do I Hear?	Connection and Description
1.	
2.	
3.	
4.	
5.	

Name _____   Date _____

Adding Texture to Writing
Using Your Sense of Touch

_____

Description of the object in the bag:

_____

What is the object?

_____

Write a comparison between the object and something else, using shape, size, or texture in your description.

Name _____ Date _____

The Tasting Party
Using Your Sense of Taste

Direction: Write about each food item and what it makes you think about.

Food Item	Description, Reaction, and Memory
1.	
2.	
3.	
4.	
5.	

Name _____ Date _____

Smelling More Than Roses
Using Your Sense of Smell

Direction: Write some memories that you have about distinct smells.

_____

1.

_____

2.

_____

3.

_____

4.

_____

5.

_____

6.

_____

7.

_____

8.

_____

9.

_____

10.

_____

Categorize the Senses

Directions: As you read the book, write all the sensory words and phrases you find.

Book Title: _____

Sight

_____

Sound

_____

Touch

_____

Taste

_____

Smell

Zoom!

The bigger the issue, the smaller you write.
—Richard Price

Key Elements of Zoom!

- Focuses on an important part or brief moment in the text
- Enlarges images like a "camera lens"
- A specific way to Show, Don't Tell
- Integrates
  - precise words
  - five senses
  - characters' feelings
- Builds intensity

Writing Standards:

2. Writing Purposes and Resulting Genres
   a. Narrative Writing: Sharing Events, Telling Stories
      - Create a believable world and use precise words and details.
      - Write a sequence of events that are logical and natural.
3. Language Use and Conventions
   a. Style and Syntax
      - Use phrases of syntactic patterns to show relationships of ideas—embed phrases and modifiers that make their writing lively and graphic.
      - Take on the language of authors—emulate literary language where appropriate.
   b. Vocabulary and Word Choice
      - Use precise and vivid words.
      - Take on the language of authors by using specialized words related to a topic.

About Zoom! ...

Zoom lenses on a camera can have a magical effect because they allow photographers to remain in one place while changing the view of an image. They can adjust the field of vision, moving from a big picture to a small area. And don't photographers always zoom in on the most interesting parts of a scene? At the instant the shutter is released, that image is frozen in time, capturing all the details of the picture.

Using a similar technique, writers can zoom in on a specific spot of writing in order to see every detail more clearly. The small place in the writing becomes enlarged through the author's descriptive words. Sometimes, authors write about the big picture; other times, they concentrate on a small part. When the writer zooms in, the scene changes from unfocused to crisp.

Not all parts of a story are equal. There are parts through which writers move quickly, and important parts where writers slow down and linger. This is a pivotal moment that the writer can stretch to intensify the action and characters' reactions. Writing about this expanded moment is the strategy we call Zoom!

The concept of enlarging an essential part of a story goes by various other names, such as Hot Spot, Explode a Moment, Magnifying Glass, Slice of Pizza, and Focus In. A rose by any other name … Whatever the name, the important idea is the same: Write in a way that expands a significant part in the story and focuses the reader's attention.

Example of Zoom! in Literature:

From *The Widow's Broom* by C. Van Allsburg:

> One afternoon two of the Spivey boys and their dog walked along the road where the broom was happily at work. When they saw what it was doing, they kicked the small stones the broom had swept aside back into its path. The broom ignored them and shuffled off to sweep another part of the road.
> But the Spivey boys would not leave it alone. They called the broom names. When it continued to ignore them, they picked up a couple of sticks and started tapping the broom's handle.
>
> Finally, it stopped sweeping. The broom turned to the two boys and knocked them both on the head so hard they fell to the ground in tears. The broom hopped off, but the Spivey dog ran after it, yapping and biting at its bristles. "Get him!" the boys yelled. The little dog leaped into the air and caught the broom by the handle. But he was not there for long. (n.p.)

How Do I Teach Zoom?

Word Study: *Zoom*!

Definitions:

- Zoom—to increase suddenly and significantly
- Zoom in—to make an object appear bigger or closer
- Zoom lens—a camera lens with adjustable focal lengths that make an object appear closer than it really is

Ask students what they think the strategy Zoom! could mean to the writing process. How can writers Zoom! in on a text? What could we do in our writing that shows a Zoom! effect? Bring in a camera with a zoom lens, if possible, for students to look through and see how an image moves from full view to close up.

Introducing Zoom! We like to introduce this strategy with a book entitled *Zoom* by I. Banyai. It exemplifies the very concept of Zoom! as we teach it. The artist zooms in on pictures in a creative way that makes the reader think and notice exact details. We use this book because it engages children to scrutinize each scene, just as we want them to zoom in as writers.

Compare Two Pictures. The premise of Zoom! is that it concentrates on a small area. Illustrate this concept by making a transparency of the Think Sheet "Compare Two Pictures" (at the end of this section). Show the Wide-Angle View and ask children what they see. Now, show how the Zoom! view moves into the picture and focuses our vision on a defined area. What do they notice now? Sometimes in our writing, we write about a big picture, a huge topic, and we get lost in telling it all. This strategy allows us to focus on one small area and write about it in a bigger, more descriptive way.

Zoom in on the Literature. Read the following excerpt from *Poppy* by Avi that zooms in on an important part of the story.

> Paddling furiously, Poppy struggled to keep her nose above water. Despite her efforts, she was swept on. She spun downstream like a whirligig. Then, abruptly, she felt herself wedged between two rocks. Water washed over her. As she gasped for air, she sensed that if she stayed put it would be only a matter of time—a short time—before she drowned.
>
> Wrenching one paw free, she groped for something to cling to. What she found was the slimy root of a water lily. She tried to hold on. The root slipped from her grasp.
>
> She reached out again and managed to find the lily's stem. Snorting to keep nose and mouth free of water, Poppy hauled in. Bit by bit she began to rise. (pp. 78–79)

Reference the Key Elements of Zoom! to guide the discussion about what Avi did to make the scene memorable. Imagine that we are zoomed in on Poppy with our camera lens:

- Why do you think Avi chose this one small place to zoom in?
- How did Avi stretch and expand this moment?
- Which precise words created pictures in your minds?
- Which words connect to our five senses?
- In what ways were Poppy's feelings shown?
- How did Avi build intensity?

Zoom! Wall Chart. Have students find examples of Zoom! in books they are reading. This writing craft is often difficult to find in the literature. Part of what makes it effective is the fact that it is used sparingly.

Examples of Zoom!

| *Sable* by Hesse | And then the strangest thing happened. Mam walked over, reached down her hand, and touched Sable. Sable held so still, like she knew how hard it was, what |

Mam was doing.

Mam's fingers spread slowly over Sable's head, taking in the bones. Her tall back relaxed a little. She moved her fingertips down, inching toward Sable's ears. Mam smiled as she touched those ears. (p. 78)

Study a Photograph. Bring in some photographs or pictures that have a scene of frozen action. Model how to study a photograph and zoom in on the most interesting part of it. Tell them about it: focus on details using precise words, five senses, and characters' feelings.

Direct students to zoom in on their own photographs and find the most interesting small part. They can write about their photographs using Zoom!

What's for Lunch? Share a lead to set the stage for writing together a zoomed part of a story. Read or tell the following, "What's for Lunch?"

> *What's this?* I thought to myself when I noticed the wrinkled brown paper bag sitting in the middle of Luke's desk. *I bet he forgot his lunch.* I reached out for the bag, but the bag jumped backwards! I froze, not daring to breathe, *but stared. Why would a bag jump?* I wondered. Gathering my courage, I picked up the bag and the soggy bottom fell out. Sitting on the desk where the bag had been was a young, green leopard frog.

Show a transparency of the Think Sheet "What's for Lunch?" (at the end of this section). Ask the questions and write student responses directly on the transparency. These are comments our students made:

What am I thinking?
- "Where did you come from?"
- "What in the world am I going to do with you?"

How do I feel?
- puzzled
- surprised
- startled
- confused
- unsure what to do next

Five senses?
- smells wet and swampy
- sounds like "R-r-r-ribb-et!"
- looks green and wet and smooth, bulging eyes, scared

What do I say?
- "Are you someone's lunch?"
- "Are you here for 'Show and Tell'?"

What is happening?
- Frog looks just as surprised as I am.
- I think he's surprised because he sits staring at me, still as a stone, not blinking.

When they have thoroughly explored the possibilities, have students continue the story, zooming in on that important part where you ended. As they share their Zooms!, have students point out the places where students applied rich language, precise words, and sensory details.

Dramatize the Moment. The talent scouts are out! Have students act out a scene from a book when an author zoomed in on a special moment. Guide children to exaggerate the movements to make the visualization clear. Discuss how we can "see" what happens through the writer's words and know how to act it out.

Poetically Speaking

Zoom! Poetry. Zoom! can be a joyous tool as poets focus in on a small subject in a big way. Look at how Paul Janeczko zooms in on the moment a batter approaches the plate.

"The Batter" from *That Sweet Diamond*:

He approaches the plate,
ponderous,
swinging smoothly
in slow motion
knowing his choice is simple:
swing or
not.

As he paws
the back line of the batter's box,
matching concentration and stare
with the pitcher,
he knows
indecision
or
hesitation
makes failure likely.

Pitcher rocks.

Batter waits.

Then, in the time it takes
a happy heart to beat,
decides.

Janeczko's poem used all the key elements of Zoom! Have students read other poems and identify the places that Zoom! Then, they pick a precise moment in their own lives, zoom in and describe every minute aspect of it, and write a poem.

What I know about ...

Zoom!

- Focuses on _____

- Enlarges images like a _____ lens.

- A specific way to _____

- Integrates:
  - _____
  - _____
  - _____

- Builds_____

- Example of a Zoom! I like: _____

_____

_____

Compare Two Pictures

© Pamela Westkott

Wide-Angle View

© Pamela Westkott

Zoom! View

What's for Lunch?

Name _____   Date _____

Zoom!

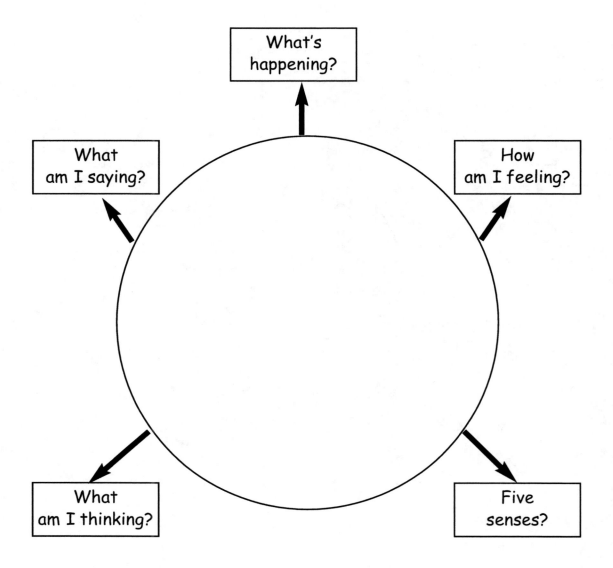

What's
happening?

What
am I saying?

How
am I feeling?

What
am I thinking?

Five
senses?

5: Teaching the Elements of Story Structure

When I start a new book, I'll noodle things over
and develop some characters.
—Dr. Seuss

Characters

Key Elements of Character:

- People, animals, and fictional characters
- Show how a character
  - looks
  - speaks
  - acts
  - feels
- Traits—features that distinguish one individual from another
- Characters drive the action

Writing Standards:

2. Writing Purposes and Resulting Genres
   a. Narrative Writing: Sharing Events, Telling Stories
      - Develop characters by providing reasons for action and how they solve problems.
      - Develop a plot or tell about an event by describing actions and emotions of characters and using story elements of dialogue, how a character feels, descriptive details, and others.

About Characters ...

"What a character!" people have often said about my father. To my dad's personality I apply the dictionary definition of *character*: "set of qualities that make somebody distinctive and interesting." I thought of descriptors, such as funny, a storyteller, thoughtful, honest, and spiritual, but I realized that these words don't give a reader a picture of him at all. But, when I tell you something specific, he becomes a real person to the reader: He whistles each morning as he gets ready for work, his hands are warm as they wrap around mine, his shoulders shake up and down when he laughs so hard, he believes that you should treat everyone with respect, and he brings my mama jonquils from the farm when they first bloom in March.

Every story has a character. Many times, when we think of favorite books, it's the character we remember and not just the story. Why is that? Perhaps it's the way we relate to characters or share similar feelings. Perhaps it's the way characters look, speak, act, and feel all blended together that makes them believable. Our challenge as writers is to show the qualities that distinguish our characters and cause the reader to care about them.

Examples of Characters From Literature:

How a Character Looks: Physical descriptions are written to show us the character's appearance.

A description of the dog, Winn-Dixie, from *Because of Winn-Dixie* by K. DiCamillo:

> He was big, but skinny; you could see his ribs. And there were bald patches all over him, places where he didn't have any fur at all. Mostly, he looked like a big piece of old brown carpet that had been left out in the rain. (p. 11)

How a Character Speaks: Characters may talk in dialect, regional speech, and/or use expressions.

Regional speech from *The Cow Who Wouldn't Come Down* by P. B. Johnson:

> Miss Rosemary marched out into the yard. She called sternly, "Gertrude! You will kindly come down this very instant. It's a known fact cows don't fly." (n.p.)

How a Character Acts: The way a character acts shows what he or she thinks, cares about, and believes.

From *Insects Are My Life* by M. McDonald:

> Amanda collected bugs. Dead ones, of course. The skin of a grasshopper, the shell of a cicada, a perfect pair of butterfly wings found after a thunderstorm. She collected bug cases. Once she hatched hundreds of tiny praying mantises right in her sock drawer. She collected mosquito bites. She counted twenty-two bites on one leg and she was proud. (n.p.)

How a Character Feels: Sometimes, feelings are not stated outright and must be inferred. Readers bring their own experiences to what they are reading, thinking and feeling.

From *Lost* by P. B. Johnson and C. Lewis

> At school I couldn't concentrate, even though we were studying Astronomy, which I really like. There was a big cactus just outside the window. It made me think of the desert.

And Flag.

Where was he?

I missed him so much. (n.p.)

How Do We Teach Character?

> **Word Study:** *Character*
>
> Lead a discussion in which students explain their own thinking about "character." Do they focus mainly on a person or an animal in a book? Do they think of characters as real people, too?
>
> Consult the dictionary and read that *character* is:
>
> - a set of qualities that make someone distinctive, especially qualities of mind and feeling;
> - qualities that make individuals interesting.

Identify Your Characters. Writer Marcia Thornton Jones categorizes story characters for young readers in three ways:

> 1. Main Character—the one the reader cares about and roots for
> 2. Antagonist—someone who makes life difficult for the main character
> 3. Secondary Characters—other people in the story

Have students identify these three types of characters in the stories they read and write. They can cite evidence to support how the writers develop each kind of character. Here are some guiding questions students can use when they are developing a story.

- Who are the main character, antagonist, and secondary characters?
- In what ways have you made the reader care about your main character?
- How did the antagonist make life difficult for the main character?
- What did the secondary characters do that added interest to the story?

Let Me Introduce You. Read aloud a passage from a book that introduces a character. Discuss the way the author shows us how a character looks, speaks, acts, and feels. Have students peruse the books they are reading independently to find how the author introduces a new character. Let them read aloud the passage(s) and discuss the interesting words and images used.

Have students select a piece of their own writing and circle where they introduce a character. Probe: What do you want readers to know and think about this character at this point in the story? Which words show the reader that? The purpose for asking the questions is to help students evaluate whether they need to give the reader more (or less) information in the introductions. Advanced writers learn to embed information about the characters gradually; it's not always desirable to put everything you know at the point of introduction. The ultimate goal is to make the characters believable.

How Does a Character Look? Writing physical descriptions may be the easiest way for students to describe characters in their stories. One way to begin is for students to find an example they like in the literature about how a character looks. Then analyze: Why do I like this passage? What words made me see the character in my mind?

For example, look at how DiCamillo describes Winn-Dixie: "Mostly, he looked like a big piece of old brown carpet that had been left out in the rain" (p. 11). Why do you think the author used a simile to describe the dog? This may be one way students could describe how their character looks—through a comparison.

Dialogue. The way that characters speak can make them believable. If you are ready to teach dialogue as part of character development, there are specific ideas listed in the "Dialogue" section of the next chapter.

Found Expressions. Let characters express themselves just like real people do. When I think of expressions associated with a person, I always smile and think about my mother. We always tease her about her colorful expressions, such as, "You've gotta roll with the punches," or "She's a lost ball in high weeds."

Guide students to think about what expressions *they* use in their everyday talk with friends. What do their friends say that may be individualistic? We tend to focus on content of conversations, rather than on style. Challenge children to listen to each other. Let them spend a few days listening and observing conversations. They may even want to tape record or jot down a few notes then share their newfound expressions with the group. Have them select or create expressions to use with a character.

Create an Idiosyncrasy. We all have them! These quirky behaviors are one way that we distinguish ourselves, unintentionally. The dictionary defines *idiosyncrasy* as "a way of behaving, thinking, or feeling that is peculiar to an individual, especially an odd or unusual one." In literature, unusual and distinctive characters stay with us long after the book is closed. For example, in *Five Dog Night,* the author uses an idiosyncrasy of the main character. Ezra doesn't use blankets on his bed to keep warm at night—he uses dogs! One dog for a cool evening and five dogs for a frosty night.

Students can have lots of fun creating idiosyncrasies for their characters to distinguish them. Encourage them to do it.

Gestures. Have you ever met someone who couldn't talk without moving his or her hands? Have students notice the various gestures people make—and when they make them. For example, twisting hair while thinking, drumming fingers on a desk when waiting, pointing an accusing finger at someone when they're mad. They may begin to notice the gestures that characters make in books. Have them give their characters some gestures.

Make a Class Chart of Character Traits. The dictionary defines *trait* as a "particular characteristic or quality that distinguishes somebody." Traits are an intrinsic part of who we are. All of our characters should have some distinguishing characteristics. The way a character speaks, acts, feels, and thinks all combine to make up character traits. Give an example of one of your own character traits and explain what behaviors make up that trait. Brainstorm other traits and list them on a chart. Discuss how we show them through our behaviors.

Example Chart of Character Traits

artistic	diligent	independent	respectful
athletic	excited	intelligent	risk taker
brave	fair	lazy	rude
careful	friendly	leader	self-confident
cheerful	frightened	lucky	selfish
clever	funny	mean	serious
curious	generous	messy	shy
courageous	gentle	nosy	sneaky
cranky	grumpy	patient	stubborn
daring	honest	proud	thoughtful
determined	imaginative	quiet	trusting

Dramatize it. There's a little ham in all of us, and we have fun dramatizing in this exercise! Select a trait, act it out, then elicit from students the behavior that showed that trait. For example:

Walking around the room with a box of cookies, I stuffed one in my mouth and said to a student, "I have some cookies and you don't. Do you want some? Well, you can't have any because they're all mine!" Then, have students identify the trait: selfish. Together write the behaviors that showed how I was being selfish.

Trait	Behaviors That Show the Trait
selfish	ate without sharing, taunted the student, rubbed it in that Mrs. W. had all the cookies

From a basket, have students draw out one character trait card (but shhhh—don't tell anyone!). Students dramatize the trait and let the class guess it. Discuss what they did to show the trait. Then, add those behaviors to a wall chart as a resource.

That Suits You to a T! Have you ever heard someone say, "That suits you to a T?" And did you wonder what a "T" was, although you probably understood that the person meant it was a perfect match? I like to introduce the concept by presenting a T-square, which architects use to precisely draw lines and angles. This exercise helps students to describe their characters precisely by connecting behaviors to specific traits.

Model the activity with a well-known character such as Little Red Riding Hood. As a class, complete the table: List several traits of Little Red and cite evidence of her behavior.

Little Red Riding Hood to a "T"

Trait	Behaviors That Show the Trait
Independent	Went by herself to Grandma's house
Trusting	Believed wolf when she met him on path
Caring	Taking food to sick Granny
Clever	Figured out that the wolf wasn't Granny

Have students refer to their list of character traits and complete a table for the main character in their own stories.

In My Character's Shoes. I can still recall the dreaded "character sketches" I was required to write in high school about a specific character. I would procrastinate because I simply didn't know how to do it. Fortunately, we have learned how to guide children to understand characters better and to put ourselves in their shoes.

As a first step, have students use themselves—the persons they know best—as the character to complete the Think Sheet "In My Character's Shoes" (at the end of this section). Next, they can use the sheet to plan characters for their original stories.

Interview the Character. Barry Lane suggests having students "become the character" in their writing as they sit in the author's chair and introduce themselves. They can dress in costume or wear an article of clothing that suggests how the character looks. The purpose is to help the writers to fully develop characters in their own stories after hearing the questions and wonders of the audience.

In My Character's Shoes

I am a character in _Jackie_'s story. In this story my name is _Arlene_, but I like to be called _Are_.
I am _6_ years old and I live with _my family_ at _88 Dentiesor Rd._
My pet _is a snake_ named _Sneaky_ lives with me too.
This is what I look like:

My best friend is _Holly_
Together we like to _play vollyball_

Shhhhh. . . I have a secret. I'll tell you, but don't tell anyone else.
I sing in the shower.

My funnest thing to do is _look at myself in the mirror and say stuf_
I never like to _do homework_
I'm really good at _coloring_
And _tracing_ is sooooooo hard for me.
My most special thing in the whole world is _my glasses_.
I have a bad habit of _scratching my nose_
One memory I have is _going to Six Flags_
I say, "_Deva vug_" all the time.
I'm very curious about _presents_
One more thing I'd like for people to know about me is

First, the interviewees share a brief summary of the stories they are writing from the perspective of the main character. Next, the audience interviews the characters. Questions students ask should be based on the Key Elements of Characters. Afterward, students may revise their stories.

Character Webs: Webbing is a striking visual way to organize information about a character. Begin with the character's name and include the key elements of looks, speaks, acts, and feels. Then, let students brainstorm evidence from the text that supports each element. Have students web a character from their own writing.

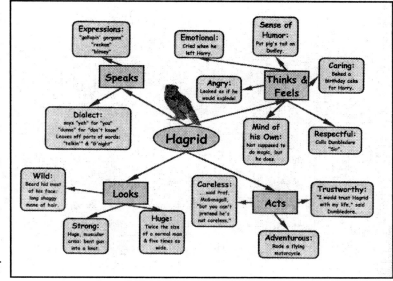

Our web example is of Hagrid from *Harry Potter and the Sorcerer's Stone* by J. K. Rowling.

Nonfiction

Use a Character Trait Model for Biography. Some books are specific in asserting character traits of famous people. They can become an excellent model for students when they write a biography or autobiography. For example, Mohammed Ali's biography, *Float Like a Butterfly* by N. Shange, provides several specific character traits (although they weren't called that) and then gives examples of Ali's actions that were evidence of these traits:

> "He believed in *excellence* …"
> "He believed in *perseverance* …"
> "He believed in *generosity* …"

If they are writing an autobiography or biography, have students follow the model and identify three to five character traits about themselves or their famous subject. They may refer to a class chart of traits that was previously developed. Then, write some behaviors that make the subject believable.

Poetically Speaking

People Poems: These poems can be about people we know or famous (or infamous!) individuals. The pattern of the five-line People Poems is as follows:

- Line 1: Name of person
- Line 2: Two adjectives connected by "and" or "but"

- Line 3: Adverb and verb describing the person's usual actions
- Line 4: Simile or metaphor to describe a personal quality
- Line 5: End with a connection between you and the person, such as "If only" or "I wish."

Emily Dickinson by Kay Kay Johnson and Pam Westkott.

Emily Dickinson
Vivid but gentle lyricism
Rhymed unconventionally
Original as a single flake of snow
If only I had her gift of words

What I know about ...

Characters

- People, animals, and made-up creatures

- Show how a character:
    - _____
    - _____
    - _____
    - _____

- _____ are features that distinguish one individual from another

- Drives the _____

- My favorite story characters are: _____
  _____
  _____

In My Character's Shoes

I am a character in a story called _____
by _____. In this story, my name is _____,
but I like to be called _____.
I am _____ years old and I live with _____.
My pet _____ named _____ lives with
me, too.
This is what I look like:

My best friend is _____.
Together we like to _____.
Shhhhh ... I have a secret. I'll tell you, but don't tell anyone
else. _____
My most fun thing to do is _____.
I never like to _____.
I'm really good at _____.
And _____ is sooooooo hard for me.

My most special thing in the whole world is _____

I have a bad habit of _____.

One memory I have is _____.

I say, " _____" all the time.

I'm curious about _____.

What I wish more than anything else is _____

_____

_____

_____

_____

_____

Some character traits that describe me are _____

_____

One more thing I'd like for people to know about me is___

_____

_____

Plot

Experience is not what happens to you;
it is what you do with what happens to you.
—Aldous Huxley

Key Elements of Plot:

- Plot = characters + situations
- Beginning
  - Characters are introduced.
  - Setting is described.
  - Problem or conflict is presented.
- Middle
  - Characters face obstacles.
  - Action builds to the high point (when the problem is about to be solved).
  - High point divides middle and end.
- End
  - Problems of conflict are solved.

Writing Standards:

2. Writing Purposes and Resulting Genres
   a. Narrative Writing: Sharing Events, Telling Stories
      - Orient the reader by establishing the time, and location and introducing the characters, or lead into the story in an interesting way
      - Create a believable world and use precise words and details.
      - Write a sequence of events that are logical and natural.
      - Develop a character by providing reasons for action and solving a problem.
      - Produce a plot or tell about an event by using story elements.
   b. Informative Writing: Report or Informational Writing
      - Use an organizational structure that helps the reader.
      - Communicate big ideas or insights that have been elaborated on or illustrated by facts, details, and other information.
      - Write a conclusion that ties it all together.
   c. Functional and Procedural Writing
      - Engage the reader by establishing a context for the writing.
      - Provide a guide to action.
      - Show the steps in enough detail to follow easily.
      - Include relevant information.

About Plot ...

Plot is noticed and studied long before students ever put pencil to paper. We teach plot as we read books aloud and pause to observe how the author moved the action along.

Anne Lamott tells us "plot grows out of character." When we write about the characters, something is bound to happen, and this action is the plot. She says not to worry about plot, just worry about the characters. Characters will confront a problem or conflict, make decisions, and navigate through obstacles to solve the problem. Finding the balance is the writer's charge. Plot is intriguing because we want to know what the characters will do and say and how they will respond in a given situation. As students write about their character's actions and adventures, plot will emerge.

It's not easy to write interesting plot, as there are many layers. We scaffold their thinking as we structure the story's development, modeling how to incorporate the necessary components of the beginning, the middle, and the end. Sometimes, plot unfolds as we follow our characters into unanticipated directions. James Howe said, "I don't know what I'll write next. But, whatever it is, I hope I'll be surprised." We may be surprised right along with our children.

Examples of Plot in Literature:

Stairstep Plot: One thing happens, then another, in a step-by-step progression that leads steadily to the conclusion.

Mirette on the High Wire by E. A. McCully:

8. He freezes, but Mirette helps him cross.

7. He tries to walk a rope across two buildings.

6. Bellini plans a way to face his fear and please her.

5. He tells Mirette he is now afraid to walk the rope.

4. Mirette hears stories about Bellini's amazing stunts.

3. She practices and learns on her own.

2. Mirette asks Bellini to teach her to tightrope walk, but he refuses.

1. Bellini, a retired tightrope walker, stays in Mirette's boarding house.

Repetition Plot: This is usually found in books for young readers. It is rhythmic and children can easily read along, memorize, or chant together.

From *There Was an Old Lady Who Swallowed a Fly* retold by S. Taback:

There was an old lady who swallowed a fly. I don't know why she swallowed a fly. Perhaps she'll die.

There was an old lady who swallowed a spider that wiggled and jiggled and tickled inside her. She swallowed the spider to catch the fly. I don't know why she swallowed the fly. Perhaps she'll die ... (n.p.)

<u>**Circular Plot**</u>: The story begins and ends in a similar way.

From *The Day That Henry Cleaned His Room* by S. Wilson:

1. Henry has a messy room.

12. Henry has a messy room again.

11. Falls asleep in messy room.

10. Henry is happy.

9. Bring back stuff.

8. Animals come back in.

7. Henry is sad and can't sleep.

2. Cleaned out his room.

3. Scientists studied dust.

4. Yard sale.

5. He spoke on TV.

6. Henry's room is clean!

How Do I Teach Plot?

> **Word Study: *Plot***
>
> Discuss how these various dictionary definitions enhance our meanings of *plot*:
>
> - the story or sequence of events in a narrated work, graph, chart, or diagram
> - a plan decided upon in secret
> - an architectural plan of a building
>
> Look at the interesting words the thesaurus furnishes: *plan, scheme, design, strategy, scenario, outline, narrative, story, storyline, action.*

Study the Literature. As you read books throughout the year, guide students to notice the plot structure of each book. Draw the structure on the board to visualize it (e.g., show stairstep or circular plot examples). When students understand how writers construct plot in the books they read, they can more easily construct plot in their own writing.

Traffic Light the Beginning, Middle, and Ending. For younger writers or those visual learners who need assistance, Tompkins uses the traffic light visuals of green, yellow, and red to connect with the beginning, middle, and ending of stories. Model putting removable green, yellow, and red dots on the pages of a picture book to correspond with the parts of the story. Direct students to use colored dots on their own writing to designate the beginning, middle, and end. They should see that the middle section usually has more text than the beginning or ending, because the middle is where most action occurs.

Visual Metaphors for Class Posters: Graphic organizers accommodate the multiple intelligences of visual learners. You can purchase class posters or make your own.

- **A Recipe for Good Writing.** This idea is a variation from a poster in Cindy Kneller's third-grade classroom. Use the metaphor of cooking as it applies to writing.

> **Recipe for a Good Plot**
> 1/3 Cup each of Beginning, Middle, and End
> a pinch of conflict
> 3 T. of Action
> 1 Scoop of S-t-r-e-t-c-h I-t O-u-t
> Blend in just enough dialogue
> Mix together with character's thoughts and feelings.
> Bake until done.
> Share it with a friend.

Here's a comparison to explain fully the metaphor to children (for those of us who don't cook!):

Cooking
When we mix the right ingredients together and give it time to cook, the result is a delicious dish. If important ingredients are left out, the dish may be bland and not fit to eat.

Writing
With the right combination of strategies, the words and ideas come together as we take time to think, plan, and write. If some important elements are left out, the piece may be bland, uninteresting, and not enjoyable to read.

- **Narrative Writing Diamond.** This illustrates visually the typical proportions of story parts, such as the beginning is short, the middle has the bulk of the writing, then the ending is brief. It is a reminder of certain elements that could be included in the writing. Post these ideas (or your own variation) on a diamond-shaped poster.

Beginning
Characters are introduced.
Setting is described.
Problem is presented.

Middle
Characters face obstacles. Action builds to the High Point (when the problem is about to be solved). S-t-r-e-t-ch out the scene to Show, Don't Tell what is happening.

- - - **The High Point divides the middle and the end** - - -

End
Problems are solved.
Extend the ending.

139

- **Cheeseburger Story Builder.** Pile it on in this graphic organizer to illustrate how the layers of plot combine to make a complete meal. At the end, the reader should be full and satisfied.

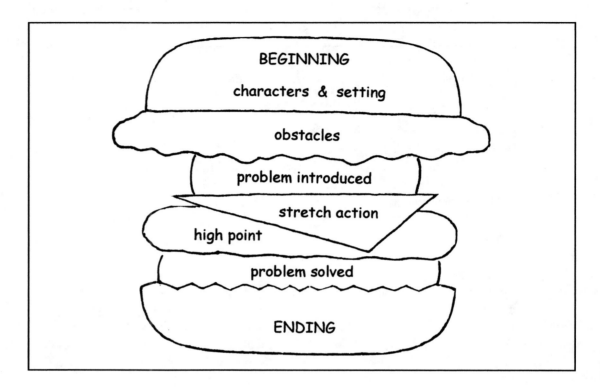

Create Some Conflict. Write a nice, little mundane story that has no conflict or problems (or use the passage below). Read it to students and have them respond to it. Ask what the conflict or problem is. When they notice that there is no problem, talk about the possibilities that the author overlooked. There are some ideas embedded in the passage that could lead to a dicey situation. In the following example, life seems peachy for Mrs. Brown, but it's terribly dull for the reader:

> Mrs. Brown lives next door to me in a large, wooden, three-story house with her kitten, Pascha. Her home is filled with antiques. Her prize possessions are everywhere, even on her front porch. Mrs. Brown loves Pascha because she has someone to care for and talk to. She is always doing something that entertains Mrs. Brown. How lucky Mrs. Brown and Pascha are to have each other.

Let each student rewrite the story, but incorporate a problem and solution. Afterward, when students share their ideas, discuss how different conflicts can arise in one story and how problems add interest and excitement.

Plotting With Pictures. Books without words can be effective ways to have students focus on plot and story structure. Their efforts can concentrate on the writing instead of the task of creating a completely new story idea. Here are some we like:

- *The Thirteenth Clue*. Review a wordless picture book, such as *The Thirteenth Clue* by A. Jonas. (The book begins with an excerpt from a diary. Each set of illustrated pages leads the main character, a girl we see in shadows, through visual clues to the high point: her friends surprise her for her birthday, but only after she's solved adventurous riddles.) Discuss the plot structure, character, setting, beginning, middle (how she solves the visual riddles), and ending.

- **Wordless Picture Books.** Distribute a variety of wordless picture books to students. Have them write a story from one of these books based on the illustrations. Some students may write a sentence for each page. Others may write a story based on the general gist of the book. Notice the different plots and storylines that emerge from looking at pictures.

- **Plot Doesn't Get** *Lost*. Similar to the wordless picture books idea, use *Lost* by C. Lewis and P. B. Johnson. It has a wonderful narrative on the right page of the book and a wordless illustrated story on the left. The narrative tells about a young girl searching for her lost dog in the desert. The wordless illustrated story shows what is happening from the point of view of the dog. Have students write a story about the dog based on what they see in the pictures. A description of each illustration could combine to create another story.

- *The Mysteries of Harris Burdick*. This Van Allsburg classic book has been utilized by many teachers to launch story ideas based on his mysterious black and white drawings and one-line descriptors. Use this book when teaching plot because students can clearly <u>see</u> a problem in each picture. Their task becomes one of elaborating on the conflict and developing a viable solution.

- **Photographs.** Imaginations can soar when we look at photographs. Collect an assortment of pictures—from magazines, old photos, advertisements, travel brochures, and so forth. Have students select one to develop into a story. Ask probing questions to get at the heart of the picture and provoke their thinking, such as:

  - What do you notice about the person or scene?
  - What do you imagine is happening in the picture?
  - What does the person's expression in the picture tell you about what might have happened?
  - List some events that you think could have led up to this picture.
  - What is the problem and some possible solutions?

Throw Three Stones Into the Plot. We adapted this idea from writer Joanne Rocklin and developed the Think Sheet "Throw Three Stones" (at the end of this section) to organize students' ideas. Sometimes called "The Magic of Three," this writing strategy has been used in literature for years, from early fairy tales to modern stories.

Discuss how events in stories frequently happen in threes. For example, in folk tales the action often focuses on three events (e.g., in "Rumpelstiltskin" the miller's daughter spun straw into gold three times, in "The Three Little Pigs" they build three houses, in "Cinderella" the three sisters tried on the glass slipper, and many, many others). Select one story and show in detail how the author developed this strategy. Plot it on the board.

Have students develop their own plots by thinking in terms of three. "Throw the first stone" can be that the protagonist tries to solve the problem by trying something, but it doesn't work. "Throw the second stone" can have the character try another way to solve the problem, with no luck. "Throw the third stone" can be the final way the character attempts to find a solution, this time with success.

After studying this strategy in the literature and practicing it in their own stories, we find that just writing the gentle question "three stones?" on their page may trigger an "Aha!" and a focused revision that develops the plot more fully.

Focus on the Middle. Robert Frost once said, "The best way out is always through." Students may have an idea to begin a story, but get bogged down in the middle as they ramble with an unclear focus. Help them to get "through" it with these ideas:

- Clarify the central plot by writing a summary paragraph to explain what is happening. Identify an important part of the story and s-t-r-e-t-c-h i-t o-u-t with the Zoom! strategy (discussed in Chapter 4).

- Or, ask a "What if …" question to help you think about something in a new way. Change something in the story that gives it a different focus. For example, what if the story were placed in a different setting? Or, what if the character were an animal trainer instead of a dancer? Or, what if the character made a different choice in the story? Could this change help make the story more interesting or improve it? Play around with a new idea to see what happens.

Plot Plan. Many writers plan their plot ideas before they begin composing. Our students do this with the Think Sheet "Plot Plan" (at the end of this section). The outline form can nudge their thinking as they deliberate about each component. Model how you consider each question posed, jot down notes of your brainstormed ideas, then circle the ones that intrigue you. Begin a story using your notes. Have students complete the Plot Plan and begin their stories.

Sticky Notes Plot Summaries. Do some children have difficulty staying focused in their writing? And do they tend to ramble? Ours do. When students are reading chapter books independently, have them post sticky notes at the top of each page or chapter telling the main plotline of that part of the book. Use the same process when they write their own stories—post notes at the top of each page to summarize the plot. This may help to keep them on track.

Act Out Tableaus. A tableau is a visually dramatic scene or situation that suddenly arises. Students depict a scene in a silent, motionless, statue-like representation. Working in groups of three, have students plan a scene about the plot of a story. Ideas for the tableaus can be written down and selected by each group, or you can assign the scenes. The tableaus are created and presented in very little time, yet they effectively engage students as they demonstrate their understanding of what's happening in the story. After each tableau presentation, discuss what that scene meant to the story and why it was important to the plot.

Sometimes, student writers use this technique to help them think through ideas when writing their own stories. Shy students often emerge as true thespians. All they need is a little help from their friends!

Draw a Mini-Movie. We can all become videographers by creating a three-frame mini-movie of our own stories. Have students draw three pictures to represent important scenes from the beginning, middle, and ending of their stories with paragraph captions underneath. Schedule a day to watch these "home movies" as students show and tell their plots. Popcorn, too?

Poetically Speaking

Narrative Poems. Narrative poetry has a plot. Read several narrative poems, such as "Casey at the Bat" and "The Midnight Ride of Paul Revere." Some rhyme and some are free verse. Discuss the character, action, conflict, and resolution. Here's a twist: Have your students compose some narrative poems based on one of their original stories.

What I know about ...

Plot

Plot = characters + situations

- Beginning
  - _____ are introduced
  - _____ is described
  - _____ is presented

- Middle
  - _____ face obstacles
  - Action leads to the high point
  - _____ divides middle from the end

- End
  - _____ is solved

Name _____   Date _____

Plot Plan

Story Title: _____

Beginning Characters? How will you introduce them? Setting? Describe place, time, weather Problem? What difficulty will the character face?	
Middle Obstacles? How does the character deal with them? High Point? What is the main event that will happen right before the character solves the problem? Action? Work backwards and decide what can happen leading up to the high point.	
Ending Solutions? How are the problems solved? Extend the ending: Choose a way to expand the closing.	

Name _____ Date _____

Throw Three Stones

Title _____

What is the character's problem?

^

How does the character try to solve it, but is unsuccessful?
1.

^

Next way the character tries to solve it, again without success.
2.

^

Final way the character tries to solve problem and succeeds.
3.

^

How does the story end?

Point of View

> *"I can't explain myself, I'm afraid, Sir," said Alice,*
> *"because I'm not myself, you see."*
> From *Alice's Adventures in Wonderland* by L. Carroll

Key Elements of Point of View:

- Who the story is told by
- First person (told by a character in the story)
  - Uses pronouns—*I, me, my, we, our, us, mine, ours*
- Third person (told by someone outside the story)
  - Uses pronouns—*he, she, it, his her, hers, its, they, their, theirs, them*
- Verb tense
  - Present (story is happening now)
  - Past (story has already happened)

Writing Standards:

2. Writing Purposes and Resulting Genres
   d. Producing Literature
      – Write stories, songs, memoirs, poetry, and plays that conform to the appropriate expectations for each.
   e. Responding to Literature
      – Discuss several works that have a common idea or theme.

About Point of View ...

Webster defines *point of view* as "a position from which something is considered or evaluated." Throughout the year, we discuss POV (as students like to call it) as we notice in the literature who is telling the story and whether it is told in the present or past tense. With young writers, we only concentrate on a first person and a general third person POV.

Most emerging writers choose to write in the first person. They often become the character and tell their own stories. First person sets up a feeling of intimacy between the writer and the reader. In this POV, we only see how the storyteller thinks and feels.

Students recognize that, when authors write in the third person, someone who is not a character is telling the story, someone outside the story. This perspective permits a great deal of flexibility for developing characters and their actions. A narrator has a broad view and can see what all characters are thinking and feeling. We hope to have young writers understand and appreciate the pros and cons of using each perspective and gain experience writing from various points of view.

Examples of Point of View in Literature:

First Person Perspective

From *Bud, Not Buddy* by C. P. Curtis:

> Here we go again. We were all standing in line waiting for breakfast when one of the caseworkers came in and tap-tap-tapped down the line. Uh-oh, that meant bad news, either they'd found a foster home for somebody or somebody was about to get paddled. All the kids watched the woman as she moved along the line, her high-heeled shoes sounding like little firecrackers going off on the wooden floor.
>
> Shoot! She stopped at me and said, "Are you Buddy Caldwell?"
>
> I said, "It's Bud, not Buddy, Ma'am." (pp. 1–2)

Third Person Perspective

From *Holes* by L. Sachar:

> He was awakened one night by a strange noise. At first he thought it might have been some kind of animal, and it frightened him. But as the sleep cleared from his head, he realized that the noise was coming from the cot next to him. (p. 83)

Present Tense. The reader is right there with the character as the action unfolds.

From *Shiloh* by P. R. Naylor:

> And this particular afternoon, I'm about half-way up the road along the river when I see something out of the corner of my eye. Something moves. I look, and about fifteen yards off, there's this shorthaired dog—white with brown and black spots—not making any kind of noise, just slinking along with his head down, watching me, tail between his legs like he's hardly got the right to breathe. (p. 13)

Past Tense. The story is told about something that has already happened. Most stories are written in past tense.

From *Tops and Bottoms* by J. Stevens:

> So Bear went back to sleep, and Hare and his family went to work. They planted, watered, and weeded.
>
> Bear slept as the crops grew. (n.p.)

How Do I Teach POV?

> ### Word Study: *Point of View*
>
> Webster says that *point of view* is:
>
> - a particular position from which somebody can look at something
>
> The thesaurus yields: *standpoint, viewpoint,* and *position*
>
> Hold an object (such as a book) up in the center of the classroom so that students can see it from different perspectives. One half of the class may see the front, the other half may see the back. Discuss the differences in what they observed and connect these experiences to POV in literature.

Pros and Cons of First and Third Person POV. There are advantages and disadvantages to writing from each point of view. After students have read books written in first and third person perspective, let them discuss their thoughts. Some may have a strong preference for one or the other. Record their ideas on a chart to compare and contrast each POV.

> ### First Person Point of View
>
> | Pros | Cons |
> |---|---|
> | • draws me in | • The characters can't "see" themselves. |
> | • feels like someone is talking to me | • I don't know how other characters are thinking and feeling. |
> | • can connect to the character | • I only know how the character who narrates is thinking and feeling. |

Think About Pronouns. Pronouns signal the point of view to the reader. Review what pronouns are: words that refer to a character(s) instead of the character's name. These words are different in first and third person perspective. First person pronouns include: *I, me, my, we, our, us, mine* and *ours.* Third person pronouns are: *he, she, it, his, her, hers, its, they, their, theirs,* and *them.* Have the class find examples of pronouns in their books to determine the POV in the story.

Examine Various Versions of a Story. There's more than one way to tell a story. Many original folktales have been retold from a different character's perspective. Read several versions of a folktale, such as "Cinderella" or "The Three Little Pigs" and identify the differences. Analyze: Who is speaking? Past or present tense? How is the version different from the original? Here are some versions of "The Three Little Pigs":

- "The Three Pigs" by D. Wiesner
- "The Three Little Pigs" by S. Kellogg
- "The Three Little Javelinas" by S. Lowell
- "The Three Little Wolves and the Big Bad Pig" by E. Trivizas
- "The True Story of the Three Little Pigs by A. Wolf" by J. Scziesca

Direct students to choose a well-known story and rewrite it from a different character's POV.

Write About a Situation—Half and Half. Give the class a situation to write about. Divide the class into halves and direct one half to write in first person and the other half to write in third person. Afterward, have students discuss what they noticed about the POV. Suggested situations:

- You are trying to convince your parents to let you have a puppy.
- You want to be a player on the school basketball team.
- Your dreaded great aunt Myrtle is coming to stay with you and your little brother for a week while your parents are out of town.

Ask 10 Questions. This is a spin-off from an exercise that many teachers use with literature. The purpose here is for students to answer questions from the POV of the character they will portray from their own stories. On separate index cards, they write 10 questions that someone would ask them about their character. They distribute the cards to classmates, who will ask the questions. The student writers answer from the POV of their characters. While they are role-playing, students can relate to the thoughts and feelings of the character they've created. They also gain experience in using appropriate pronouns that go with first person POV.

Review the Literature for Verb Tense. Select a few books that are written in present tense and a few that are written in past tense. Have students read the first page and determine which tense is used and report the verbs that let them know the tense.

Write With Consistent Verb Tense. Elementary school writers often wander unintentionally between past and present verb tense within a piece of writing. We find that an occasional mini-lesson during Writer's Workshop helps clear up some confusion and focuses their thinking on this important element. We review:

- <u>Present</u> tense tells that something is happening now and uses verbs such as *is, are, write, come, draw.*
- <u>Past</u> tense focuses on events that have already happened, often in a particular time period in the past, such as *was, were, wrote, came, drew.*

Write an assortment of present and past tense verbs and put them on separate index cards. Make a present tense and past tense chart on the board. Have students pick a verb from a basket and tape it in the correct column. Discuss some of the patterns that emerge that might give them clues about whether a verb is showing present action or something that has already happened (e.g., -ed).

Children need to decide at the start of their writing piece what tense to use and stick with it. Have students read aloud their story to a partner as they both listen for consistency in verb tense. Then, make changes where needed.

Poetically Speaking

Two Voices. The award winning book *Joyful Noise: Poems for Two Voices* by P. Fleischman is a collection of poems to be read aloud by two people, sometimes together and sometimes alternating. Some are poems from two different perspectives. For example, "Honeybees" tells a story from the POVs of a queen bee and a worker bee—two completely different tales of experience, each from its own perspective.

Play around and dramatize with these poems as students enjoy the dual readings. Then, have them work with a partner to write their own poems for two voices as they compose from two different POVs.

What I know about ...

Point of View

- Who the story is told by
  - _____ Person is told by the character in the story
  - _____ Person is told by an outside narrator

- Verb Tense
  - _____—story is happening now
  - _____—story has already happened

First Person Pronouns	Third Person Pronouns
_____	_____
_____	_____
_____	_____
_____	_____
_____	_____
_____	_____
_____	_____
_____	_____
_____	_____
_____	_____

Setting

I haste now to my setting.
From *Henry VIII* by Shakespeare

Key Elements of Setting:

- Place—where the story happened
- Time of day or season—when it happened
- Time period
  - past
  - present
  - future
  - passage of time
- Weather

Writing Standards:

2. Writing Purposes and Resulting Genres
   a. Narrative Writing: Sharing Events, Telling Stories
      – Orient the reader by establishing the time, and location and introducing the characters or lead into the story in an interesting way.
      – Create a believable world and use precise words and detail.
   b. Informative Writing: Report or Informational Writing
      – Introduce the topic and provide a context.
   c. Functional and Procedural Writing

About Setting ...

Where are we? In real life and in reading, we must be somewhere, and we like to know where we are. We think of *Charlotte's Web* and picture the farm; we remember *The Wall* and visualize the black slab of shiny granite; we recall *Sarah, Plain and Tall* and envision the western plains. In these books, the setting is integral to the story and helps to drive the plot and develop characters. In other stories, however, the setting is simply a backdrop and is of minimal importance to the story. In those stories, the plot and characters don't hinge on the location or time period.

Remember when you were little and the storm knocked out the electricity? You groped through the darkness to find the candles and the flashlight. You huddled by the dim light, anticipating that next clap of thunder. If you were scared, you didn't admit it. Later, you made hand animals in the shadows, played games, and told ghost stories. Maybe you made tents out of blankets thrown over chairs and everyone crawled in. It turned out to be a fun experience after all, and you felt that tinge of disappointment when the lights came back on. In this anecdote, the storm helped set the mood, but it is the personal experiences and characters' reactions that create the story. Weather, time, and place influence the way writers shape a setting.

Examples of Setting in Literature:

Place: The location where the story happens.

From *Ruby Holler* by S. Creech:

> Boxton was a tired town, a neglected place that looked as if it was in danger of collapsing in on itself. A tangle of old homes and shacks clustered around small stores and buildings that had seen better days. One of these buildings was the Boxton Creek Home for Children, a ramshackle house that tilted toward the train tracks and hills beyond. (p. 4)

Time of Day or Season: The timeframe in which the story happens. Writers either come right out and tell us or give us visual clues, if that's important to the story.

From *The Relatives Came* by C. Rylant:

> It was in the summer of the year when the relatives came. They came up from Virginia. They left when their grapes were nearly purple enough to pick, but not quite. (n.p.)

Time Period: Some books subtly give us information about the time period in the text. Others provide specific dates.

From *The Watsons Go to Birmingham—1963* by C. P. Curtis:

> The windshield on the Bomber wasn't like the new 1963 cars, it had a big bar running down the middle of it, dividing it in half. (p. 7)

Weather: In some stories, weather is an essential element to the plot. However, in many stories, weather is not mentioned because it has little bearing to the storyline.

From *Thunder Cake* by P. Polacco

> On sultry summer days at my grandma's farm in Michigan, the air gets damp and heavy. Stormclouds drift low over the fields. Birds fly close to the ground. The clouds glow for an instant with a sharp, crackling light, and then a roaring, low, tumbling sound of thunder makes the windows shudder in their panes. (n.p.)

How Do I Teach Setting?

Word Study: *Setting*

Have students find *setting* in the dictionary and thesaurus. Study the definitions and root word. How do these definitions apply to the story element of setting?

- surroundings or environment in which something exists
- the period in time or the place in which the events of a story happen
- set—location, props, and scenery where actors perform for a film or play

Look at the varied words that are listed in a thesaurus that connect to our ideas of setting—*location, surroundings, scenery, situation, background, set, locale, site, venue,* and *backdrop*. These synonyms provide clarity.

Where Are We? Let's take a look at where authors take us through literature. Help students get a "sense of setting" by studying the books they have read this year. On chart paper, begin a list of book titles and write beside them the setting(s) of the story. For example:

Settings

The Relatives Came	Farmhouse in West Virginia; a car on the road
A Single Shard	Seaside village in 17th-century Korea
Lost	Desert in Arizona

Ask Five Questions. We all have special places in our lives, and these could be good starting points for focusing on setting. Have students write about their own special place. (This could range from their bedroom, to a spot in their neighborhood, to a place they traveled—and anywhere in between.) Help students create the sense of place and time with these questions:

- Where are you?
- When do you go there?
- What do you do in this place?
- What makes the place special? Use your senses and think about the sights and sounds around you, textures of things you touch, memorable tastes and smells.
- What are your feelings when you are there?

Just Like an Author. Professional writers often borrow from the masters. We can, too. Put an interesting phrase from literature or poetry on a transparency and let students emulate the phrasing in their own setting. Example:

Original Text:	It was a dark and stormy night. (*A Wrinkle in Time*, p. 3)
Student Texts:	It was a bright and sunny morning.
	It was a gray and foggy day.
	It was a hazy and sluggish afternoon.
	It was a dim and dreary dawn.

Focus on Wordless Picture Books. Wordless picture books can be a fertile resource for noticing and describing specific places. Because there are no words to tell the reader information, everything we learn must be explicitly shown in illustrations. We can make these books an opportunity to stretch our descriptive writing.

For example, in *Anno's Journey,* every page is rich with setting. Study one page together to get an overall impression of the setting, then hone in on the details. Model how you might write a paragraph describing this setting. With student input, include some of the elements, such as location, time of day or season and weather. Add some descriptive language to make the setting visible. Assign each child a page for writing a descriptive setting.

Home is Where the Heart is. Writers can create rich settings from their imaginations and their memories. But first, they must get in tune with how to call up sensory images.

Use guided imagery: Have children close their eyes and create pictures in their minds as you "walk" them slowly through their homes. It could go something like this:

> You walk up to the front door of your home and turn the doorknob. You push the door open and step inside. Notice the familiar smell. You walk to your room and drop your backpack on the floor. Sit on your bed and look around. Observe the sounds around you—the noise your bed makes as you settle onto it, the sounds that you hear from outside. Run your hands over your bedspread. How does it feel to your touch? Look around you and become aware of what you see in your room: colors, favorite objects, furniture, rug or floor, books, toys, pictures, something on the walls. Think about what is special to you in this room and how you feel when you are here.

Have students write a descriptive paragraph about their room using their memories. Collect these papers. Then, for homework, ask students to write a second descriptive paragraph when they can sit right there in their own room and use all of their senses.

The next day, compare these two paragraphs. How well were they able to write from memory? In what ways was sitting in their room helpful as they wrote? Was the second paragraph more fully developed? Can they close their eyes again and imagine the room even more clearly now? Good writers try to develop their sense of imaging so that they can describe what they are picturing in their minds.

Research a Place. We don't always have to write about some place we know. We can travel in our thoughts to anywhere! But, if we write about a place we have never visited, we must find out about that place somehow. A trip to the library or Internet can help students take notes about new places. They can use the information in their own writing, as many authors do, such as Mary Pope Osborne with her *Magic Tree House* series. Guide student planning and researching:

- What are some special geographical features of the place?
- List some interesting details that would give readers an image.
- How would characters dress here (influenced by time period and weather)?
- What do you notice about the climate or weather?
- What could people do here for fun?
- How would your characters feel about living here?

Mapping Our Neighborhood. Some authors include maps in the front of their books to illustrate where characters travel or to show the passage of time. My son intently studies the maps in front of every *Redwall* book, as Jacques' drawings carefully detail the setting. While reading, he refers to the map to get a sense of where characters are traveling. Have students draw a map of the neighborhood they are writing about, and like Jacques, include the map in the front.

Change the Setting. Use a "What if …" question to move a character to a different setting. What if the character is visiting her grandmother in a cottage on the beach instead of living with her family of five in a city apartment?

Have students play around with settings for their stories. Direct them to list five different settings, choose one, and ask, "What if …?" This is exactly what some authors do when they create a series. The characters remain the same, but the setting changes, and a new storyline emerges.

A Picture's Worth … Collect and laminate pictures or postcards that show various settings, time periods, and weather. To demonstrate how to use these, show a picture and have students describe the setting. Discuss how a setting might lead to a story idea, plot, or character. Guide with questions such as:

- What's in the picture?
- Describe the place.
- What could be happening there?
- I wonder what I would do in this setting?

These picture cards can also be used for nonfiction writing. I have different collections for the various topics I teach, such as animals and their settings for a Habitat Unit. The visuals help students to be more descriptive when they write about animals in their natural habitats.

Sensory Settings. Using our five senses can help to bring a setting to life. Model how you could use your senses to list possibilities for describing this classroom. Look around and record a list, such as my example:

- <u>see</u> the "Helping Hands" wall chart,
- <u>hear</u> the scratching of chalk on the board,
- <u>smell</u> the waxy scent of broken crayons,
- <u>taste</u> the woody pencil as I gnaw on a once-was tree,
- <u>feel</u> the sun on my face as it brightens my room.

Incorporate the list you made into writing your own descriptive paragraph. Have students return to their writing with the five senses in mind. Direct them to list some sensory words that connect to their story's setting.

Weather Can Create a Mood. Authors evoke moods by incorporating descriptions of various weather conditions into their stories. Notice the words and phrases they write. Point out how weather often changes throughout a book, which could transform the mood. Students enjoy searching the literature for examples, which are easy to find:

Book	Weather	Words Authors Used to Create a Mood	Mood
A Wrinkle in Time	stormy beginning	trees tossing, frenzied lashing, clouds scudded frantically, moon ripped, wraith-like shadows	unsettling disturbing
Holes	hot and dry	dry, flat wasteland, town shriveled and dried up, temperature hovers around 95 degrees in the shade, you're going to be thirsty for the next 18 months	discouraging distressing hopeless oppressive

Have students add some weather conditions to their writing. To do this, guide them to decide what mood they want to develop in one part of the story. Brainstorm words and phrases describing the weather that might create a mood in the setting.

Nonfiction

Nonfiction Settings. Select a number of nonfiction books that have strong visual settings. Read some passages that describe the setting, such as Yolen's *Welcome to the Sea of Sand*:

> It was a wash of blue sky, the splash of terra-cotta sunrise, the dash of a speckled roadrunner, a cache of kangaroo rats busy in their burrows, a scuttle of tarantulas, a muddle of centipedes … (n.p.)

Talk about how Yolen writes this nonfiction book as if it were fiction, full of rich descriptions and visual images. Challenge student writers to use the techniques they have learned in their fiction writing and apply them to their nonfiction settings.

Poetically Speaking

Home Town Settings. Walter Dean Myers' award-winning picture book *Harlem* is filled with poetic setting. When I first read that book, I was inspired to write about Lexington, KY following his poem's format. When I read it to students, they wanted to write about their hometowns, too. And what images emerged!

© Heather Ferraro

After reading and discussing *Harlem*, have students use the Think Sheet "Home Town Settings" (at the end of this section). They can plan and compose one about their own hometown.

What I know about ...

Setting

- _____ where the story happened

- _____ when the story happened

- Time periods:
    - _____ (has happened)
    - _____ (is happening)
    - _____ (will happen)

- <u>Weather</u>—what it is like outside

Home Town Settings

Directions: After reading and analyzing *Harlem*, use this sheet to plan a poem about your town using the same categories of Myers' poem. Write your own free verse poem.

Harlem

_____
(Your Town's Name)

Places People Came from:
Waycross, Georgia, East St. Louis
Holly Springs, Gee's Bend, Memphis
Trinidad, Goree Island, Ghana/Mali/
Senegal, Niger

Places in Harlem:
Smalls, Striver's Row, Lenox Avenue
Cotton Club, Abyssinian Baptist, Apollo
110 Street

Colors:
Black, Yellow/tan/brown/black/red
Green/gray/bright, Sun yellow shirts,
Burnt umber bodies, Black skins, Indigo

Music:
Song, Tambourine rhythms, Clarinet
New sound, raucous and sassy, Hallelujah
Own sweet songs, Coming of the blues
Weary blues, Countee sung
Lilt, tempo, cadence, Sing a capella
Sunday night gospel "precious Lord …
Cracked reed/soprano sax, Learn the tunes
Poem/rhapsody, Metric, Horns, A note

People:
Jack Johnson, Joe Louis, Sugar Ray,
Langston, Countee, Du Bois, Baldwin,
Shango, Jesus, Asante, Mende, Lady Day,
Marcus, Malcolm

Food:
Summer herbs
Mangoes
Bar-b-que
Fried fish

Places People Came From in My Town:
_____
_____
_____
_____

Places in My Town:
_____
_____
_____

Colors:
_____
_____
_____

Music:
_____
_____
_____
_____
_____
_____
_____
_____

My Special People:
_____
_____
_____

Food:
_____
_____
_____
_____

Theme

*No themes are so human
as those that reflect for us.*
—Henry James

Key Elements of Theme:

- Main meaning within a story
- Beliefs about human nature
- Two kinds of theme:
  - Explicit = stated directly in the text
  - Implicit = suggested

Writing Standards:

2. Writing Purposes and Resulting Genres
a. Producing Literature. Students should:
   - Build on a story idea by extending or changing the storyline.

About Theme ...

Theme is a message about life that writers reveal to us in their stories. Sometimes, authors' words speak explicitly to the heart of the theme and state it directly to the reader. Other times, readers must draw their own conclusions about the implicit theme the writer has suggested. We look at how these universal truths emerge, often through characters' emotions.

Marcia Thornton Jones said, "If you tell a good story, theme is there" (p. 134). That's a comforting thought since we usually don't begin our writing with a theme in mind. We often "find" the theme as the piece develops. Then, we can continue to weave in the important reason for the story.

Although theme is sometimes difficult for readers and writers, we recognize that deep understanding is an evolving process, but an important one. All year we work on developing awareness of theme as we study literature and write our own stories. We are establishing a foundation that will be built upon in subsequent grades.

Examples of Theme in Literature:

Theme of "determination" in *How Angel Peterson Got His Name* by G. Paulsen is summed up in this passage:

> ... we also believed in ourselves and what we could do or thought we could do. It didn't matter that it hadn't been done before. It was still worth trying. It was, always, worth the try. (p. 111)

Theme of "living a good life" in *John Henry* retold by J. Lester is summarized in this excerpt:

> Then something strange happened. Afterward folks swore the rainbow whispered it. I don't know. But whether it was a whisper or a thought, everyone had the same knowing at the same moment: "Dying ain't important. Everybody does that. What matters is how well you do your living." (n.p.)

Themes of "loss and renewal" in *Out of the Dust* by K. Hesse are listed below:

<u>Loss</u>

Loss of Billie Jo's Ma and baby brother in the fire
Loss of the use of her hands that got burned and scarred
Loss of the wheat crop in the drought
Loss of spirit, hope, and dreams

<u>Renewal</u>

Cherishes mother's memory, but accepts Louise
Hands heal and she begins to play piano again
Dad diversifies crops
She forgives herself and makes peace with her father.

How Do I Teach Theme?

> **Word Study:** *Theme*
>
> Definitions of *theme* are:
>
> - a distinct, recurring, and unifying quality or idea
> - an idea, point of view, or perception embodied and expanded upon

Ask Universal Questions. We've all experienced hope or fear or joy. These are universally accepted feelings that each of us understands. Writers use the literary element of theme to write about theses ideas. It may be a little easier to understand the concept of theme by asking overarching questions. With younger children, we simply point out these ideas in the text and name the theme. Over time, they may answer these kinds of questions themselves.

- What is the overall idea (or theme) of this story?
- Where is there evidence in the text of this recurring theme?
- What text-to-self connection can you make with the feelings?

Explore a Theme in Literature. Guide students to identify and name one specific theme in a book. Look up the theme word in the dictionary and thesaurus to deepen their understanding. Dig into the text to support how the writer developed that theme through words, character, and plot. Example of how we scaffold their thinking using *Mirette on the High Wire*.

We identified "persistence" as one theme. Then, investigate the root word, *persist* in a thesaurus and dictionary with this guiding question: "Which words will help us to better understand the theme of persistence?" They might discover that *persist* means "to stick with something, to hold firmly to a purpose, to be tenacious, refusing to give up."

Next, have students delve back into *Mirette on the High Wire* and put sticky notes on places where Mirette holds firmly to an idea, sticks with it, and refuses to give up. Explore how McCully developed that theme through her word choice, such as:

- "Excuse me, Monsieur Bellini, I want to learn to do that!" she cried.
- Mirette watched him every day.
- Finally she couldn't resist any longer ... she jumped up on the wire to try it herself.
- Surely she could do it too if she kept trying.
- In ten tries she balanced ...
- Finally, after a week of many, many falls, she walked the length of the wire.
- "In the beginning everyone falls. Most give up. But you kept trying."
- She got up two hours earlier every day ...

Have students return to a piece of their writing and determine what theme has emerged. Look up the theme word in a dictionary and thesaurus. List synonyms from the definitions and piggyback on these ideas. Find places in the text to embed words that will continue to weave the theme throughout.

Using Theme to Develop Plot. Tompkins (1990) suggested that we expand a multidimensional theme by expressing phrases and sentences, rather than simplistic one-word themes. First, have students select a theme word, study it in a dictionary and thesaurus, then list plot ideas associated with the theme. Finally, they can draft the story.

Just as they saw the theme of "persistence" in *Mirette on the High Wire*, they can consider other possible storylines using the same theme. Example theme word and definitions: *Persistence*—perseverance, doggedness, determination, stick-with-it-ness, diligence, endurance, fortitude.

Theme	Various Plot Ideas
persistence	• She was determined to find the lost map in her grandmother's attic. • She stuck with the ballet lessons and was asked to play the role of Cinderella as an understudy. • Although he was the shortest member of the basketball team, he practiced hours a day on the three-point shot and became a high-scoring point guard and a team leader.

Name That Theme. There are a few major themes that recur in numerous books. Ask students to bring a favorite book to this lesson and share the various themes from these books. Brainstorm and record other universal themes. Post this list so students can add new themes as they find them. Examples:

friendship	belief in oneself	acceptance
courage	loss	survival
independence	trust	love
imagination	making new friends	hope
overcoming fear	perseverance	getting along with others
change	bravery	conflict
determination	responsibility	betrayal

Use Wordless Picture Books to Center on Themes. It may be easier to identify the theme when our eyes are focused on the pictures without the interference of words. Show a wordless picture book to the class. Together, identify and discuss a specific theme. Have students find the pictures that support the theme.

For example, in *Good Dog, Carl* by A. Day, we identify the theme "caring" as we watch the dog, Carl, take care of the baby. Students can point out how specific pictures of Carl feeding and cleaning the baby demonstrate that theme.

Extension: Expand the theme of "caring" and further define it to include:

- We care for people we love.
- We like to have people care for us.
- We enjoy doing nice things for people we care about.
- Caring for others makes us feel good.
- Looking out for others is part of being a good citizen.
- We care for each other in our classroom.
- We put other people's needs ahead of our own.

Books That Have Common Themes. There are a few universal themes that are revisited throughout literature. Discuss the way that many authors use the same theme, but write it in different ways (e.g., courage). There is physical courage and mental/emotional courage. Here are a few books that celebrate courage as an overarching theme: *Hatchet, The Single Shard, Holes, Maniac McGee, Dr. Desoto, Mirette on the High Wire, Number the Stars, Call it Courage, The Courage of Sarah Noble.*

This lesson studies some ways that a writer builds a theme throughout the text. First, model the process: Read (or reread) a book or chapter, name and discuss the theme, and find passages to support it.

Divide the class into groups to read a book together and search for evidence of themes. Distribute books on one topic, such as "friendship with a dog." Here are a few dog books of varying reading levels and length: *Lost, Officer Buckle and Gloria, Love That Dog, Sable, Because of Winn-Dixie, Shiloh.* Have students read the books or chapters aloud, keeping in mind the theme of friendship and companionship with a dog. Then, have them return to the text to reread and locate specific passages that support the theme. They may further define or expand the theme through their discussion, such as: Dogs can enrich our lives, it's important to have a buddy, we love our dogs just like part of the family, dogs are loyal to us no matter what we do, and so on. As a whole group, discuss:

- What expanded themes have emerged from each text?
- How have the authors developed the theme through characters' thoughts, feelings, actions, and reactions?
- Cite excerpts from the stories that confirm the theme.

List What We Know About a Theme. The process of listing gives students ideas about how they can develop theme in their stories. After students write a first draft, have them identify one theme. Brainstorm and list what they know about that theme. For example, friendship—what do we know about friendship?

- like to do things together
- share our thoughts and secrets
- stick up for each other
- ask each other for help
- like to do things and play together
- takes time to be a friend
- can find friends in unexpected places
- get mad and have fights
- say "I'm sorry"
- sometimes it hurts and we cry

Guide students to return to their stories and incorporate some of their listed ideas to expand their theme further.

Study a Symbol. For more experienced readers and writers, discuss the symbols in books and how they enhance the theme. For example, to study the owl in *Owl Moon*, you might look at the characteristics of owls by reading some nonfiction information. (They are nocturnal, silent fliers, have special feathers that don't make any noise, can sneak up on prey without being heard, have good night vision, can turn their head nearly all the way around—about 280 degrees.) Yolen used this understanding of owls to write the book and give her words more impact. Have children examine the symbol of the owl and how it connects to the theme of hope in this final passage from *Owl Moon*:

> When you go owling
> you don't need words
> or warm
> or anything but hope.
> That's what Pa says,
> The kind of hope that flies
> on silent wings
> under a shining
> Owl Moon. (n.p.)

Guide students to develop this sophisticated concept of symbolism in their writing. They may analyze how fine writers select a symbol or metaphor, make connections, and apply to in their writing.

Poetically Speaking

Concrete poems. Concrete poems are shape poems. Students find they can be playful and fun to create. Yet, they can be quite sophisticated. There are two kinds of concrete poems:

1. Poems use features and descriptors of the theme or topic to fill the area of a shape.

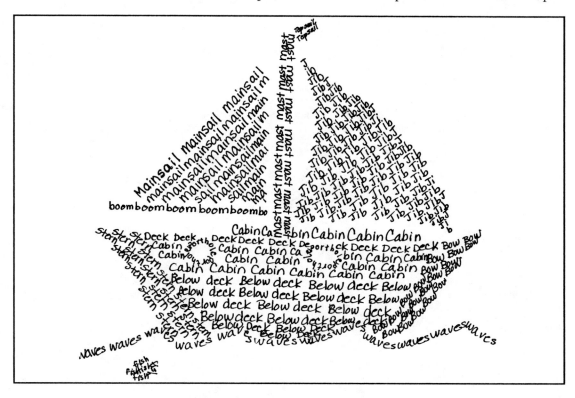

2. Poems use poetic verse to create a shape.

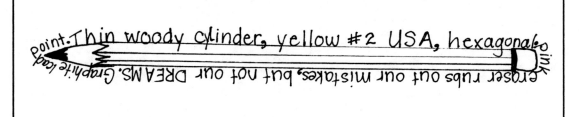

Have students write one type of concrete poem. Select a theme or topic, brainstorm features or characteristics, or write a free verse poem, then play around writing the feature words to fill or create the shape.

6: Teaching the Craft of Writing

The Speech of man is like embroidered tapestries.
—Themistocles

Dialogue

Key Elements of Dialogue:

- Word Study:
  - *dia* = two or part
  - *logue* = speak
- Conversation between two speakers
- Balance talk and action
- Show characters' thoughts and feelings

Rules for Writing Dialogue
- Indent with each speaker.
- Put quotations around speakers' words.
- Use tag words to name the speaker.
- Begin speech with upper case letters.
- Place ending punctuation inside quotation marks.

Writing Standards:

2. Writing Purposes and Resulting Genres
   a. Narrative Writing: Sharing Events, Telling Stories
      – Create a believable world and use precise words and detail.
      – Develop a plot or tell about an event by describing actions and emotions of characters and using story elements of dialogue, how a character feels, descriptive details, and others.
3. Language Use and Conventions
   a. Style and Syntax
      – Use their own language in writing.
   d. Punctuation, Capitalization, and Other Conventions
      – Use capital letters at the beginning of sentences.
      – Use periods, question marks, and other end punctuation most of the time.
      – Begin to use quotation marks.

About Dialogue ...

We spend much of our lives in dialogue as we converse, laugh, tell stories, play, and communicate with others. We are inundated with talk. We see written dialogue in books, magazines, newspapers—everywhere. Yet, when students begin to write dialogue it's a real struggle trudging through the tedious idle chatter they love to write, such as "Hi. How are you?" "I am fine." "What do you want to do?" and so on and on and on. This is where developmentally these emerging writers are at this point in time.

Our charge is to scaffold this development and help them become proficient in using the craft of dialogue. They view writing dialogue as a transition to "big kid writing," similar to their feelings about learning cursive writing. Alisa even announced, "I'm doing <u>real</u> writing now." They are eager to write like authors do in the chapter books they are reading. We, as teachers, have the responsibility to provide them with examples of fine dialogue in literature so they begin to notice the balance of dialogue and action, characters' thoughts and feelings, and individual expressions. Eventually, many students begin to use dialogue in these ways.

Examples of Dialogue From Literature:

<u>Conversation Between Two Characters</u>

<u>Example of tag words at the beginning of a sentence or paragraph</u>: Tag words used at the beginning or the ending of the speaker's words are the simplest way for students to begin writing dialogue. It's clear who is talking.

From *Waiting for the Evening Star* by R. Wells:

> I said, "Grandmother, I wish all our vegetables would be as big and fat as the ones on the packages."
>
> She said to me, "Berty, keep your eye on that spot in the sky just over the mountains and wait for the evening star. When it comes out, we'll wish on it. Wishes on the evening star are bound to come true." (n.p.)

<u>Example of tag words in the middle of a sentence or paragraph</u>: More experienced writers may be ready to attempt split dialogue with tag words in the middle.

From *Maniac McGee* by J. Spinelli:

> "Sure you do," Maniac prodded. "About yourself. You know about you. Everybody has a story.
>
> "Not me," Grayson was edging for the door. "I ain't got no story. I ain't nobody. I work at the park." (p. 89)

Example of a special dialogue style using indentation of text, rather than quotation marks, to separate two characters' speech: This is an uncommon feature, and students may identify others they want to emulate.

From *Knots on a Counting Rope* by B. Martin and J. Archambault:

> Tell me the story again, Grandfather.
> Tell me who I am.
> > I have told you many times, Boy.
> > You know the story by heart.
> But it sounds better
> when you tell it, Grandfather.
> > Then listen carefully.
> > This may be the last telling. (n.p.)

Balance Talk and Action—Too much dialogue can make the story drag. We encourage students to use dialogue with care, striving for balance and communication.

From *Thy Friend, Obadiah* by B. Turkle

> Obadiah stopped. The bird stopped. The fishhook bobbed in the wind.
> "If thee is quiet, I'll try to get that off thy beak."
> The sea gull didn't move.
> "I won't hurt thee," Obadiah said.
> The bird allowed him to come nearer and nearer. In a moment, the fishhook was in Obadiah's hand … (n.p.)

Characters' Thoughts and Feelings—This is another form of Show, Don't Tell. It guides students to show a character's thoughts through words, rather than just telling what they were thinking or feeling.

From *A Toad for Tuesday* by R. E. Erickson:

> It was dark inside and smelled musty. The owl sat the toad in a corner and stepped back. He gave him a piercing look.
> "What's your name?" he said.
> "Wharton."
> "Wharton?" said the owl. "Well, I think I'll call you … Warty."
> "I don't care for that very much."
> "You don't? Well that's too bad … Warty?"
> The little toad got up all his courage and looked right at the owl. "Are … are you going to eat me?" (p. 23)

How Do I Teach Dialogue?

> **Word Study:** *Dialogue*
>
> On the board, write *dia-* and tell them it means "two or part."
> Then, write *-logue* which means "speak." Put those two parts together and ask,
> "What could the word *dialogue* mean? "Two characters speaking, having a conversation."
>
> **Extension:** List a few other words they may know that begin with *dia-* and connect how studying roots and affixes helps us to understand many unfamiliar words. For example:
>
> - *diameter*—*line* that goes through the center of something and separates it into two parts
> - *diagnose*—identifying what is wrong by studying various parts. For example, a doctor looks at different parts of you before determining what is wrong
> - *diagram*—shows a whole object and labels its parts
> - *dialect*—speech that's unique to a specific part of a country

Listen Like a Writer. Many writers collect and record words and phrases from real conversations to write believable dialogue. Students and teachers can work this way, too. Pause long enough to listen and notice what people around us say to each other. Write some phrases you overhear in conversation and share these with students.

I kept a journal of my boys' emerging language when they were little and still love to read it. Some of the entries, such as "I was brooming the sidewalk," eventually find their way into my short stories. Only because I took the time to write down this phrase, I was able to access it later. Have students write interesting expressions in their journals. Later, they may use them in characters' dialogue.

We "Said" It! There's more than one way to say something. Sometimes we holler and other times we whisper. Writers search for precise words to communicate clearly. As we encourage students to think of varied ways people talk, have them open a book and see how characters speak. Ask:

- How many times was *said* used on one page?
- What other words, or synonyms, were used in place of *said*?
- How many times were those synonyms used?
- How did the synonyms help us hear the dialogue in a different way?
- Why do you think the author chose to use the synonyms?

We find *said* is used more often than its synonyms. And there is a reason for this. It is such a common background word that we don't have to think about it. Our minds focus on what's most important: the conversation. However, when a synonym for *said* is used effectively, it helps the reader see <u>how</u> something is being said, such as *whispered* or *hollered*. But, often *said* is sufficient.

List on a wall chart some of these synonyms for "said" that students found. Have them continue to add to it. It becomes a quick resource when they write dialogue. Reference the example chart "We 'Said' It" (at the end of this section).

No Idle Chatter. Good writers know that dialogue must move the story action along. If there are words that are there for no reason, it makes the story drag. Written dialogue is different from our actual talking. We must leave out many of the words we might say in real life. Put some rambling, chatty dialogue on an overhead and have students eliminate all the words that don't contribute meaning to the story.

Add Dialogue to Text. Sometimes, we need to add dialogue in places to create interest and drive the action. Make a transparency of "The Food Volcano" (at the end of this section). Read it aloud to the class and identify several spots in the story where dialogue could help. Direct students to keep the original text, but embed dialogue within it. Name their characters and add tag words to the dialogue. Show characters' feelings, thoughts, and wonders. Have students share their rewrites. Discuss how the added dialogue provided interest and balance.

Create Dialogue From Pictures. Pictures can provide an opportunity for writing dialogue. Bring in some picture books that have narrative, but no dialogue, such as *The Relatives Came* by C. Rylant. Discuss how the books tell stories, but the characters don't talk. Have them pair with another student so they can role-play conversations. Have students select a picture of people talking. They will become characters in the picture and create a conversation. They can give the characters names and then write the dialogue.

Balancing Words and Action. If you have balance scales in your room, place a block on one side that says "dialogue." Put the same size and weight block on the other side that reads "action." Effective writing often has a balance between talk and action. Select a passage from a book that exemplifies this writing craft. Then, have students revise a piece of their own writing for the purpose of balancing dialogue with action.

For the visual or kinesthetic learners, provide a set of unifix cubes (or other items). After reading each sentence of their stories, let them put a cube in either a dialogue pile or an action pile. Although balance does not mean that there needs to be an equal number of sentences of dialogue and action, this visual exercise can show obvious imbalances.

Dialect. Writing in dialect is a rather sophisticated skill, and some children may enjoy playing around with it. But first, let students become aware of it in the books they read and understand how different people talk in various parts of the country and world. Dialect can use a kind of invented spelling of sounds and words, as well as the way words are phrased. Cushman's medieval book *The Midwife's Apprentice* has interesting British dialect: "... are you drownt? I'd open the sack and let you out, but I be sore afraid of the eel" (p. 8). Creech used some colorful expressions in *Walk Two Moons* to give the characters a "Kentucky" flavor: "caboodle of houses" (p. 1), "couldn't read maps worth a hill of beans" (p. 4), "a hog's belly full of things to tell about her" (p. 8). Have them research how people express themselves in a particular part of the country and jot down ideas. Show how to weave some of these phrases into dialogue as the story develops.

Writing Conventions for Dialogue:

What Does Dialogue Look Like? All writing conventions are there for a purpose: to help the reader understand when talking begins, when a different character speaks, and when talking ends. Have students peruse a trade book and make observations about how the author showed dialogue. Discuss how the dialogue conventions help the reader to understand the conversation better. Several students were amazed that there was a new paragraph every time someone different spoke! Make a list of their observations. Hang a dialogue mobile (taken from Key Elements) in the room for easy reference. When they see it in published books, they believe it and emulate it.

1—2—3, Tag: Tag words are sort of like price tags you see when you go shopping. They give information. For example, price tags on tee shirts tell the buyer how much the items cost. Tag words in writing dialogue tell the reader who is talking and how the words are spoken. Look at books that have dialogue. How did children know who was talking? (Usually, somewhere in the sentence or paragraph the writer identifies the speaker. Other times, they must infer who the speaker is from previous paragraphs.) How did this help the reader?

How Do Authors Use Conventions? Discuss the general rules for dialogue, punctuation, and capitalization. Word process passages from a book, leaving out the punctuation and other conventions of dialogue. On a transparency or handout, let the students punctuate and capitalize the dialogue, and then check it against the author's dialogue. This shifts the responsibility from the teachers to the students for making corrections.

Poetically Speaking

Dialogue Poems. Read the picture book *Yo! Yes?* by C. Raschka, which is really poetic dialogue in its purest form. Have students notice how much is said in so few words. Talk about the characters' thoughts and feelings behind the words. Of course, the expressive pictures contribute a lot to the meaning. Pair students to create a brief

"In our class we did an experiment with goo that we called Oobleck," said Devin.

Lucy continued, "we smelled, looked at, touched, and some of us tasted the Oobleck, but we didn't hear anything."

"When we got the Oobleck it was in a tin piepan covered with tinfoil," explained Laine.

"First, we looked at the Oobleck. Then we smelled it, and then we touched it," Anthony told us.

Allie remarked, "When I first looked at it the Oobleck looked watery, but when we touched it, I was surprised it wasn't.",

Eric added, "when we put it in our hands the Oobleck dried out, but when we put it back with the rest it became moist again."

Mrs Westkott asked the question Why do you think the Oobleck keeps on changing?"

scenario with dialogue. Then, read and dramatize the conversation before the group.

What I know about ...

Dialogue

"What is dialogue?" she asked.

- Word Study:
  - *Dia-* means _____ or _____
  - *-logue* means _____
- Conversation between 2 characters
- Balance _____ and _____
- Show characters' _____

"How does dialogue look?" he asked.

- _____ with each speaker
- Put _____ around speaker's words
- Use _____ words to show who is talking
- Write a dialogue between you and your friend.

We "Said" It!

Precise Words for *Said*

asked	blurted	laughed
suggested	snarled	urged
announced	added	expressed
whispered	chuckled	mimicked
continued	bellowed	yakked
sniffled	exaggerated	snapped
yelled	confessed	declared
exclaimed	growled	sniffed
begged	boasted	reminded
cried	boomed	cheered
wailed	squeaked	wheezed
shrieked	complained	sputtered
screeched	hissed	giggled
squawked	stuttered	choked
groaned	yapped	howled
directed	commented	conversed
explained	remarked	stated
screamed	shouted	whined
demanded	muttered	pointed out
moaned	called	interrupted
barked	admitted	scolded
thundered	whimpered	mentioned
gasped	chatted	discussed
warned	sang	peeped
piped	sighed	questioned

The Food Volcano

by a Third-Grade Student

Help this author make the writing more interesting by balancing the narrative with dialogue.

1. Rewrite this story and add dialogue with two or more characters.

2. Give characters names and add tag words to show who is talking.

3. Put quotation marks around the spoken words.

4. Show a new paragraph when a different person speaks.

Once there was a little town that had a volcano smack dab in the middle. Every morning, afternoon, and evening, the volcano erupted lots of food. People in the town dashed out of their houses carrying plates, forks, knives, and spoons. They ate as much as they wanted. One day, people ran out of their houses to collect food, but they didn't get any. People started digging to see what happened. They finally reached a huge tree root. Food couldn't get past it. A person got a saw and cut through the root. The town got lots of food again.

Endings

How do you know when you're done?
You just do.
—Anne Lamott

Key Elements of Endings:

- Closing part of a story:
  beginning, middle, *ending*
- Extended endings are from the high point to the final word.
- Gives closure to the story
- Some kinds of endings
  - circular
  - surprise
  - wrap up
  - conclusion/summary
  - personal reflection
  - final wonders
  - (and others)

Writing Standards:

2. Writing Purposes and Resulting Genres
   a. Narrative Writing: Sharing Events, Telling Stories
      – Wrap it up with a conclusion.
   b. Informative Writing: Report or Informational Writing
      – Write a conclusion that ties it all together.
   d. Producing Literature
      – Build on a story idea by extending or changing the storyline.

About Endings ...

Early in the year, students flail their hands and proudly announce, "I'm done!" I notice that "The End" is written in big bold letters at the bottom of the page because the writer believes that those two words are all it takes to finish a story. Endings involve far more than the words "The End" or even a final sentence. Young writers learn how vital endings are to the story, equally as important as the lead. Each kind of ending has its own distinctive characteristics, which we study and figure out how to structure our endings in similar ways.

A well-written ending leaves readers with a sense of closure, sometimes surprise, or maybe a hint of how the story or character might continue. Even my 7-year-old neighbor expects another *Stuart Little* movie because the ending of the screenplay suggests the possibility! And how many readers close the last page of a *Harry Potter* volume with satisfaction, anticipating the next one? We teach students how to write extended endings that leave the reader (and the writer) satisfied.

About Nonfiction Endings: I picked up five brand new nonfiction books recently with the intent of examining the writer's craft throughout the texts. Only two had effective extended endings, while the remaining three left me wanting more. In reaction to my discovery, my students and I searched for the various ways nonfiction writers ended their work. After a group analysis, we noticed these strategies worked best in ending nonfiction: Summary, Final Wonders, and Reflection.

Sometimes, children think writers must know how the story will play out from the very beginning. It's not necessary to know what is going to happen. As the story unfolds, they can make decisions about the ending.

Examples of Endings in Literature:

<u>Circular Ending</u>: It brings the story back to the way it began. It often restates or paraphrases the lead.

From *Haystack* by B. Geisert:

> (First two lines of the book): In a time not so long ago, before machines made hay in convenient bundles, haystacks stood high, long, and wide on the prairie. Across the prairie in the spring, the grass grew tall. (pp. 3–4)

> (Last line of the book): And the grass grew tall in preparation for the cycle to begin again. (p. 32)

<u>Surprise Ending</u>: The unexpected ending leaves the reader surprised. It often has foreshadowing.

From *First Day Jitters* by J. Danneberg:

> (In *First Day Jitters* Sarah is nervous about her first day in a new school. We never actually *see* Sarah until the conclusion of the book that ends in this surprising way):

> The class looked up as Mrs. Burton [the principal] cleared her throat. "Class. Class. Attention please," said Mrs. Burton.

> When the class was quiet she led Sarah to the front of the room and said, "Class, I would like you to meet …

> (Final page): … your new teacher, Mrs. Sarah Jane Hartwell." (n.p.)

<u>Wrap-Up Ending</u>: It ties the story together and gives closure and resolution. This usually leaves the reader satisfied.

From *Vampires Don't Wear Polka Dots* by D. Dadey and M. T. Jones. It ends with the title line:

> On the last day of school, the kids met under the oak tree.

"I can't believe the year's over," Liza said.
"I can't believe we lived through it," Eddie moaned.
"But, you know," Melody said, "Mrs. Jeepers wasn't so bad."
Howie said, "She's really not *that* weird.
Melody laughed. "I can't believe we ever thought she was a vampire!"
"After all," Lisa agreed, "vampires don't wear polka dots!" (p. 78)

Conclusion/Summary Ending: A brief summary statement restates the main points of the information learned. Many nonfiction writers conclude their work in this way.

From *So You Want to Be President?* by J. St. George:

If you want to be President—a good President—pattern yourself after the best. Our best have asked more of themselves than they thought they could give. They have had the courage, spirit, and will to do what they knew was right. Most of all, their first priority has always been the people and the country they served. (p. 47)

A Final Wonder: We noticed how some authors leave us with a question or impose a responsibility on the readers. They leave us without closure; they provoke our thinking about the subject.

From *Mammals* by G. Stevens:

You've now read all about mammals and how far they've come, how they've adapted, and their amazing diversity. It's time to ask, "What would the world be like without them?" (p. 32)

How Do I Teach Endings?

Word Study: *Endings*

Brainstorm all the things that have endings. Consult a dictionary for definitions of *endings* to broaden our understanding. Discuss several, such as:

- where the action stops;
- the point where something cannot go beyond;
- opposite of the beginning;
- conclusion; and
- to reach a specific point or place, finale.

Linking the Middle to the Ending: The summary is the sum of the parts. This can be set up as an addition problem (the beginning + the middle + the ending = the complete story). There is often a connection that links the middle section to the ending. This link can be a single connecting element that propels the story toward the conclusion. In the example below from *Lost* by P. B. Johnson and C. Lewis, the old prospector is that link.

1 Beginning	Flag was lost in the desert
+ 2 Middle	They search and search for him …
	They meet the old prospector.
	(This is what linked the middle to the ending.)
+ 3 Ending	Old prospector finds Flag and brings him home.
= Complete story	Whole book is completed with a satisfying ending.

In a new story, have students physically separate each part of their writing, such as using a separate page(s) for each section (beginning, middle, ending). Have students highlight something in the ending that could become a link. Then, add that link to the middle of the story.

All's Well That Ends Well. Help students to become more aware of how authors craft their story endings. Have students list some books they have read. Beside each title, write the kind of ending the book has. Which ending is used most frequently for fiction books? For nonfiction books? Students may discover some overlap. We've listed a few categories on the chart, but keep going …

Book Title	Circular	Surprise	Wrap-up	Conclusion/Summary

Have students work with a partner to choose a book from the chart. Ask this focus question: "How can you rewrite this book's ending using a different type of ending than the author used?" Afterward, students can share and discuss how the new ending impacts the storyline as a whole.

What is an E X T E N D E D Ending? Raise your children's level of awareness: One sentence does not an ending make. We work a lot on extended endings as we study how published authors wrap up a story and discuss exactly what happens from the high point of the story to the final words. Share some extended endings of books, which may be several paragraphs in picture books or several pages in chapter books.

To develop their own extended endings, students should reflect on how the main character has grown, changed, or reached a decision. Using these questions, have them reconsider an ending they have already written, then extend it.

- What worked well about the ending?
- What memories or feelings might your character reveal?
- What did the character hope would happen (or not happen)?
- In what way did the main character resolve the problem?
- In what ways did you tie the ending back to something that happened earlier?

Authors Tie It All Together. Good writers like to have connections and repeated elements to give continuity. Throughout the year, have students notice how some books tie the ending back to something that happened at the beginning. For example, if a character took a trip, the story could end by unpacking his bags and link it back to the beginning where he packed his bags. Often, writers will have to revise the beginning after the piece is finished. Here are some examples of books that tie it all together, which students may emulate:

Come a Tide by G. E. Lyon begins with snow and rain in the spring. It ends with the anticipation of more snow and rain in the spring.

Poppy by Avi begins with the mice going to Bannock Hill to dance and eat hazelnuts. It ends with the mice dancing on Bannock Hill under a hazelnut tree.

Officer Buckle and Gloria by P. Rathmann begins and ends with a safety tip from the officer.

Making Ends Meet: Circular Endings. Our students enjoyed writing circle stories in kindergarten and first grade. They continued writing them throughout the elementary grades with increasing sophistication. Laura Numeroff's "Mouse" stories are favorites that can lead to spin-offs.

Have students follow the circle story structure to give a character an adventure, but always come full circle in the action, ending the way the story begins. There are many nonfiction possibilities for circular stories, such as the life cycle of animals or plants.

How Could it End? Surprise! Discuss how writers must problem solve and make decisions about how to end their stories—their choices are many. And each kind of ending has its own set of characteristics and ways for developing it. This lesson focuses on how to craft a surprise ending.

Read aloud a brief book and stop before you reach the ending. Have students tell how they think the story will end. Then, read the author's actual ending. These are a few short books that work well, some with real surprise endings!

- *Big Bad Bruce* by B. Peet
- *The Widow's Broom* by C. Van Allsburg
- *The Cow Who Wouldn't Come Down* by P. B. Johnson
- *The Incredible Painting of Felix Clousseau* by Jon Agee
- *The Thirteenth Clue* by A. Jonas

Analyze what the author wrote that surprised us. How was the ending different from what you expected? Study the word *surprise* and think about the definitions of "to encounter suddenly or unexpectedly, caught unawares, to cause to feel wonder or astonishment, to cause or do or say something unintended." How did the author craft that surprise? Go back and find hints the author wrote that let us know what might happen (foreshadowing).

Have students list five possible ending ideas for a piece of writing they may want to end with a surprise. They can look over their ideas and eliminate the most predictable endings. Then, select the one that is the least expected to develop more fully into a surprise ending.

A Chip Off the Old Ending. We all react to endings of books or movies. Guide students to become young critics. Robert Munsch's *The Paperbag Princess* is a good book to share that surprises readers with an unexpected ending. The author takes the classic fairy tale formula and writes an atypical ending that can generate a whole class discussion. Challenge those readers who are dissatisfied to suggest how they could have written the ending differently. It is not always "happily ever after"… or is it? Now, have students select a folk tale and rewrite the ending—with a new twist!

Endings Can Reveal Feelings. To appreciate how a writer gets to the heart of a character, we can look for these feelings in the classic *Charlotte's Web*. E. B. White writes,

> Wilbur never forgot Charlotte. Although he loved her children and grand-children, none of the new spiders ever quite took her place in his heart. She was in a class by herself. It is not often that someone comes along who is a true friend and a good writer. Charlotte was both. (p. 184)

Have student writers share how they showed their character's feelings in their endings or have them go back and revise the endings, if appropriate, to reveal feelings.

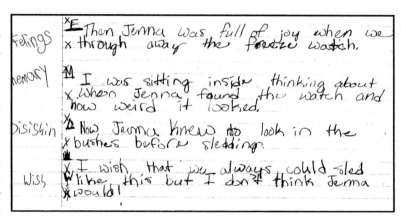

A Few Well-Chosen Endings. When students are ready to write their endings, have them write notes about several possible ideas. Next, they decide which one to develop fully into an extended ending. This is what writers do—list, consider, and decide.

Poetically Speaking

Piggybacking Off the Pros. Read an assortment of poems and discuss the various ways poets end their poems. Distribute a few published poems and cover or omit the last verse or lines. Continuing the form of the poem, have students write their own endings. Afterward, show them the poet's actual endings for a comparison.

What I know about ...

Endings

- Closing part of a story:

  > Beginning
  > + Middle
  > + Ending
  > = _____ Story

- Some kinds of endings:
  - _____
  - _____
  - _____
  - _____

Leads

First sentences are doors to worlds.
—Ursula K. Le Guin

Key Elements of Leads:

- Word Study: *lead*
    - To show the way by going first
    - to begin or open
- Grabs the reader's interest
- Sets the tone and creates a first impression
- Kinds of leads
    - setting
    - action
    - dialogue
    - sound word
    - character introduction
    - final wonders
    - (and others)

Writing Standards:

2. Writing Purposes and Resulting Genres
    a. Narrative Writing: Sharing Events, Telling Stories
        - Orient the reader by establishing the time and location and introducing the characters or lead into the story in an interesting way.
    b. Informative Writing: Report or Informational Writing
        - Introduce the topic and provide a context.
        - Use an organizational structure that helps the reader.
    c. Functional and Procedural and Writing
        - Engage the reader by establishing a context for the writing.
        - Identify the topic.

About Leads ...

Shocking incident? Quiet setting? Heated conversation? Each one of these leads can make a powerful difference in the way the reader is engaged at the beginning of a story. "In what way do I want to invite the reader into my story?" is one question writers ask themselves before they craft their leads. There are many varied ways that authors lead us into their stories, and each one has its own distinct characteristics.

Sometimes, writers can feel stumped about beginning a story as they stare at the looming blank page. They think they should know what is going to happen in the whole story before they write the first word. Untrue! As students learn techniques for crafting leads, they decide how to begin writing. Later, they may reconsider another kind of lead to best fit that particular story.

About Nonfiction Leads: All writers must reach their audience at the beginning of their non-fiction writing. When we need to research a topic, we have a specific purpose to our reading. Writers of nonfiction have the same responsibility as fiction writers to grab our attention, or we may lay the book aside and continue searching elsewhere. These are strategies young nonfiction writers may find helpful: Summarize the Topic, Ask a Question and Set the Scene.

Examples of Leads From Literature:

These are a few effective ways that some authors begin their stories. But, there are many other possibilities. See if your students can notice and name a few others they find as they read.

<u>Setting</u>—Helps the reader to picture where and when the story takes place.

From *A Toad for Tuesday* by R. E. Erickson:

> On a windy, wintry night, as countless stars were shining bright, deep in the ground, far under the snow, two little toads were having an argument. The toads lived by themselves in their cozy home. (p. 9)

<u>Dialogue</u>—Puts the reader in the middle of people's conversations.

From *Sarah, Plain and Tall* by P. MacLachlan:

> "Did Mama sing every day?" asked Caleb. "Every-single day?" (p. 3)

<u>Character Introduction</u>—Lets the reader know from the start something about the main character.

From *Tales From the House of Bunnicula: It Came from Beneath the Bed!* by J. Howe:

> Uncle Harold—who is a dog, like me, and not even my uncle, I just call him that—got me this real cool notebook from under Pete's bed …
>
> I want to be a writer just like Uncle Harold …
>
> Well, being a wirehaired dachshund and all, one thing I know about is the Floor. I could write a story called "The Floor."
>
> Or not. (p. 1)

<u>Action</u>—Begins right in the midst of what's happening, immediately pulling the reader into the story.

From *The House of Wings* by B. Byers:

Sammy crouched in the metal culvert that ran beneath the highway. His head was bent forward over his dusty knees. His shoulders were hunched, his eyes shut. He was listening. (p. 7)

Sound—Lets the reader "hear" the writing, using words that are spelled like they sound. This is a favorite way for young writers to begin their stories—and they do it so well!

From *Bridge to Terabithia* by K. Paterson:

Ba-room, ba-room, ba-room, baripity, baripity, baripity, baripity—Good. His dad had the pickup going. (p. 1)

Leads Often Used in Nonfiction

Ask a Question—Starting with a question is one way to get readers wondering about a topic. They will read on to learn the answers.

From Here *We All Are: A 26 Fairmount Avenue Book* by T. dePaola:

Have you ever moved into a new house? A whole house with a basement, a first floor, a second floor, and an attic? (p. 1)

Summarize the Topic. Some leads can sum up the main idea at the beginning or even combine a couple of the strategies.

From *Skateboarding in Action* by J. Crossingham:

What is Skateboarding?

Skateboarding, or "skating" is a sport that involves performing tricks, or moves, on a board that has four wheels. (p. 4)

Set the Scene. This method lets the reader imagine a topic and the setting where it takes place.

From *The Planets* by C. Nicolson:

Imagine living without TV, videos and electric lights. What would you do on dark nights? People long ago watched the stars. They noticed a few strange dots of light that moved through the stars. They called these moving lights planets, a word that means wanderers. (p. 4)

How Do I Teach Leads?

Chart It. This exercise helps students discover the types of leads in books. Limit the number of leads you introduce at one time. Identify books that have three different kinds of leads, such as setting, dialogue, and character introduction.

Distribute selected books to students. Direct them to read the first page and write the lead paragraph(s) on paper strips. Have a few students share the leads from their books and post their papers on the charts.

Dialogue	Character Introduction	Setting
From *2095: The Time Warp Trio Series*	From *Henry Huggins*	From *Come a Tide*
"Hey buddy, what's your number?" said a metal voice with a Brooklyn accent. "I think that vacuum cleaner is talking to you," said Fred (p. 1).	Henry Huggins was in the third grade. His hair looked like a scrubbing brush and most of his grown-up front teeth were in (p. 1).	Last March it snowed and then it rained for four days and nights (p. 1).

Discuss the findings on the charts. Ask some of the following questions:

- Which kind of lead did most books use?
- Why do you think authors begin with these leads?
- What if the author had used a different lead?
- What mood do the various leads create?
- Which were your favorites?
- Which leads would you like to try in your own writing? Why?

Grabbers That Make Readers Want to Know More. Don't you love for a book to seize you from the first paragraph so that you absolutely can't put that book down? Some good leads immediately grab the readers' interest and pull them into the story. Select a few books that have a variety of leads, some grabber leads and some not.

Read a few leads aloud to the students and discuss what the writer did in the first few lines. Does the lead grab their attention or not? Students could judge it with thumbs up or thumbs down. If it does grab them, what did the author do to snag their interest? Let students come up with a list of criteria for a good grabber lead. Post this list for reference when they are beginning new stories.

Can You Guess? We can raise students' awareness of the various ways authors begin books. Read leads from familiar books and let children guess the book it begins. How did they know? What were the clues? If you're looking for ways to meaningfully fill a 5-minute block of time, try this exercise.

Write Another Lead. Published books provide us with examples of already strong leads. The content is established, so children can easily focus on writing another lead.

This is the way we might teach how to write a different lead using *Charlotte's Web*. Read the lead and discuss it: "'Where's Papa going with that ax?' said Fern to her mother as they were setting the table for breakfast." Ask, "Why do you think the author chose to use dialogue?" Discuss in what ways dialogue is effective. Together, choose a different kind of lead, such as setting. We might write, "A light breeze whispered through the curtains as Fern sat down to eat the bacon and eggs Mrs. Arable set on the table." Talk about how this new lead worked or didn't work and why. How did the mood change?

Have students choose books they love and write different leads. Let students see that there is no single way to begin a story. Our job as writers is to explore the possibilities and evaluate and select the one we like best.

Vary the Lead. The purpose is to have students rework the beginning of a story by using various types of leads. Make a transparency of a lead from your own writing or from a published book.

Assign students a writing partner. Have them develop a different kind of lead for the story. Students can share their leads and evaluate how the new beginning altered the mood. Survey the class about which leads worked.

Lines of Leads. On a clean sheet of paper, have students write the lead sentences to one of their stories and draw one line underneath it. Next, have them write a different kind of lead and separate it with another line underneath it. Repeat this process for two or three additional writings. Have them evaluate their leads and decide which one is the precise lead for that story. Reiterate that it's not what lead they use that's important, but finding the lead that fits their story.

Contrast Moods for Impact. When writers place two contrasting moods side by side, it provokes a dramatic reaction, hooking the reader. Read the excerpt from Van Allsburg's *The Stranger*:

> It was the time of year Farmer Bailey liked best, when summer turned to fall. He whistled as he drove along. A cool breeze blew across his face through the truck's open window. Then it happened. There was a loud "thump." Mr. Bailey jammed on his brakes. "Oh no!" he thought. "I've hit a deer."
>
> But it wasn't a deer the farmer found lying in the road, it was a man. (n.p.)

Notice how Van Allsburg begins with a mood of contentment in a setting. There is an abrupt and striking change as readers gasp in shock as we learn "it wasn't a deer ... it was a man." Discuss how the reader was lulled into a quiet, peaceful beginning, then shaken into sudden horror. Have students analyze how Van Allsburg created this impact with the juxtaposition of contrasting moods. Encourage students to experiment with this convention when writing their own leads.

Nonfiction

Nonfiction Leads. "This report is about ..." Does this lead grab your interest? Yawn, yawn, yawn is our reaction if we had to read 25 reports beginnings like this. Many nonfiction writers realize that they need to write leads that pull the reader in, just as fiction writers do. Review some nonfiction literature and let students decide which ones hooked them from the start. They can name and categorize the types of nonfiction leads they find.

Poetically Speaking

Lead Lines. Many forms of poems begin with a specific lead line that may launch poets into the creative process.

Kind of Poem	First Line Begins With ...
"I Wish" Poems	I wish ...
"If" Poems	If I were ...
"I Like" Poems	What I Like About _____ is ...
"Trouble" Poems	The trouble with _____ is ...
"Used to" Poem	I used to ...
Limericks	There once was a ... (Follow the limerick structure.)

What I know about ...

Leads

Setting

_____ and _____ the story takes
place.

- "Dialogue"
People _____ something interesting.

- Action!
Begins right in the _____ of an event.

- Sound Word
A word that is _____ like it sounds.

- Character Introduction
Tells something about the
_____.

- Question?
Question/answer format, often used in _____,
guides the reader through lots of information.

Precise Words

The difference between the right word and the nearly right word
is the same as that between lightning and the lightning bug.
—Mark Twain

Key Elements of Precise Words:

- Words that create an image
- Word choice—the exact word for the context
  - verbs
  - adjectives
  - adverbs
  - sound word
  - invented words
  - brand names

Writing Standards:

2. Writing Purposes and Resulting Genres
   a. Narrative Writing: Sharing Events, Telling Stories
      – Create a believable world and use precise words and details.
   b. Informative Writing: Report or Informational Writing
      – Introduce the topic and provide a context.
      – Use an organizational structure that helps the reader.

About Precise Words...

If we had to choose only one craft to teach students about effective writing, it would be precise words. It means saying exactly what we want to say. Precise words lead to clear communication, the ultimate goal of writing. If children practice this craft, it could steadily raise their level of writing. To accomplish this, teachers model, model, and model some more: playing with various words, choosing the most appropriate words for the context, and writing and rewriting passages. Together, teachers and students notice the way published authors use language, which always leads us back to—precise words!

Strong verbs may be the easiest part of precise words for children to understand. They can hear the difference between *talking* and *whispering*. And see the difference between *walking* and *tiptoeing*. If they can picture these precise actions in their minds, they can learn to write them. It's not just about using <u>strong</u> verbs, but the <u>right</u> verb, the most appropriate verb—*the* precise word. It's the exact image that we want readers to see in their mind's eye.

Examples of Precise Words From Literature:

<u>Words That Create an Image</u>. We can picture the scene as if we were sitting there watching it.

From *How Angel Peterson Got His Name* by G. Paulsen:

> The trainer and I pulled Orvis onto a stool in the corner and wiped the dust
> out of his eyes and the trainer gave him a towel to use to clean himself up a
> little. Orvis looked like he had been pulled through a knothole backward. (p.
> 94, a description of how Orvis looked after wrestling a bear)

Exact Verbs. These are such important words in a sentence because they show the action. We work on expanding students' vocabulary so they will have many choices of active verbs at their fingertips.

From *Coyote* by G. McDermott:

> Old Man Crow plucked a feather from his left wing.
> He told his flock to do the same. They stuck the feathers in Coyote.
> Coyote winced. His nose twitched.
> The crows chuckled. (n.p.)

Exact Adjectives and Adverbs. Although most fine writers use strong nouns and verbs and avoid relying on adjectives and adverbs, there are times when nouns or verbs need clearer descriptions. Expressive adjectives are abundant in the literature; adverbs are harder to find.

Adjectives from *Pictures of Hollis Woods* by P. R. Giff:

> One raw Tuesday morning I awoke and pulled the shade aside; the trees were
> charcoal smudges against an iron gray sky. (p. 62)

Adjectives from *Listen to the Rain* by B. Martin, Jr. and J. Archambault:

> Listen to the rain,
> the roaring pouring rain,
> the hurly-burly
> topsy-turvy
> lashing gnashing teeth of rain,
> the lightning-flashing
> thunder-crashing
> sounding pounding roaring rain,
> leaving all outdoors a muddle,
> a mishy mushy muddy puddle (n.p.)

Adverbs from *The School Story* by A. Clements:

> Mom read calmly, evenly, thoughtfully. Even if the story was exciting or scary
> or sad. (p. 8)

Invented Words—These are words students create to give the exact image of what they want to communicate.

From *Catherine Called Birdy* by K. Cushman:

> Ordinarily I do not mind Perkin's granny's <u>muddle-mindedness</u>, for she is the most <u>roomy-hearted</u> person I know, but sometimes she forgets to make her cakes and we are all disappointed. (p. 43)

<u>Brand Names or Specific Names</u>—We all know the name brands of many products. That's why using them can be more precise than using a general term—we can picture them, precisely.

From *Maniac McGee* by J. Spinelli:

> Maniac shrugged, took the <u>Mars Bar</u>, bit off a chunk, and handed it back. (p. 34)

How Do I Teach Precise Words?

> **Word Study:** *Precise*
>
> Webster says that *precise* means
> - clearly stated or depicted;
> - definite or exact;
> - fine details distinguish it from others.
>
> Roget says, "exact, accurate, definite."

Precise Verbs. Many writers agree that using strong verbs is one of the easiest ways students can improve their writing. Together, convert weak verbs with adverb modifiers to strong verbs (e.g., "said softly" to "whispered"; "jumped far" to "leaped"). Copy and distribute the Think Sheet "Precise Verbs" (at the end of this section) to give students practice in thinking and writing more precisely. Precise verbs give the reader a clearer picture instead of using adverbs to describe mediocre verbs.

All Verbs Are Not Created Equal. The most important actions should be precise and expressive. Copy a piece of writing onto a transparency. Have students circle the verbs. Which ones were strong and expressive? Which ones were not? Discuss how all the verbs don't necessarily have to be strong, but they should fit the context. Send students to review their original writing, circle the verbs, and decide if those are the most precise words to use.

Walk on By. Dramatizing strong verbs helps students visualize how different each action word looks. On the board or chart paper, write, "She <u>walked</u> into the room." Have someone act it out. Ask, "What do we know about the scene based on this verb *walked*? (Not much perhaps she wasn't in a big hurry, she's not a baby because she walks instead of crawls ...) Use a different verb to tell how she got into the room. For example, "She <u>tiptoed</u> into the room." Have someone act this out and discuss, "Now, what do we know about the scene?" (She came in quietly, maybe she didn't want to be seen or heard, and maybe she didn't want to wake anyone.) Comment on how the reader can picture her differently now. Both words tell of a way that a person went into a room. But, they create different images in the reader's mind. Some possibilities:

Synonyms for Walked

tiptoed	sauntered	flew	stomped
snuck	edged	dashed	slipped
meandered	hopped	stepped	scampered
bounded	limped	skidded	lunged
leapt	dragged	swam	slid
twirled	tumbled	galloped	wove
fell	danced	moseyed	staggered
drifted	bolted	trudged	wandered
inched	ambled	dived	sprung

Using the brainstormed list of synonyms for *walked*, play a form of Charades. Have a student silently select one of these words, and then act it out. Everyone else guesses the synonym for *walk*.

Sports Action. Sports pages are great resources for precise verbs. They are visual and full of action and use interesting verbs in fresh ways.

Bring in a collection of sports pages. Point out the way journalists use precise verbs to show the action in a game. Using the example headline "Wildcats Claw Their Way Past Bulldogs," discuss what we notice and what probably happened in this game. (It was close. Wildcats had to play hard to win. An exciting game. Choice of word *claw* goes with the name *Wildcat*.) Ask why this is a more interesting headline than saying, "The Wildcats Beat the Bulldogs." (We have more information in the first one, we know it was a close game, it gives the reader a mental picture.)

Distribute newspapers to groups of students. Let individuals highlight headlines that use precise verbs. Include some headlines that do not have precise verbs so that they can see the difference. **Caveat:** If you think that the entire sports page will be distracting to students, then cut out the headlines only.

Critter Action. Because many children write about their pets and wild animals, have them focus on specific words that describe actions for animals. When they are ready to write, they have a resource of words available.

Animal	Action
bird	hop, perch, fly, flap, soar, glide, peck, swoop, dive, chirp, tweet
cat	
horse	

Alphaboxes. This alphabet grid provides a way to organize the precise words students find in the literature they read. Talk about precise words, show a list of words, and have students identify which ones are precise, eliminating the words that are general. Then, put these precise words into the correct boxes on the sheet. Distribute the Think Sheet "Precisely Alphaboxes" for students to follow the same process as they read silently, being cognizant of the author's precise language. These sheets become resources, kept in their Writing Binders and referenced when they need words for their writing.

Swap Those Overused Words. Are you tired of reading in Jason's story for the 14th time that the girl was "nice"? Ho-hum. Guide students to study their own writing and determine which words are overused. Your class can begin to create charts with fresher and more precise alternatives.

Examples of overused words: cute, went, bad, lots, good, big, said, saw, make or made, nice, did, neat, little, fun, and funny.

Title of book: Because of Winn-Dixie
The reader: Haley

A aimed, actually, applauded, appear	B Barbecue, Baptist, Barreling, bald	C collar, certainly, consisted, combination	D (Name) Dunlap (Name) Dewberry
E Elvis, expensive, embarrassed, experience, explained	F (Name) Franny, furious, faint	G grand (Name) Gertrude	H healthy, hollering, Herman, hind h'000
I irritating, imagined, intends, introduced, installment, identical	J	K knelt	L (Name) littmus, limp, leash, leather
M Memorial, Mistaking, Mention, Mosquitoes	N (Name) Nordley, Naomi, Nervouslike	O (Name) Opal (Name) Otis	P properly, potluck, peculiar, prideful, positive, preparing
Q	R Retriever, raised, recalls	S stray, skidding, squinting, selecting, serious, sprouting	T tucking, trembling, terrorized, tease, typhoid
U unit	V vermin	W (Name) Wilkinson (Name) Winn-Dixie	XYZ

Synonym Chart for Nice

satisfying	pleasant	sympathetic	perceptive
good-hearted	polite	gentle	gracious
thoughtful	insightful	enjoyable	understanding
caring	considerate	courteous	tender
unselfish	agreeable	generous	affectionate
lovely	selfless	warm	amusing
accepting	sensitive	entertaining	respectful

Make Friends With a Thesaurus. The thesaurus is one of the best tools a writer can have. They not only help writers locate the exact word, but they assist authors in using a variety of words. I use a thesaurus when the word is on the tip of my brain. It provides the writer with choices and allows us to find those exact, precise words.

Have many age-appropriate thesauruses available in your classroom. Model how you use a thesaurus to look up a word, which is just like searching a word in a dictionary. Demonstrate how you jot down a few of the synonyms you find. Put a passage of writing on an overhead and circle the word you looked up. Discuss with students if one of the words found in the thesaurus is more precise. If so, cross out the word on the transparency and write the new word above it.

Play With Precise Adverbs and Adjectives. There are many times when the right adverb or adjective makes the writing clearer. Read some examples of precise adverbs and adjectives and talk about how they made the sentence stronger and the verbs more visual.

Adjectives from *Joey Pigza Loses Control* by J. Gantos:

> "Pablo and I were digging into the dirt with the <u>splintered</u> handle of a <u>broken</u> baseball bat and collecting good <u>throwing</u> rocks." (p. 11)

Adverbs from *Sable* by K. Hesse.

> The dog wagged her tail <u>weakly</u>. (p. 6)

> <u>Cautiously</u>, the dog came over, her nose stretched way out in front of her, sniffing. (p. 7)

> Sable sat <u>patiently</u> as I tightened the ends around her neck into a square knot. (p. 14)

Have students collect examples of adverbs and adjectives in literature. Notice if these words were exact and if they added to the communication of an idea.

The true test of whether the adverb or adjective is needed and if it is the precise word is to remove it and read the sentence without it. Try it. For example, "The dog wagged her tail" does not give us the same picture as "The dog wagged her tail weakly." With the adverb, *weakly*, we understand that the dog was starving and frail.

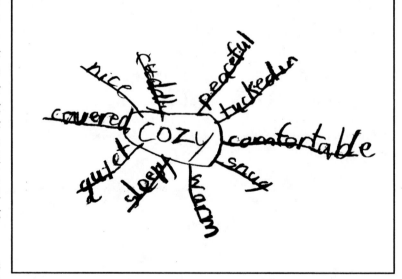

Contrast these examples of precise adverbs and adjectives to some stuck-on modifiers that we often see children write, such as: "The cute big brown hairy dog went home." More does not equal precise.

Be Specific. Think of what a difference the choice of words can make. Compare "a tree," to "a weeping willow." Or "a flower" to "a tulip." Or a "cat" to a "Siamese." Direct students to notice when published authors use specific words. Have them go back to their own writing, circle some general words, and make them more exact.

Variation: Brand names specifically identify products, and readers can connect to them without further description. For example, instead of saying, "He ate a snack," write, "He munched on *Cheetos*," and the reader hears the crunch and pictures his cheesy orange fingers. Encourage your young writers to build descriptions by using some brand names.

Use Invented Words. When we see invented words in literature, they often put a smile on our faces! Keep a class chart available for students to post invented words they read. (Make sure they write the entire sentence to show the word in context and note the source.) Help them to notice how expressive our original words can be. This is a way to add voice to our writing.

Categorizing Precise Words. During literature studies, you could organize words by parts of speech. Here is an example of a lesson Rebecca Boxx taught using *Out of Darkness: The Story of Louis Braille* by R. Freedman:

Person, Place, or Thing (Noun)	Action (Verb)	Descriptions (Figures of Speech, Adjective, or Adverbs)	Unusual Words
harness	echoed	topsy-turvy	awl
tuberculosis	pitied	bolder	wriggled
infection		yoke of oxen	francs
institute			embossed
punches			stylus

Have students fold a piece of paper into four sections and write the headings at the top. Then, they review a piece of their writing and identify some words that fit into these categories. This is a quick analysis of their word choice.

Word Study Charts. Have students work in groups to generate a list of many words that have the same roots or affixes. Together, study the similarities in the way a word looks and the subtle differences among their meanings. This activity is a life skill that will serve them well from now on. Example:

Mem—from the Latin word that means to remember, or memory

- *memory*—a thought from something in the past
- *memorize*—to know something by heart
- *memorial*—a special honor given to someone who is dead
- *memorabilia*—objects that remind us of something
- *remember*—to recall something in our minds
- *memo*—a note we send to remind people of something
- *memoir*—a written piece from someone's memory
- *memento*—an object kept as a reminder of something

Poetically Speaking

Action Poems. Have students select something that they enjoy doing. Brainstorm a list of all the actions that go with it, and then write these actions in verse form. They may write a short form with verbs only or an expanded form that elaborates on each action. These two garden poems were written by Robin Phillips based on B. Meyer's poetry found in *The Secret Life of Words* by B. Franco and M. Damon:

i garden (Short version)	a day of gardening (Expanded version)
i clip	i peek open an eye
i prune	i leap out of bed
i cultivate	i sip hot coffee
i scatter seeds	i race to my garden
i mulch	i reach for a shovel
i deadhead	i dig a new hole
i water	i transplant a bush
i edge	i sprinkle with water
i fertilize	i admire my work
i rake	i kick off my rubbers and head home
i compost	
i fluff soil	
i tend	
i top-dress	
i plant	
i watch	
i'm exhausted and sink into bed	

Basketball Player by Cliff (fifth grade)
I shoot
I take long threes
I make short lay ups
I dribble
I walk (sometimes)
I catch.
I block
I rebound
I pass
I pivot
I jump
I steal
I fastbreak
I love the Wildcats
I play basketball

What I know about ...

Precise Words

- Words that create an _____

- Word _____—select the exact word for that place in the story

  - verbs
  - adjectives
  - adverbs
  - invented words
  - brand names

- List some precise words from the book you are reading.

Name _____   Date _____

Precise Verbs

Directions: Write one precise verb beside the adverb phrase.

Example:

- came happily = _danced (or skipped, pranced ...)_

- said softly = _____

- ran quickly = _____

- walked slowly = _____

- went angrily = _____

- laughed loudly= _____

- threw hard = _____

- looked quickly = _____

Precisely Alphaboxes

A	B	C	D
E	**F**	**G**	**H**
I	**J**	**K**	**L**
M	**N**	**O**	**P/Q**
R	**S**	**T**	**U**
V	**W**	**X/Y**	**Z**

Repeated Words

Curiouser and curiouser!
—Lewis Carroll from *Alice's Adventures in Wonderland*

Key Elements of Repeated Words:

- Word Study: *Repeat*
  - To seek again (*L. repetere*)
- Gives emphasis to something important
- Provides continuity
- Kinds of repetitions:
  - concepts
  - sentences and phrases
  - words and word parts
  - initial sounds — alliteration

Writing Standards:

2. Writing Purposes and Resulting Genres
   d. Support an interpretation by referring to specific examples in the text.
      - Discuss several works that have a common idea or theme.
      - Make text-to-text connections as they notice and discuss where they have seen the writing craft or ideas in other literature.
3. Language Use and Conventions
   a. Style and Syntax
      - Take on the language of authors—emulate sentence structures from various genres.

About Repeated Words ...

Many writers, poets, and lyricists employ the writing craft of repeated lines. While young children love the repetition and predictability of recurring phrases, older students appreciate the emphasis of something important. Children grow up learning poems, nursery rhymes, songs, refrains, and choruses. We are familiar and comfortable with lines we know and love—and can remember! My father used to tease me about listening to rock music. He joked that if you took away one line of the lyrics, there wouldn't be a song left! But, isn't that part of what we enjoyed? The song was easy to learn so we could chime in. Even now, we can sing along with the radio to a song we haven't heard in 10 or more years. (But, we can't remember most of the dates we studied so hard for the history exam!)

Even though children have read various texts with repeated lines, they may not be aware of how authors use this writing craft. We first build an appreciation and awareness of the strategy by Reading Like a Writer. Begin with our curiosity—Why were words repeated? What does the repeated line do for the story? Would it impact the reader in the same way if it did not repeat?

When we study literature passages that use repeated lines, it becomes clear that they have a common base. All have one identified important idea to emphasize to the reader. Repetition is their way of doing this. With each repetition, the meaning is enlarged, giving increased attention to the word or phrase. Good writers make choices about using a specific writing craft—when it strengthens and enhances the writing, never as a contrived convention.

Examples of Repeated Words From Literature:

Repeated Concept. Notice how Creech stresses the concept of smallness by repetition of diminutive words. She repeats the concept, not just a single word, for emphasis.

From *Walk Two Moons* by S. Creech:

> We walked through the <u>tiny</u> living room into the <u>miniature</u> kitchen and upstairs into my father's <u>pint-sized</u> bedroom and on into my <u>pocket-sized</u> bedroom and into the <u>wee</u> bathroom ... Half of the <u>tiny</u> yard was a cement patio and the other half was another <u>patch</u> of grass that our imaginary cow would <u>devour in two bites</u>. (p. 11)

Repeated Sentences or Phrases. These repeated lines emphasize how neighbors looked out for each other and worked together during hard times.

From *Come a Tide* by G. E. Lyon:

> "Did you hear the whistle? Do you want to go with us?" (This was spoken three times in the story) (n.p.).

Repeated Word (or Parts of Words). Paulsen's repetitions accentuate the character's feelings.

From *Hatchet* by G. Paulsen:

> He was <u>alone</u>.
> In the roaring plane with no pilot he was <u>alone</u>.
> <u>Alone</u>. (p. 12)

Alliteration. This is the repetition of initial sounds in two or more words that often gives rhythm and emphasis.

Nonfiction—From *Red Wolf Country* by J. London:

> The <u>s</u>tartled wolves <u>s</u>kitter and <u>s</u>kate on the <u>s</u>lippery ice ... and <u>s</u>cramble off into the trees. (n.p.)

How Do I Teach Repeated Words?

> **Word Study:** *Repeat*
>
> The dictionary tells us that the word *repeat* comes from the Latin word, *repetere*. It means:
> - to say or write something again;
> - to say again what somebody else has said;
> - to recite something that has been learned;
> - to do something several times.
>
> After reading a passage of text that uses repeated lines, discuss how these definitions build understanding.

Study How Authors Use Repeated Lines. Read aloud several examples of passages from favorite published books that use repeated lines. For each one, discuss why the writer might have chosen those particular words to repeat. Notice how they used repetition—emphasizing something important and how the words take on added significance with each repetition.

Synonyms Make it Stronger. This activity focuses on using synonyms to develop a concept. Retype the paragraph from Sharon Creech's *Walk Two Moons* (in Examples of Repeated Lines). But, in place of the underlined words, type the word *little* and make a transparency, such as:

> We walked through the <u>little</u> living room into the <u>little</u> kitchen and upstairs into my father's <u>little</u> bedroom and on into my <u>little</u> bedroom and into the <u>little</u> bathroom… Half of the <u>little</u> yard was a cement patio and the other half was another <u>little</u> piece of grass that our imaginary cow would devour in <u>little</u> bites.

Read the paragraph aloud and talk about how the writer emphasizes the smallness of the new home. But, look how boring the paragraph is by repeating the same word! Together, brainstorm synonyms for *little*. Then, have each student rewrite the paragraph substituting other words.

Share a few and see how the paragraph changes. Then, read them the real text, the way Creech wrote it. In their own writing, is there a place where multiple words could be utilized in a paragraph to give stress to a particular concept? This exercise develops vocabulary and expands our word choices.

<u>Variation</u>: To appreciate the concept of repetition, I return to a familiar story that students know and love. I can always count on *The Teeny Tiny Woman*, possibly because of its comfortable predictability in the story's repeated phrases. Contrast how Creech uses the same concept of size, but in a varied and unique way in *Walk Two Moons*.

Alliteration. Another form of repeated words is alliteration, in which the initial sounds are repeated. In primary grades, students begin writing alliteration by creating lengthy lists of words beginning the same way, such as "Ingenious iguanas improvising an intricate impromptu on impossibly impractical instruments" (from the alphabet book, *Animalia* by G. Base, n.p.). A more sophisticated form is to use two or three alliterative sounds sprinkled across a line of text to add rhythm and movement to the passage.

Have students make a list of alliterative words that describes what a character is doing in a part of their story. Experiment with embedding some of these words into a paragraph to see if it adds rhythm.

Alliteration can also be used across content areas, such as this example by a second grader during a dinosaur unit:

> Sam Stegosaurus played softball and drank strawberry smoothies on Saturday.
> On Sunday he sat on a stone in a storm and stubbed his toe.

They Said it Again! We often remember characters by their repeated expressions. Go to the literature and find expressions that characters use again and again. How did the writer use these expressions to create a memorable character? Examples:

- Toad from *Frog and Toad* says, "Drat!"
- Charlie Brown from Schultz's cartoon says, "Rats!"
- Henry Huggins from *Henry Huggins* says, "Golly."
- Kenny from *The Watsons Go to Birmingham—1963* says, "They might as well tie me to a tree and say, 'Ready, Aim, Fire!'"
- Rabbit from *Tops and Bottoms* says, "It's a done deal, Bear."

Then, have students list some expressions they use or have heard. They can give a character one of these expressions to use repeatedly throughout their story.

Add a Word, Add a Phrase. Have students identify a place in their own writing where a repeated word or phrase could add emphasis or continuity. After they make their revisions, let them check in with a writing partner to get some feedback. This can help them determine if the addition makes the writing stronger.

> 5 heaps of wool
> 5 heaps of wool
> All as white as snow
> It's turning and turning and turning
> And spinning and spinning and spinning
> It's turning and spinning and turning
> In the spinning wheel
> 5 heaps of wool
> 5 heaps of wool

We Each Have a Song in Our Heart. Play or sing a song that has a repeated line or refrain. Let students feel the rhythm of it by tapping it out with their hands. Familiar simple rhymes, such as *Row, Row, Row Your Boat* or *Hickory, Dickory Dock* could be sure choices for success. Have students work in pairs to compose new lyrics following the exact rhyme scheme and rhythm. Then, of course, perform the new songs. This works well across content areas, such as science or social studies topics. Stephanie Ha and Sara Goldenberg's fifth-grade class developed and performed some rocking Colonial American verses to the rhythm of *Three Blind Mice*.

Identify a Place to Add Repetition. When we want to emphasize an important idea, repetition is a clear way to give attention to it. Put a passage on a transparency. Identify an idea that could be accentuated and revise the passage by adding a repeated word or phrase. Read the following text by a fifth-grade student. The repetition emphasizes the cool, fresh night air and makes the simile even more striking.

> *Original text*: The night was as crisp as a cookie.
> *Revision*: The night was crisp, as crisp as a cookie my Mama baked.

Poetically Speaking

Refrains. Many poets use repeated words and phrases in their poems to create rhythm and alliteration. Explore this writing craft in various poems as students find repeated lines and study how and why they were used. They may create their own poems modeled after those they like.

Together you can create a poem based on a topic you are studying and demonstrate how you can identify an important line or phrase, then repeat it for a stronger impact. I might start with a lively poem such as *Old Black Fly* alphabet rhyme by J. Aylesworth. Discuss how the repeating phrase gives continuity and rhythm to the poem. Students can chant the chorus line together throughout.

> … He ate on the crust of the **A**pple pie.
> He bothered the **B**aby and made her cry.
> > Shoo fly!
> > Shoo fly!
> > Shooo. (n.p.)

There are certainly many ways to use repeated words: opening lines, internal repetitions, in a chorus, or within each verse. And, of course, each poet must determine if repeated words are an appropriate idea for the poem.

What I know about ...

Repeated Words

- Gives _____

- Focuses on something _____

- Provides continuity to story

Examples from books I've read:

Sound Words

> *Trit-trot, trit-trot.* That is the sound of Piggins,
> the butler at 47 The Meadows, going up the stairs.
> —Jane Yolen from *Piggins*

Key Elements of Sound Words:

- Words that read like real sounds
- Words are spelled like they sound
- Sound words are called *onomatopoeia*

Writing Standards:

3. Language Use and Conventions
   b. Vocabulary and Word Choice
      - Use precise and vivid words.

About Sound Words ...

As I was listening to "Prairie Home Companion" Saturday night, I was fascinated by the clever and humorous sound effects in the background of Garrison Keillor's stories. First, the sound effects person had to determine <u>what</u> the appropriate sound should be, then figure out <u>how</u> to make the sound to enhance the story. This is exactly what our students do when they write onomatopoeia in their stories. They focus on the sense of hearing as they determine <u>what</u> the sound could be. Then, they decide <u>how</u> they want to spell the sound so that the reader can "hear" it.

Children love finding sound words in the literature. But they love writing these words even more! You can feel the excitement in the air as children hunker down over their desks creating, inventing and sounding out their newly invented words! Sound words make us feel like we're right there in the middle of their stories.

Example of Sound Words From Literature:

<u>Onomatopoeia</u>. This long, impossible-to-spell word simply means that the words are spelled like they sound. Sometimes, these words are found in the dictionary and sometimes they're not—some are invented words.

From *John Henry* by J. Lester:

The road crew planted dynamite all around the rock and set it off.

KERBOOM BLAMMITY-BLAMMITY BOOMBOOM BANG-BOOMBANG!!! (n.p.)

How Do I Teach Sound Words?

Word Study: *Sound*

Ooh, what descriptive words rest in the thesaurus beside *sound*. Each one of these words could create a distinct sound image:

- noise, resonance, hum, echo, thud, reverberation, crash, jingle, swish, clatter.

The dictionary defines *sound* as,

- something that can be heard.

Have students brainstorm some sounds that they have heard and spell them phonetically, just like they "sound."

Notice the Sounds. Guide students to observe sound words and their spellings in the literature. Find examples in books ahead of time to put on their desks. Here are some features they may point out:

- something a person says;
- animal noises;
- invented spellings;
- spelled like it sounds, not a real spelling;
- often in italics, caps, or bold letters;
- often has an exclamation point following;
- sometimes shows action; and
- found only in parts of the story.

Analyze Sounds From a Book. The previous exercise, "Notice the Sounds," dealt with sound words in general. This activity focuses on one particular passage from a book and invites children to study the sound words more closely. This excerpt from *A Cricket in Times Square* lets the reader overhear a conversation about the cricket's sound.

> "Some people say a cricket goes 'chee chee chee,'" explained Chester. "And others say, 'treet treet treet,' but we crickets don't think it sounds like either one of those."
>
> "It sounds to me as if you were going 'crik crik crik,'" said Harry.
>
> "Maybe that's why they call him a 'cricket,'" said Tucker. (p. 30)

Ask questions, such as:

- Which sounds do you think are most like a cricket's chirp?

- Does this remind you of another text? (Some may refer to Carle's *The Very Quiet Cricket* and comment on the tape-recorded cricket chirp in the end.)
- Can anyone share a text-to-self connection? (If someone has heard a real cricket, have them make the sound they remember.)
- What are other ways you might spell a cricket's sound?

Create an Onomatopoeia Board. *Onomatopoeia* is a word that is spelled like it sounds. It is a word we can either find in the dictionary or write our own invented spelling to match the sound.

On a classroom chart, have students list sound words they find. The listing becomes even more useful when students tweak the spellings just a little bit to make them more aural, such as spelling *beeeep* or *twannng*. Here are some we compiled:

Onomatopoeia
Words That Spell the Sounds They Make

bang	dash	moan	ssssmack
beep	ding-dong	mumble	snarl
blab	drip	ping	snicker
blubber	flap	pitter-patter	snort
boom	fling	plop	splash
bow-wow	flip	pop	squeak
burp	flop	puff	squeal
buzzzz	flub	rasp	squish
caw	flump	ricochet	swish
chirp	glug	r-r-ring	thud
chomp	groan	roar	thump
chug-chug	growl	rumble	thwack
clatter	grumble	rustle	tick-tock
click	grump	scamper	tinkle
clip	grunt	scoot	twang
coo	gulp	screech	whack
cough	hiss	shatter	whine
crack	honk	sigh	whisper
crackle	hoot	slice	whiz
crash	howl	slink	whoosh
creak	hummm	slither	zip
crunch	meooow	slurp	zzzoom

Sound Bites. Just a word or phrase will do it! Have students create individual collage posters filled with action pictures they snipped from magazines. Let them write the sound effects underneath each picture to show the sound. For a picture of a soccer player kicking a ball, a sound word might be *sshhhwhop*! The reader can hear the foot slicing through the wet morning grass as the cleat strikes the ball. Display posters for students to reference when adding sound words.

Write it Like it Sounds. This exercise brings sound words to life as students act out the sound and then spell what they hear. First, demonstrate some actions in front of the class. Let students write sound spellings and share them. Here are a few sound descriptions:

- dropping rocks onto the floor;
- tearing paper;
- ringing a bell or chime;
- jumping a rope; and
- scraping a chair across the floor.

Have students draw some sound descriptions out of a basket. Let them act out the description and then write a sound word on the board that would represent this sound. For example, for a mosquito whining, a student could make a high-pitched nasal sound, then write on the board, *nnnnnn*.

Spell it Like it Sounds. Students can become sound effects specialists and create sounds to enhance stories. Share a book and have students create sounds, all variations of sounds, to match the text or pictures. Afterward, write some of these into sound words. Demonstrate how you write invented spellings to represent the sounds. Ask students for other possible spellings. This is one time in writing where there may be no correct spelling—just spell it like it sounds!

This is an example that my students have used enthusiastically: The book *Barefoot* by P. D. Edwards provides a stimulus for reading, listening, and discussing the sound descriptions that are written on each page.

We discuss the phrase from the book, "the sounds were a salute to courage" (n.p.). There are no actual sound words written in this book, only sound descriptions. Students create their own spellings for particular sounds they imagine.

Text of Sound Descriptions	Sound Words Students Wrote
warning cry of heron	cuccawwwl
croaking of a frog	rrrrupp
mockingbird began to sing	tshweet, and whi whu
exhausted sigh	ih-haaa

Have your students identify the places in their own texts where sound occurs and then create invented spellings to represent the sounds.

Stump the Teacher. Teachers, you're in the spotlight on this one. Have students tell a sound description and you model how to write the word. For example, if "slam a door" was the sound description, you might write on the board *whhamp*! You might think aloud as you explain how you decided on the spelling. For example, you could say that the double "h" was put there because of the air sound the door made as it closed. You could also write the word, *wham* beside it and ask which word is more expressive—*wham* or *whhamp*? Which one gives the reader a sharper image of a slammed door?

Carry it to the extreme and write *wwwwhhhhammmppp* and discuss how it is a bit too hard to read and actually interferes with communication. We found that students can easily get carried away with wild, drawn-out spellings that are fun to write, but lose the meaning. Writers must make decisions on how to spell the words to best express the sound and enhance the meaning.

Poetically Speaking

Poetic Sound Words. Many poets play with sound as they create new words that add rhyme, rhythm, and visual imagery to their poems. Look at how S. Silverstein uses rhyming onomatopoeia in "Squishy Touch" from *A Light in the Attic*:

> Everything King Midas touched
> Turned to gold, the lucky fellow.
> Every single thing I touch
> Turns to raspberry Jell-O.
> Today I touched the kitchen wall (squish),
> I went and punched my brother Paul (splish).
> I tried to fix my bike last week (sploosh),
> And kissed my mother on the cheek (gloosh).
> I got into my overshoes (sklush),
> I tried to read the Evening News (smush),
> I sat down in the easy chair (splush),
> I tried to comb my wavy hair (slush).
> I took a dive into the sea (glush) –
> Would you like to shake hands with me (sklush)? (p. 53)

Have students create their own King Midas poem with everything turning to _____ when they touch it. The sound words can gush (or goosh!) onto their papers as they compose their versions.

What I know about ...

Sound Words

- Words that read like real _____

- Words are _____ like they sound

- Sound words are called onomatopoeia.

- Sound words I like: _____

  _____

  _____

  _____

  _____

  _____

  _____

  _____

  _____

  _____

  _____

  _____

  _____

  _____

  _____

  _____

Titles

Does the title give a hint or taste of the topic?
—Nancie Atwell

Key Elements of Titles:

- • Connects to the story
- • Invites the reader in
- • Kinds of titles
  - – Names of characters
  - – Who a character is
  - – Place or setting
  - – Idea, word, or phrase from story
  - – Alliteration
  - – and others

Writing Standards:

3. Language Use and Conventions
   b. Vocabulary and Word Choice
      – Use precise and vivid words.

About Titles …

Titles are the windows through which we get a brief glimpse into stories. They are the first words that readers see. Since we may "judge a book by its cover," the title alone can draw readers in or make us place it back on the shelf unopened. We want to help our young writers consider the importance of titles as they invite the reader into their written world.

We want to uncover what the title means to the story—whether it is a character's name, the main idea, or the setting. Titles can also reflect a bit of mystery, requiring the reader to search for the author's meaning to emerge. Nonfiction titles, in contrast, are usually more obvious because they need to announce the topic.

Mariah began by writing the title first, then created a story around it. Although she did it well, this process is atypical of what most writers do. We encourage our students to draft first, discovering how a title emerges from the work. Writers may give stories working titles until the piece is completed and then change it several times until the exact title speaks to us.

Examples of Titles From Literature:

Names of Characters
   Wilfred Gordon Macdonald Partridge by M. Fox
   Snowflake Bentley by J. B. Martin (Nonfiction)

Lincoln: A Photobiography by R. Freedman (Nonfiction)

<u>Who a Character Is</u>
>*The Kid in the Red Jacket* by B. Park
>*My Great Aunt Arizona* by G. Houston
>*Astronaut: Living in Space* by K. Hayden (Nonfiction)

<u>Place or Setting</u>
>*Harlem* by W. D. Myers
>*Tar Beach* by F. Ringgold
>*26 Fairmont Avenue* by T. dePaola

<u>Idea, Word, or Phrase from the Story</u>
>*Frindle* by A. Clements
>*Everything on a Waffle* by P. Horvach
>*Taking Flight: The Story of the Wright Brothers* by S. Krensky (Nonfiction)

<u>Alliteration</u>
>*Creepy Crawly Caterpillars* by M. Facklam (Nonfiction)
>*The Z Was Zapped* by C. Van Allsburg

How Do I Teach Titles?

> **Word Study: *Title***
>
> Look up *title* in the dictionary:
>
> - a name that identifies a book, movie, play, or other literary work;
> - a descriptive heading for something such as a chapter, a magazine article, or a speech.
>
> Discuss these meanings with students in relation to their story titles.

What Do Good Titles Do? Every child knows what a book title is. However, they may never have thought about what makes a good title and why they are drawn to some titles and not to others. Have them share a few titles of their favorite books. Ask the question, "What do good titles do?" We think that good titles:

- engage the reader and make us want to read the book;
- tell us the topic, idea, setting, character's name or who the character is; and
- are remembered long after the book is read.

Categorizing Book Titles. Understanding the various categories of titles will help to give student writers more defined ways to title their own stories. In our own search of titles, we found five categories that emerged most frequently. Place these or others on a chart.

Collect a few books that have titles that fit into the categories. Have the class look at books together, identify the categories, and write book titles where they belong. They may find additional categories. Create a class chart, as shown below.

Book Title Categories

Character's Name	Who a Character Is	Place or Setting	Idea, Word, or Phrase	Alliteration

Take the class to the library for a scavenger hunt. Have students work as pairs to search for book titles in the five categories. They are to scour the library for fiction, nonfiction, picture books, chapter books, and poetry to find as many titles as they can in each group within a given time period. Direct them to write one title per sticky note to categorize on the class chart when they return.

Post the results and analyze:

- What do we notice about how authors title their books?
- Which is the most common way to title?
- What books had the most intriguing titles?
- How can these ideas help us create our own titles?

Title Collections. Sometimes, just a phrase can provoke an idea for an entire story. When my son Cliff was 2, people commented on how much he loved to play with trucks or trains. "That's not the half of it," I said. He loves everything on wheels." What a great title, I thought, and I wrote a story called "Everything on Wheels."

Have students create a page in their idea journal entitled "Ideas for Titles." When they hear or read phrases they like, students can record them on this page. Who knows? They may decide to create a whole story around that title.

Finding Titles in Our Writing. For students who are struggling to develop a title, this exercise may help. Have them read over their stories and use a highlighter to identify words or phrases that are important to the story. Using a different colored marker, have a partner read over the story and highlight for the same purpose. They notice what they highlighted and talk about what emerged. The author will decide if any of these would be ideas for a suitable title.

Quick Summaries Can Lead to Titles. Tell students to write what their story is about in a brief paragraph. Then ask, "Could any of these words or phrases work as a title?" They can make a decision to use a title from this exercise or another method.

Writing Alternative Titles. In this mini-lesson, children write alternative titles for books they like and share their rationale for creating them. For example, I might read aloud *Wolves* by Seymour Simon. Then, we would discuss some of the main ideas, generate several possibilities, and select one. Possible titles might be:

- *Wolves: Our First Dogs*

- *Man's First Best Friend*
- *Wolves: Friend or Enemy?*

Have students select one book they have read and write several alternative titles for the book. This may lead them naturally into following the same process when developing titles for their own stories.

To Title or Not to Title Chapters. Many authors create a little fun and attention with catchy chapter titles that can become page-turners. When I'm reading aloud a book to students, they plead "just one more" when the next chapter's title snags their interest. Show students some books that have interesting and intriguing chapter titles. Here are two book examples:

Study the way Curtis named chapters in *The Watsons Go to Birmingham, 1963*:

- And You Wonder Why We Get Called the Weird Watsons (p. 1)
- Every Chihuahua in America Lines Up to Take a Bite Out of Byron (p. 86)
- Tangled Up in God's Beard (p. 138)

Notice the way Lowry titled chapters with a question pulled directly from the text in *Number the Stars*. Students find themselves reading with a purpose that answers an important question.

- Who Is the Dark Haired One? (p. 39)
- Why Are You Lying? (p. 74)

Have students pull quirky phrases or questions from their own stories to create chapter titles that engage the reader.

Conventions for Titles. Using book titles as our guides, have students observe the conventions:

- Capitalize first, last, and important words in-between.
- If it has a colon, capitalize the first word following the colon.
- Center the title.
- Can put the title on the top line of the first page.
- Skip a line between the title and the text.

Students may have a working title from the start and change it at the end or whenever they find the exact title they want to use. Many published authors change their titles even after they have gone to the publisher. They are allowed to change it right up until the time it goes to press (and many do!) We hope our students commit themselves earlier than that!

Nonfiction

Nonfiction Titles: Guide students to notice how authors title their nonfiction books. Let students play around with titling their writing by emulating these three options:

1. Name the topic, such as *Manatees* by J. Palazzo-Craig.

2. Extend with a catchy phrase, such as *From Seed to Plant* by G. Gibbons.
3. Expand with a subtitle, such as *Hiawatha: Messenger of Peace* by D. B. Fradin.

Subheadings in Nonfiction Literature. Headings and subheadings are essential organizational components because they help readers to sort through substantial amounts of information. Headings are titles at the head or beginning of nonfiction chapters that announce the general topic. Subheadings are listed below the headings to separate information into smaller, more manageable segments. Study the prefix *sub-*, which means "under." Make the connection that writers place detailed information <u>under</u> the main heading.

Distribute a wide variety of nonfiction books for students to examine. Have them notice the way information is organized and how headings and subheadings are used. As they write nonfiction pieces, they can choose subheadings that are questions or phrases. Guide students to structure their nonfiction writing into subheadings before they begin. As they find information, they can record their notes under the subheadings.

Poetically Speaking

Newspaper Poems. Nancy Willard has penned an entire book of poems, *Water Walker*, using random newspaper headlines as titles for poems. Her collection is written for adults, but children can use the same technique and play, play, play! When taken out of context, the headlines can make intriguing fodder for poetry.

Quickly and randomly, snip out some headlines from newspapers. Almost any headline can become a title of a poem. Distribute these and let their imaginations guide the graphite to write a poem with a headline title.

DISAPPEARING ACT

Five goldfinches hanging on.
Full cylinder spin.
Four goldfinches hanging on.
Wonder which will win?
Three goldfinches hanging on.
Chirping chorus aflutter.
Two goldfinches hanging on.
A flash like yellow butter.
One goldfinch hanging on.
No thistle, that's a fact.
No goldfinches hanging on.
Disappearing act.
—PVW

What I know about ...

Titles

- Connects to the _____

- Invites the reader in

- Some kinds of titles:

  _____
  _____
  _____
  _____

- Book titles I like: _____

  _____
  _____
  _____
  _____
  _____
  _____
  _____
  _____
  _____
  _____
  _____

Transitions

Every single phrase is a string of perfect gems.
—George du Maruier, *Trilby, pt. VI*

Key Elements of Transitions:

- Word Study: *Transition*
  - *Trans* = "across"
- Word or phrase to indicate change:
  - From one point in time to another
  - From one place to another

Writing Standards:

3. Language Use and Conventions
   a. Style and Syntax
   - Use their own language in writing.
   - Incorporate transitional words and phrases to show the reader a sense of time and place.

About Transitions ...

When writers change time or place, transition words cue readers to where they are in the story so they can follow without confusion. Transitions can be about the shift of time or place, or about the change of speakers. Transitional words can move the reader along, speeding up or going back in time.

We've all used the fast forward and rewind buttons on a VCR when we wanted to skip over a section and quickly get to another part. Sometimes transitional words can help us fast forward or rewind the text, such as "the next summer" or "last week." They permit us to move the story to an important part and not drag the reader through every tedious detail of how we got there. In this section, we guide students' thinking to become aware of how authors use transitional words and phrases so they can apply them in their own writing.

Examples of Transitions From Literature

From *Sophie's Masterpiece* by E. Spinelli (n.p.):

"When Sophie arrived ... "
"The first thing she did was ..."
"Her first project was ..."
"Day after day she whizzed along ..."
"Then one day ..."
"When she finally settled down ..."

"By this time, many spider years had passed."
"After the booties were finished …"
"Then the yarn was gone."
"That night …"

How Do I Teach Transitions?

> **Word Study:** *Transition*
>
> Direct students to explore the word *transition* in their children's dictionaries.
>
> - *trans* means "across" or "change"
> - a word, phrase, or passage that links one subject or idea to another in speech or writing
> - a passage connecting one subject to another
>
> Discuss the meanings "across" and "change" and how these relate to transitions in their writing.
>
> Extension: What are other words they know that begin with the prefix *trans-*? Find and discuss some, such as:
> - transform - to change form or shape (they may connect to the Transformer toys that change from one object to another);
> - translate - to change from one language into another; and
> - transplant - to dig up and plant again in another location.
>
> Ask, "How can all of these familiar *trans-* words and meanings help us to better understand *transition*? How do the definitions of "across" and "change" apply to *transition*? Have students make the connection that story transitions mean to move across time or place or to change the time or place?

Circle the Transitions. Select a brief story or chapter that contains varied examples of transitional words and phrases. Read the entire story aloud for comprehension, then go back to analyze the text, searching for where transitions occur.

Show a transparency of a page that you just read. Have students come up and mark transitional words. We've used the picture book *Sophie's Masterpiece* because there are several examples of transitional words on each page:

When she finally settled down, she looked around and saw nothing but gray. Gray shirts. Gray pants. Gray sweaters.

The captain needs a new suit, Sophie decided. *Something bright. Blue. Like sky.* She began to spin patiently. A sleeve. A collar.

<u>One day</u> the tugboat captain caught Sophie at work.

He screeched, "A spider!"
<u>Then he climbed</u> onto the windowsill and out to the roof.

Sophie did not want anyone falling off the roof on her account. She scuttled out of the closet, down the hall, and into the cook's bedroom slipper. (n.p.).

Point out that transitional words indicate where transitions occur. Discuss how these words help readers understand how time and place in the story change. Send them on a search for transitional words in their own writing. Share these examples with the class.

Found Phrases. Transitional words and phrases will be found in every book that children read. Let them notice how authors use transitions for change of time or place. Students may record their findings on the Think Sheet "Transitions" (at the end of this section). Example:

Book/ Author	Transitional Words or Phrases	Change of Time or Place
My Great Arizona by G. Houston	When spring came … (n.p.)	Time
Bluebird Summer by D. Hopkinson	We came home with beans, zinnias, snapdragons … (n.p.)	Place

How-to Projects. One clear way to focus on time-order words is to teach someone a new skill. Have children write a how-to piece that gives directions using the ordinals first, second, and so on. Then, have them teach their classmates how to do something or role-play it. Examples: How to read a compass, how to build a snowman, how to trap a soccer ball, and so forth.

Where Are the Transitions? Retype a few paragraphs of a published text and leave out the transitional words and phrases. Copy onto a transparency and work together to find where the transitions occur. Then, add in the needed transitional words. Now, compare the original text (before you omitted the transitions) to see how the author used the transitional words. In what ways were they similar to or different from our words?

Ask students to return to their own writing and see if there are places where transitional words and phrases could be helpful. At the end of the Writer's Workshop, have a few students share their transitions, explaining how they helped their piece of writing.

What I know about ...

Transitions

- *Trans* means _____

- Word or phrase that shows change
    - to a different point in _____
    - from one _____ in the story to another

- Write some words that show a change in time or place: _____

_____

_____

_____

_____

_____

_____

_____

_____

_____

_____

_____

_____

_____

_____

_____

Transitions

Book/ Author	Transitional Words or Phrases	Change of Time or Place
How Angel Peterson Got His Name by G. Paulsen	So we went to the army surplus store … (p.12)	Place

Visual Imagery

Listen. Close your eyes and listen. See! Words are the poets' paint.
They're like musicians' notes.
—Mem Fox

Key Elements of Visual Imagery:

- Word Study: *Visual Image*
  - *Vis* = to see
  - *Image* = a mental picture
- Word choice:
  - Vivid descriptions
  - Precise verbs and nouns
  - Exact adjectives and adverbs (used sparingly)
- Figures of speech
  - simile
  - metaphor
  - hyperbole
  - personification

Writing Standards:

2. Writing Purposes and Resulting Genres
   a. Narrative Writing: Sharing Events, Telling Stories
      - Create a believable world and use precise words and detail.
   b. Informative Writing: Report or Informational Writing
      - Use diagrams, charts, and illustrations appropriate to the text.
   c. Functional and Procedural Writing
      - May use illustrations to give detail to the steps.
3. Language Use and Conventions
   a. Style and Syntax
      - Use their own language in writing—embed phrases and modifiers that make their writing lively and graphic.
   b. Vocabulary and Word Choice
      - Use precise and vivid words.
      - Take on the language of authors by using specialized words related to a topic.

About Visual Imagery ...

When Jane read *Bluebird Summer*, she was struck by the passage, "I miss watching her roll out piecrust smooth as an eggshell. And how she perched on a stool beside the tub and read us stories until our fingers pruned up." She bobbed in her seat, hand flailing, to call me over to share it. "Oh, that's just like my grandma. I can just picture her in my mind, can't you?" she said. I can, because this excerpt is visual imagery at its finest! Jane put a sticky note on the page as a reminder to add it to our class chart "Favorite Examples of Visual Imagery."

The writing craft *visual imagery* says exactly what it is: an image we can visualize or picture in our minds. Fine writers accomplish visual imagery when their exact phrases help readers "see" a character or the scene through their words.

Growing up in the South, hearing colorful and visual language in everyday conversations was so commonplace that I took it for granted. I never appreciated these figures of speech until I moved away. I feel right at home with books by Sharon Creech, George Ella Lyon, Cynthia Rylant, and Jerrie Oughton. I've heard my mother use the exact same expressions that their characters say. I realize that this regional language is filled with metaphor, simile, personification, and hyperbole, a textbook lesson in visual imagery. But, what is important in writing effective figures of speech is that the words relate to the content of the story; they are never just stuck in. The picture it gives the reader must fit the situation so that it flows naturally into the story. The language writers use distinguishes the truly fine pieces of literature from ones that are just good stories.

Examples of Visual Imagery From Literature:

<u>Vivid Descriptions</u>: An author's precise words create pictures in our minds. There may not be a specific phrase, but the entire passage engages us. Other examples and activities related to precise verbs and nouns and exact adjectives and adverbs are found under "Precise Words" in this chapter.

From *Red Wolf Country* by J. London (nonfiction):

> "She climbs a low rise, and as the sun sinks into clouds of gold and silk, the coats of the two wolves flare up like bright red flames." (n.p.)

<u>Simile</u>—*Sim-* means "similar or like." A figure of speech that makes a comparison between two unlike things and often uses the words "like" or "as."

From *What Jamie Saw* by C. Conan

> Jamie's first sight of the trailer, from a distance, made him think of a <u>big silver toaster</u>. The sunlight hit on it and made it <u>gleam like a jewel</u>—a silver jewel set down at the end of the logging road, slightly tilting toward the trees and the base of the mountain. (p. 41)

<u>Metaphor</u>—*Meta-* means "change, transferred, or transformed." Metaphor is a figure of speech in which one thing is transferred from one object to another through comparison. It's not meant to make a literal comparison. By saying something *is* something else, it creates a strong visual image.

From *How the Stars Fell Into the Sky* by J. Oughton:

Behind a low tree Coyote crouched, watching her as she <u>crafted her careful mosaic</u> <u>on the blackberry cloth of night</u>. (n.p.)

Hyperbole—The prefix *hyper-* means "over, above, beyond; excessive, abnormally high." When we write hyperbole, we say something that is deliberately exaggerated to make a point. It is used in all tall tales, as well as many fiction stories, particularly humorous ones.

From *How Angel Peterson Got His Name* by G. Paulsen:

> And if a boy's last name is Orvisen, and his parents are silly or addled or just plain cruel enough to give him the first name of Orvis so he has to say, "Hello, my name is Orvis Orvisen," they might as well just <u>rub him with raw liver and throw him into a pit of starving wolves</u>. (p. 56)

Personification. *Person* is the root word. *Personification* means "qualities of a person given to objects or creatures." Early literature was filled with personification, from *The Little Engine That Could,* to modern award-winning books such as Avi's *Poppi.* Young children use personification as they pretend their stuffed animals talk and have adventures.

From *Georgia* by J. Winter:

> I painted the <u>arms of two red hills reaching out to the sky and holding it</u>. (n.p.)

From a poem by Lillian Moore from *Winter Poems* by B. Rogasky:

> Winter dark comes early
> mixing afternoon
> and night.
> Soon
> there's a comma of a moon,
>
> And each street light
> along the way
> puts its period
> to the end of day.
>
> Now
> a neon sign
> punctuates the
> dark with a bright blinking
> breathless
> exclamation mark! (p. 31)

How Do I Teach Visual Imagery?

> **Word Study: *Visual* and *Imagery***
>
> There are lots of words to study involving visual imagery. As you introduce each figure of speech, give students the background information (in "Examples of Visual Imagery From Literature") that will help them more fully understand the word meanings. These words will become part of their literacy vocabulary.
>
> *Visual Imagery* root study:
>
> - *Vis*: to see
> - *Image*: a mental picture

Carefully Crafted Sentences. During read-alouds, pause at a vivid image or figure of speech to let students visualize the words. Briefly discuss what picture comes into their minds. Talk about how the writer planned the image to fit perfectly into the entire context of the writing, not just added a snazzy tag-on.

Select some favorite books filled with images. Let pairs of students read a few pages together and mark with sticky notes the visual images they find. Afterward, categorize by types of imagery (simile, personification, etc.). Here are some of our favorite image-filled books.

- *Owl Moon* by J. Yolen
- *Emily* by M. Bedard
- *Guess Who My Favorite Person Is* by B. Baylor
- *Sophie's Masterpiece* by E. Spinelli
- *Mirette on the High Wire* by E. A. McCully
- *Walk Two Moons* by S. Creech
- *Because of Winn-Dixie* by K. DiCamillo
- *Pictures of Hollis Woods* by P. R. Giff
- *Welcome to the Sea of Sand* by J. Yolen

Have students return to a piece of their own writing and identify where they can add a full description of something or someone to give the reader a clearer picture.

Colorful Writing. Tennis ball yellow? Pine needle green? Can't you imagine these exact colors? This exercise focuses on noticing and writing color detail to give the reader an exact visual image.

Ask students what their favorite colors are and write these on the board. (Most children will say general colors, such as red, yellow, blue.) Have students write a paragraph to describe the color they named. Then, read aloud the book *Guess Who My Favorite Person Is* by B. Baylor or at least use the following excerpt from it that relates a conversation between a man and a precocious girl who meet in a field one day:

She said, "Tell your favorite color."

I said, "Blue."

But she said, "See, you've already done it wrong. In this game you can't just say it's blue. You have to say what *kind* of blue."

So I said, "All right. You know the blue on a lizard's belly? That sudden kind of blue you see just for a second sometime—so blue that afterward you always think you made it up?

"Sure," she said. "I know that kind of blue."

The she told me *hers* and it was brown.

Maybe I looked surprised because she said, "Not many people appreciate brown but I don't care. I do. And the one I like the best is a dark reddish brown that's good for mountains and for rocks. You see it in steep cliffs a lot."

I said, "I know that kind of brown." (n.p.)

Point out how Baylor describes the blue on the lizard's belly and the rocks that are dark reddish brown. Discuss how we can clearly picture the colors because of her descriptions. What text-to-self connections did they make?

Now, have students return to the paragraph they wrote on color and underneath it write another passage describing their favorite color. But, this time, play around with the techniques that Baylor used to give readers a visual image. Share these and have students compare their first and second writing passages.

Act it Out. Drama can bring writers' words alive for students to see the descriptions in action, not just in their minds. There are many ways to structure this exercise. Here are a few suggestions:

Act I. Have pairs or groups of students select some visual images from books they are reading and plan a way to show this imagery through their body actions. Discuss how the words gave them the ideas of what to dramatize.

Act II. Each student can select a passage from their own writing to dramatize. The writer can direct a group of children what to do. Afterward, read aloud the written passage. Were there any actions students saw through the drama that could now be expressed more clearly?

Act III. Teachers can select some favorite visual images from books and list these on the board. Collect more than you will act out, and if possible, make them similar images. It's necessary to have more selections than needed so the audience has more than one choice for the last act. Then, whisper one of these images to each acting group to act through mime. The rest of the class can guess which selection from the board the group is performing. Discuss what movements gave clues to the image. Here are a few from *Tuck Everlasting* (and there are a thousand others—no hyperbole intended!):

- The first week of August hangs at the very top of summer, the top of the livelong year like the high seat of a ferris wheel when it pauses in its turning (p. 1).
- The August sun rolled up, hung at mid-heaven for a blinding hour, and at last

wheeled westward before the journey was done (p. 40).

- The sky was a ragged blaze of red and pink and orange, and its double trembled on the surface of the pond like colors spilled from a paint box (p. 54).
- The sweet earth opened out its wide four corners to her like the petals of a flower ready to be picked and it shimmered with light and possibility until she was dizzy with it (p. 38).

Good, Better, Best. Have students become aware of the specific language we can use in our writing by playing with general words to make them more specific. Write a general word, then have students write a more specific word, and then write the most specific word. The third, most specific word gives the reader the clearest picture, so that may be the word they choose to use. Example:

General	More Specific	Most Specific
dog	bird dog (or black dog)	Labrador Retriever

Here are a few ideas of general words to get them going: girl, shoe, book, car, tree, road, song, movie, utensil, tent, pet.

Model: Describing an Object. Writers develop visual imagery that fits into their stories by using the five senses to notice special features, brainstorming a list of descriptors, selecting a few, and writing a description.

Show students how you think of ideas to give readers a picture through your words. Select an object they can see, such as a pencil. Using your five senses to notice special features, brainstorm ideas together a list, such as:

- painted school bus yellow;
- #2 Ticonderoga, USA;
- six-sided;
- short, stubby;
- shiny silver cylinder;
- soft, pink eraser with smudged black tip from erased words;
- black pointed lead;
- shaved, wooden cone-shaped tip; and
- teeth marks indenting the sides.

Select a few descriptors and write a paragraph in front of the class about the pencil. (Whatever object you choose, plan ahead of time by brainstorming and writing down your own ideas to be prepared.)

Suki reached into her desk and grabbed a well-used stub to finish her story. She thought about what to write as she touched the letters –d-e-r-o-g-a #2. Suki remembered that Ticonderoga was a place she had visited in New York State. Her hand moved into writing position, ready to begin, only to feel the row of indentations in the woody surface. Teeth marks? Disgusting! Suki blurted, "Hey, this isn't my pencil!"

Discuss with students how every idea listed was not used. The brainstormed list gave us ideas to get us going and to add enough detail to give the reader a picture.

Journal Entries. Give students a small strip of paper that has a focus question about visual imagery from a class book they are reading. They paste the strip in their journal and write an answer. Example:

**Why did Lester in *John Henry* use personification
instead of just saying, "The boulder shook?"**

The hammer hit the boulder. That <u>boulder shivered</u> like you do on a cold winter morning when it looks like the school bus is never going to come (n.p.).

Answer:

Hype the Hyperbole. Read a tall tale and list examples of hyperbole on the board. Show the contrast between what was exaggerated and what was realistic. Have students fold a page in half and set up two columns. Label these "Hyperbole" and "Reality." After reading tall tales, list all the hyperbole they find in the first column. Write the realistic counterpart in the second column.

Example is from *Davy Crockett Saves the World by* R. Schanzer:

He <u>combed his hair with a rake</u>, shaved his beard with an ax, and could run so fast that, whenever he went out, the trees had to step aside to keep from getting knocked down (n.p.).

Hyperbole (Exaggeration)	Reality (Actual)
"combed his hair with a rake"	combed hair with a brush

Draw a Picture. Connect this writing lesson to a social studies unit on a particular geographical area, such as deserts or mountains or plains. Discuss the features of that region. Tell students to imagine that they are sitting inside of a house looking out a window. Have them write a descriptive paragraph of what they would see in that geographical setting. Then, have them switch papers with a partner, and each will draw what the other's paragraph said. When they finish, discuss:

- In what ways was the drawing like what the writer had envisioned?
- What visual images did the writer use to help you draw the pictures?
- What words could be added or changed to make the artist visualize the scene more like the writer had in mind? (Give the writers an opportunity to revise.)

Replacing Overused Expressions. Expressions are most effective if they fit into the context of their story, rather than being just added on. Have students make a list of simile expressions they have heard. Many dictionaries have lists of trite expressions in the front or back. If children are familiar with these figures of speech, chances are they are overused and could be considered cliché. Students may <u>not</u> want to use these in their writing because it makes for predictable and uninteresting reading. They will want to make fresh, new comparisons that go with the setting, character, and mood of the story. Take the beginnings of each expression and have them create new similes. Examples:

- hot as a firecracker could become hot as _____
- cool as a cucumber could become cool as _____
- run like the wind could become run like _____
- quick as a wink could become quick as _____
- pretty as a picture could become pretty as _____

Poetically Speaking

Visualize. Poetry is filled with visual imagery. Read selections of your favorites for a class discussion. Have students select something they can visualize, drawn from their own experiences with a narrow focus (e.g., a cardinal, rather than bird). Jot down some ideas about it, fully exploring the topic. Have them compose a free verse poem that gives the reader a rich visual image. Example:

"The Willow Tree" From *The Great Frog Race* by K. O. George:

I waited all summer
for my weeping willow
to weep. It sighed.

Its shoulders drooped
and branches sagged.
It never cried.

When autumn came
my willow wept
piles of tears for me to rake.

What I know about ...

Visual Imagery

- Word Study
  - *Vis* means _____
  - *Image* means _____

- Vivid _____

- _____ verbs and nouns

- Figures of Speech
  _____ - comparison that says something <u>is</u> something else because they share a common quality (She <u>is</u> a cheetah.)
  _____ - comparison using like or as (She runs <u>like</u> a cheetah.)

Voice

Sound like yourself.
—Kurt Vonnegut

Key Elements of Voice:

- Sounds like you!
- Words sound natural, like a real person is behind the words
- Distinctive quality to the tone

Writing Standards:

3. Language Use and Conventions
   a. Style and Syntax
      - Use their own language in writing—embed phrases and modifiers that make their writing lively and graphic.
      - Take on the language of authors by using specialized words related to a topic.

About Voice ...

I know about voice. I'm always aware of voice, having that rare Southern dialect in New England. People recognize my voice without even looking at me. My first realization at how different I sound to others was the first week we moved to Rhode Island. I went right away to get a public library card and met the entire friendly staff. The next day, I called the library with a question. I had only said, "Hello," when Liz, the librarian, said, "Hi Kay." I was shocked. "How did you know it was me?" I asked. "I'd recognize your voice anywhere," she said.

Voice in literature is not so different from my voice experience—it is that recognizable sound that authors have that distinguishes their writing from all others. You know it when you hear it. It's authentic, it's earnest. We talk about voice all year long with many kinds of writing and continue to ask, "What is voice? What gives this piece a distinctive tone?" Students will first recognize it from their reading and then be aware of it in their writing.

Many young children write naturally with a lot of voice. Research tells us that student writing changes over time because children are expected to conform to the conventions and writing formats. As a result, their voice can be diminished or even lost. In our writing classrooms, we have become more conscious of voice in the literature we read and in the stories we write. We include voice in our expectations and celebrate it when we hear it in children's writing.

Examples of Voice From Literature:

<u>In Fiction:</u>

From *Because of Winn-Dixie* by K. DiCamillo:

From the minute me and Winn-Dixie got in the library, he hogged (the fan). He lay right in front of it and wagged his tail and let it blow his fur all around. Some of his fur was pretty loose and blew right off of him like a dandelion puff. I worried about him hogging the fan, and I worried about the fan blowing him bald; but Miss Franny said not to worry about either thing, that Winn-Dixie could hog the fan if he wanted and she had never in her life seen a dog made bald by a fan. (pp. 98–99)

<u>In Nonfiction:</u>

From *Lincoln: A Photobiography* by R. Freedman:

At first glance, most people thought he was homely. Lincoln thought so too, referring once to his "poor, lean, lank face." As a young man he was sensitive about his gawky looks, but in time, he learned to laugh at himself. When a rival called him "two–faced" during a political debate, Lincoln replied: "I leave it to my audience. If I had another face, do you think I'd wear this one?" (p. 1)

How Do I Teach *Voice*?

Word Study: *Voice*

Study the dictionary meanings and read aloud the two definitions that best fit our interpretation of *voice*:

- a sound that makes you think of someone's speech;
- a specific quality of a vocal sound.

Discuss with students how this same idea can be applied to their writing.

Tape-Record Recognizable Voices. Before class, tape-record a few people's voices that they know (librarian, principal, another teacher, yourself). Play one voice recording. Let them guess who is speaking. Then, ask how they knew. Discuss what features that voice has that let them recognize it. Play another and discuss and so on. They couldn't see any of the people, yet it is likely they knew right away whose voices were recorded. Each voice has an individual sound, a distinctive quality that identifies it. That is just like it is in writing.

Awareness of Voice in Literature. Select read-aloud books that echo a voice you like. Let students begin to notice characteristics of voice—that it sounds like a real person's thoughts and feelings. Distinguish it from "dialogue." <u>Dialogue is the actual talking between two characters, and voice is the particular sound of an author's writing.</u>

Type and make a transparency of the above passage from *Winn-Dixie* by K. DiCamillo (from Examples of Voice From Literature). Students mark some phrases they like. Discuss how the author uses zinging visual imagery and striking word choice. The natural sounding voice of

Opal seems just like she's sitting there talking to us. Examples:
- "me and Winn-Dixie"
- "hogged the fan"
- "right off of him like a dandelion puff"
- "never in her life"

Acknowledge Their Voice. It's a big leap from finding voice in the literature and then writing with voice ourselves. When Brendon read aloud his new story, I was struck by a phrase, "There it was, smack-dab in the middle of the room ..." I said, "Oh, I like that word *smack-dab*. It sounds just like you. It rings with voice!" He looked surprised and said, "It does? Wow. I didn't know that." He stared at his paper a few minutes, amazed that he had written with voice. I realized how critical it is for teachers to let students know when and where they are using the craft we spend so much time teaching them. Tell students when you hear voice in their writing. Suggested phrases to help students make the connection:

- That sounds just like you.
- This phrase speaks to me.
- I like the sound of that sentence.
- Such voice right here.
- Where do you see the voice in this passage?
- Can you tell what my favorite phrase is in this paragraph?
- I get a clear image in my mind.
- Good choice of words here.
- I can tell you are excited (or others).
- I'm dazzled by this phrase.

Finding Our Own Voices. Donald Graves said, "Voice is the imprint of ourselves on our own writing" (p. 227). To help students recognize that their writing has voice, have them identify certain words and phrases in their writing that are "their own." Trade pages and have each partner identify places where they see voice emerge. Do they need to add more of their own natural phrasing throughout the piece?

The Writing's on the Wall. Raise student writers' awareness by having them post their favorite examples of voice from the literature on a wall chart. Periodically during Writer's Workshop, you can reference some of the passages and discuss what authors did to make the voice so engaging.

Introducing Myself. Robert Olmstead said, "When you think of voice, think of participating in what has come before, while at the same time contributing what is of your own making" (p. 183). Select a passage from a book you like that has strong voice. Write a passage on the board and let students notice and discuss what is distinctive about the structure and word choice. Let students practice writing some sentences to emulate that author's style, phrasing, rhythm, or sentence structure.

In an autobiography or first person narrative, characters must introduce themselves to the reader. Using the excerpt from *Everything on a Waffle* by P. Horvath, look at the interesting way Primrose Squarp introduces herself.

> I live in Coal Harbour, British Columbia. I have never lived anyplace else. My name is Primrose Squarp. I am eleven years old. I have hair the color of carrots in an apricot glaze (recipe to follow), skin fair and clear where it isn't freckled, and eyes like summer storms. (p. 3)

Have students discuss this introduction. What did they learn about Primrose? What did they think of this introduction? And ooh, look at that last sentence, a bit of a surprise, and what a graphic description of her appearance!

Now, guide them to use the Think Sheet "Introducing Myself" (at the end of this section) as a sort of template to introduce themselves. We can learn a lot about sentence structure and effective ways of turning a phrase by first emulating accomplished writers, then playing with the text until it becomes our own.

Recreated text I wrote based on Horvath's model:

> I live in a house in the woods in Kingston, RI. I've lived in so many other places that it would take two hands to count. But, mostly in Kentucky. My given name is Kathryn Lee Johnson, but my favorite name is Mom, which can only be used by my two young men. I'm old enough to use a bunch of hands to count my age. I have hair the color of the silver locket my mother wore that enclosed a picture of my father. My eyes are the color of ripe gooseberries.

I would never have thought of introducing myself in this way had I not followed the structure of Horvath's model. Of course, before using this in my own story, I would rework it and make it my own, not a copy of Horvath's. The writing the students created was fresh and used visual imagery as they made comparisons. This shows how we can use the basic model as a guide, but elaborate to make it our own, our voice.

Celebrate Our Own Voices. We all have certain ways of talking that distinguish ourselves from others. It might be a regional accent, particular words or phrases we like to use, or expressions. Even the way we use our hands as we talk are part of our talking style. Have students put themselves in their stories by giving a character some of their traits they know so well.

From 'Voiceless" to "Voiceful." It's not hard to find examples of writing that are dull, dry, and boring. Put a voiceless piece on a transparency and see how voiceful your students can make it. Have them share their rewrites and discuss the strategies they used to revive the piece. Spandel (2001) says that voice is the presence of the writer on the page. Direct students to notice each writer's presence in their rewrites. Determine the distinguishing characteristics of each piece.

Write to Someone You Know. When we converse with a friend, even in writing, we may use our most natural voices. Have students write a letter to their best friend telling about a special memory. Encourage them to describe vividly what they remember and to share their feelings. Afterward, have students highlight certain phrases they used that gave it voice.

Special Features. Sometimes, when I notice a special feature in an author's writing, I jot down the idea in my notebook so I'll remember the strategy and where I saw it. Then, I try it in my own writing to see if it adds anything to my text. Encourage students to notice special features and bring them to share with the group. Listen to what they liked about the features and why they might want to use them in their own writing.

Use of colons—These vertical dots cue the reader to take note that something is going to follow. It can be a list of items, an explanation, or a clarification. Examples:

> The cat: He was called Dragon. (p. 21, from *Mrs. Frisby and the Rats of NIMH* by R. C. O'Brien)

> The first thing to understand is: Chester Cricket is a very talented person. (p. 107, from *The Cricket in Times Square* by G. Selden)

Use of single words:

To stress an important idea:

> And now if I just had something to eat.
> Anything. (p. 58, from *Hatchet* by G. Paulsen).

To use in the real way we wonder—natural, and informal:

> A goldfish?
> Turtle?
> Snail?
> Worm?
> Flea? (p. 14, from *Love that Dog* by S. Creech)

Emphasis: *Emphasis* is the convention that is a visual counterpoint to onomatopoeia: The words *look* like their meaning (rather than sound like their meaning). Important words can be accentuated in various visual ways: all caps, italics, squiggly lines, bubble letters, tall and thin, short and squatty, spread out.

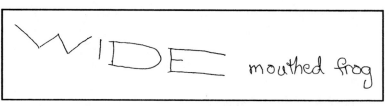

Develop a Voice Rubric. Developing a rubric or guide sheet with students helps us better understand what voice is and what to strive for. First, have students individually do a quick-write on what they think voice is in writing. Have students report out and list their phrases on the board. Together, select the most expressive ones that best describe the various aspects of voice. The rubrics we find most helpful are those that just list a few of the most desirable traits:

- It sounds like me.
- It has personality.

- You can tell that I wrote this.
- My reader can feel what I feel.
- I write with confidence.
- My writing is lively and engaging.

Nonfiction

Write Nonfiction Like Fiction. Some nonfiction authors today write in such an interesting way that it reads like fiction. They use visual imagery, engage the reader, and write with voice. Review some of texts by writers such as Seymour Simon, Faith McNulty, and Russell Freedman. Consider the strategies they use that enliven their books. How can students best emulate some of these ideas and apply the strategies when they write nonfiction?

Nonfiction Voices: Compare and Contrast. When we read various passages on the same topic, the diverse voices of each piece become immediately apparent. Study the differences in these two passages about galaxies: an encyclopedia and a well-crafted nonfiction book. Ask students what they notice about the way the writing sounds. Can they determine the sources without your telling them which was which? Ask someone to describe the voice in each one. Have students try Seymour Simon's techniques when they write nonfiction, including visual imagery, a connection to the reader, and precise words. (This idea was adapted from Portalupi & Fletcher, 2001.)

From *Grolier Multimedia Encyclopedia*:
The giant spiral assemblage of several billion stars that is home to the Sun and its family of planets, including Earth, is only one of the billions of star systems known to exist in the universe. Because it is our star system, however, it is usually called the Galaxy. The Milky Way, another name for it, is the portion visible to the naked eye.

From *Galaxies* by S. Simon:
On a clear, moonless night, you can often see a hazy band of pale light stretching across the sky. This luminous band, called the Milky Way is made up of millions and millions of stars. These stars are so far away from Earth that the tiny points of light blend into one another and you see only a faintly glowing ribbon of light. (n.p.)

Personal Favorites: Books with Voice.

Picture Books
The Babe and I by D. A. Adler
Come a Tide by G. E. Lyon
The Cow Who Wouldn't Come Down by P. B. Johnson
Guess Who My Favorite Person Is and others by B. Baylor
Higher on the Door by J. Stevenson
Owl Moon by J. Yolen
The Relatives Came by C. Rylant
So You Want to Be President? by J. St. George
Sophie's Masterpiece by E. Spinelli

Thunder Cake by P. Pollacco
The True Story of the Three Little Pigs by J. Schieska
When I was Nine by J. Stevenson
Why Mosquitoes Buzz in People's Ears by V. Aardema
Wilfrid Gordon Macdonald Partridge by M. Fox

Chapter Books
Because of Winn-Dixie by K. DiCamillo
Bunnicula by J. Howe
Catherine Called Birdy by K. Cushman
Everything on a Waffle by P. Horvath
Hatchet by G. Paulsen
Holes by L. Sachar
How Angel Peterson Got His Name by G. Paulsen
Joyful Noise: Poems for Two Voices by P. Fleishman
Lincoln: A Photobiography by R. Freedman and other Freedman books
Love That Dog by S. Creech
Maniac McGee by J. Spinelli
Out of the Dust by K. Hesse
Pictures of Hollis Woods by P. R. Giff
Tales from the House of Bunnicula by J. Howe
26 Fairmount Avenue books by T. dePaola
Walk Two Moons by S. Creech

Poetically Speaking

Expressions All Our Own. Many of us have favorite expressions we use that are distinctively our own—they're part of our voice, part of what sounds like us. This poem asks students to think about the one special word or phrase they use and show-case it. If they don't have one, create one that appeals to their senses. They may choose any structure of poem since the focus is on the expression, not the form. The example "Fried Calamari" is a cinquain written by a fourth-grade student, who ends with her unique expression.

What I know about ...

Voice

- Sounds like _____!

- Words sound _____.

- Examples of Voice from Books I've read:

_____

_____

_____

_____

_____

_____

_____

_____

Introducing Myself

I live in _____. I have (<u>Tell about</u> <u>where else you've lived.</u>) My name is _____ (<u>Put full name and what you</u> <u>like to be called.</u>) I am _____ years old. I have hair the color of _____ (<u>What?</u> <u>Compare it to something.</u>), skin (<u>What can you say</u> <u>about it?</u>), and eyes are (<u>What? Compare to</u> <u>something!</u>).

(based on character introduction of Primrose from *Everything on a Waffle*)

Introducing Myself

I live in _____.

My name is _____

I am _____ years old.

I have hair the color of _____,

skin _____

and eyes are _____

7: Assessing Writing

What is Assessment?

When you look at those 20-plus faces at the beginning of the year, you may wonder, "What does it mean to be a competent writer in the middle elementary grades? In what ways can I judge if a student is an accomplished writer? What can I learn from assessment that will help me teach each diverse learner to write well?" Standards become the framework for our assessment of writing. They are strands that weave through every assessment tool and practice.

The standards we focus on throughout this book help us to analyze writing skills and to set goals for learning, such as literacy habits and processes, writing purposes, and language use and conventions. The complete writing standards are listed in Chapter 1. Specific standards that connect to each topic are listed at the beginning of the sections.

Assessment is the careful study of student writing. It comes from the Latin word, *assidére*, which means "to sit by." It seems like an odd meaning for a word that educators define as "to appraise or evaluate." But, it is, in fact, what we do with students all through Writer's Workshop. We "sit by" them as we examine their writing pieces. We "sit by" them as they measure their own progress. We "sit by" them as we notice what they do well and what we still need to teach. This scaffolding supports the student thinking and learning that is at the center of our teaching.

We view assessment in these ways:

- Assessment <u>measures and documents progress and growth</u> by comparing writing samples over a period of time.
- Assessment <u>improves instruction</u> through careful examination of student writing. We identify areas where help is needed and use that information to plan our lessons. It is essential and integral to our teaching.
- Assessment <u>views the whole child</u> through a balance of carefully selected methods. No one tool can fully assess student progress.
- Assessment <u>informs students, parents, and the school community</u> about writing achievement.
- Assessment <u>reflects the standards-based curriculum</u> of instruction.

What and How Do We Assess Writing?

It's important to consider the entire writer, not just what is written. So, we assess three essential aspects, each providing a different view of the writer and the writing:

1. **Process**—the way students use strategies and their disposition toward writing.
2. **Products**—the various texts children create.
3. **Fluency**—the smooth flowing rate and ease of expressing ideas in writing.

Writing teachers may ask, "What tools and practices are available to assess writing?" and "How do I know which ones to use?" There are several methods for assessing the three components of writing. Assessment data combines to give us a more complete understanding of children's progress over time. We hope to provide in this chapter some choices and guidance for assessing process, products, and fluency.

Process	Products	Fluency
Observations	Teacher Responses	Individual Analysis
Anecdotal Records	Error Analysis	Class Chart
Checklist	Rubrics	
Student Self-Evaluation	State/National Assessment	

Writing Sample for Demonstrating Assessment Practices

As we present each assessment tool, we will demonstrate specific applications by assessing one writer and her writing. Our intent is to provide a comparison. By assessing the same writing sample using different tools and practices, we can see the distinctions that exist among them.

Example of a writing piece with the open-ended prompt of "Write about a special memory:"

My Frist swim meet!

by Katelyn (a third-grade child's first draft)

My sashal mamaer is my frst swim meet. It was at a hie school. It is a very big School! My famle and my casints came with me. They cheed me on. My avant's wher 25 back and 25 free. In the back I came in frst in my heet. I got a ribbon for it! In the free I came in thrd in my heet. Afder the swim meet me and my frand Cristena and I want to the hole tell. Whan we got there we whent to are rooms and orderd peza and chines me and chrsten had peza and played cards. The game we playde was wor. I whan! It was my brathers brithday the nexted day! My Mom droped my brather and his frand at a move then my mom want to biy a kace. When my brather came back we started siging happy brthday! This is my spashal mamary because it was my frst swim meet!

Process Assessment—
The Way Students Write

Writing is more than a piece of written work that you are evaluating. It is the way children utilize strategies they have practiced during Writer's Workshop. It is also their disposition toward writing—initiative, curiosity, risk taking, determination, and a willingness to learn from others.

Observations

We can learn a lot about how children write by making careful <u>observations</u>. This is an informal way to assess how, not what, students write. Are they becoming more proficient at generating ideas or creating a lead? Are they using strategies introduced in workshop?

Tompkins (1990) suggested that teachers assess the process of writing throughout each stage of writing. In the following chart, we made observations about how Katelyn was writing during each stage of her piece, "**My Frist swim meet!**"

Writing Stage	Observations About Katelyn's Process
Prewriting	Organized her ideas by making a web
Drafting	• got right to work • included a title • skipped lines • emphasized content over mechanics • used a strategy she learned in class on how to write a lead sentence
Conferring	No conference during this piece
Revising	Scratched out some words and made changes
Editing	Made some spelling corrections, completed an Editing Checklist
Publishing	Rewrote the piece into a final copy

Anecdotal Records

When we write the observations down in an organized manner and review them periodically, they are known as <u>anecdotal records</u>. These are specific notes that detail how the writer was working and/or what was evident in the writing. This documentation helps us to be aware of writing strengths, as well as identify areas that need attention. We plan instruction based on what we learn as we review the notes.

Anecdotal record of Katelyn during the writing of "**My Frist swim meet!**"

> 9/29 "First Swim Meet" — Katelyn webbed lots of ideas + got right to work. Did not check Quick Word Book for spelling high frequency words; spelled phonetically.
>
> 10/3 "My Big Sister" — Observed Katelyn using her QWB for spelling help; Word Wall, too. Developed lead using setting. She's beginning to "Show" more. Lots of voice about her sister, Laura!

Checklists

Checklists are succinct lists that can be used in two ways. Students use these as guides to determine what they need to do as they write. Teachers use checklists to inform them whether observable skills have been applied. They are easy to develop and quick to use. Checklists can be tailored to any need: genre, project, specific writing stages, conventions, and so forth.

Student Self-Assessment

Donald Graves said, "Children spend 99 percent of their time with the book they read or the piece they write. If they do not understand their own evaluation role, they lose many opportunities for learning" (p. 186). And, indeed, the ultimate goal for all writers is to become self-reliant and evaluate their own writing when we are not around. But, these are skills that must be taught.

This is the way we scaffold. We model self-evaluation through an example of revising a first draft.

1. Select an appropriate tool to guide our thinking, such as a Revising Checklist.

2. Reread the entire piece while using the Revising Checklist. Review the checklist to notice what was done well (those statements have checkmarks). Determine what still needs to be done by looking at the statements that do *not* have checkmarks.

3. Reread again to focus on one part of the story that needs revision. Place sticky notes directly on the writing with comments to show where and how you plan to revise.

4. Review how the process of using the assessment tool focused your thinking and guided the revisions.

5 Then, invite students to follow this same process as they evaluate their own writing.

Product Assessment— The Text Students Write

The focus of Product Assessment is on the written work. We can view the piece of writing in two ways: (1) the whole piece to get an overall impression (holistic assessment) and (2) the parts of the piece (trait assessment). Traits are the particular characteristics that distinguish fine writing.

In this section, we present four ways to assess writing products: teacher responses, error analysis, rubrics, and state/national writing assessments. Each one of these tools serves a different purpose and focuses on various aspects of the writing students produce. But they all communicate information about what writers do well and identify what writers need to learn. An analysis of the information helps students and teachers become more aware of what makes fine writing and guides us in ways to improve it.

Teacher's Response to Student Writing

Our response to students' writing tells them a lot. It conveys what we are looking for and what we value. Our comments are powerful and will influence what students write next.

It is our responsibility to give feedback in some way that not only supports, but instructs, first as a person, then as a developing writer. Sometimes, we see sparks of writing that make us cheer as we realize they "got it." It's easy to respond to that piece. Other times, the writing is less than we expected and riddled with problems. That response is harder. We must make some choices about what to say or write to that student. Remember that we are thinking about how to help the writer over time, so all corrections don't have to be made in every piece.

Think about the kinds of comments that are helpful to you as a writer: those that support, acknowledge, guide, instruct, and nudge. Then, make those kinds of remarks to your student writers. Examples of responses I would make to Katelyn about "My Frist swim meet!" are listed in italics. These could be written or told in a conference. We follow the similar format of Read Like a Writer, with which both students and teachers are familiar.

- <u>What do you notice</u> about the writing? First, always begin with a positive comment, celebrating something you recognize that has been done well.

    Katelyn, I can tell you had a great time at your first swim meet! Lots of voice in this piece.

- <u>Focus on one area</u> that the writer needs to develop. Revising only one part is do-able, so the student doesn't become overwhelmed and discouraged. Make small corrections in conventions as you read, but avoid marking up the whole page.

    The first few sentences are the only ones about the meet, which was your title, and I wanted to know more! I wondered exactly what was happening when you were swimming. Can you show me more with your words?

- <u>Make connections</u> to the writer's text. Does the writing remind you of another story (text-to-text), a personal experience (text-to-self), or something you know about the world (text-to-world)?

    This story reminded me of the swim meets I went to with my sons and cheered them on. We had such fun!

- Note how the individual <u>used what was learned</u> during Writer's Workshop. In what ways has the writer developed through this piece?

    The last sentence wraps up the piece—just like we've been practicing in class! You tied it back to the beginning sentence.

Error Analysis of Writing

Just as we learn about a child's reading from taking running records (miscue analysis) and identifying specific areas of difficulty, we can also learn about some aspects of writing by using a similar technique: writing error analysis. When we analyze, we list the writing errors, categorize them, and look for patterns. Discuss some of the errors with the student to get an insight into why they were made. Then, we decide how we can use this information in our instruction.

First, read holistically to get a general impression of the piece. Then reread to:

- notice what the writer does well;
- find specific problems in the writing; and
- list and categorize specific areas, what the student actually wrote, and the correct form.

Analyze the errors and identify what the writer needs to learn to improve the writing. Then, identify <u>two or three</u> areas to teach that will have the most impact on the writer.

To analyze **"My Frist swim meet!,"** use the previous five guidelines:

- *Notice what Katelyn does well.* (clear idea of a special memory, phonetic spelling, beginning words sounds, most capitalization and punctuation, topic sentence and some details, attempted an ending sentence that tied back to beginning, sequence of events, showed excitement, starting to write beginning-middle-end, has voice)

- *Find specific problems in her writing.* (she listed events with little development of story, spelling interfered with ease of reading, consistent errors in medial vowel sounds and "wh" words, misspelled many sight words, lacks three clear parts of a story: beginning-middle-end, tells rather than shows)

- *List and categorize specific areas.* (List the errors in the written work, then categorize into broader areas; see "Error Analysis of Conventions.")

- *Analyze the errors and identify what Katelyn needs to learn.* (development of beginning-middle-end; leads; extended endings; transitions and signal words—first, next, then, finally, etc. vowel sounds; affixes; high frequency sight words; precise words; descriptive language)

- *Identify two or three areas to teach that will have the most impact on Katelyn as a writer.*
  1. Story structure of beginning, middle, end. Work on the lead and focusing more on how to show the events to the reader.
  2. Precise words. Help Katelyn use precise words to show the reader in clear pictures what she is telling.
  3. Because there were so many vowel sound errors, I would spend time on this. If she learns a few vowel rules, it could eliminate many errors and make the writing communicate more clearly.

Rubrics

Rubrics are tools used to interpret and evaluate students' writing performance. They are structured into three components: writing <u>traits</u> that are valued, <u>levels</u> of performance, and <u>criteria</u> that describe the performance. Teachers use rubrics to guide their instruction and to communicate with students and parents. Rubrics serve four purposes:

- *Help students and teachers see what is expected.* Criteria describe the skills for each designated level and trait. Share benchmark papers for each level to help students identify and understand what writing looks like that "meets the standard."

- *Document student progress.* Rubrics can show the strengths and weaknesses of

Error Analysis of Conventions in "My First Swim Meet" by Katelyn

Area of Errors	Student Wrote	Correct Word
short vowels	avant's	events
	want	went
	droped	dropped
	Whan	When
	whant	went
	want	went
long vowels	hie	high
	heet (2)	heat
	biy	buy
irregular vowels	frst (3)	first
	brithday	birthday
	are	our
	brather (2 X)	brother
	frand (2)	friend
	siging	singing
	casints	cousins
	whor	war
"wh" words	wher	were
	whan	when
	whant	went
	whan	won
-ed endings	cheed	cheered
	orderd	ordered
	playde	played
	nexted	next
capitalization	inconsistent caps in title	cap all title words
	loal hie school	Lowell High School
	School	school
	chines	Chinese
	inconsistent names	consistency of names
	cristen	Christina
	this	cap beginning of sent.
punctuation	avant's	use of apostrophe (plurals)
	brathers	brother's
	no paragraphs	use of paragraphs
	no period at end of sent	use of periods
other words	sashal	special
	spashal	special
	mamary	memory
	mamaer	memory
	loal	Lowell
	famle	family
	hole tell	hotel
	peza (2)	pizza
	chines	Chinese
	Afder	After
	cristen	Christina
	move	movie

specific aspects of individual writing pieces, as well as indicate progress over time.

- *Analyze progress of whole class to guide instruction.* Review the rubrics to see what the whole class does well and what they need to learn. Look for patterns to emerge that show areas that need to be taught and/or retaught.

- *Provide evidence for reporting progress.* You can show performance on a particular piece of writing or on several pieces to show growth over a period of time.

Many districts nationwide have embraced *Spandel's 6: Trait Writing Assessment and Instruction.* It is organized by six key traits of writing that are important elements to assess and teach (p. 26): Ideas, Organization, Voice, Word Choice, Fluency, and Conventions. In her book, *Creating Writers,* Spandel walks teachers through the process of developing rubrics based on these six traits. Then, she suggests ways to use this assessment information to make teaching more focused and purposeful.

Review Katelyn's **"My Frist swim meet!,"** through the lens of an adapted six-traits rubric:

Narrative Writing Rubric
Based on Spandel's 6 Traits

Student: **Katelyn**   Title: **My First Swim Meet** Date: `

Circle the bullets that best describe the writing.

	Outstanding Exceeded Standard	Proficient Achieved Standard	Developing Approaching Standard	Needs Assistance Below Standard
Ideas	• Fully developed ideas • Well suited to audience • Connections & insights	• Ideas fit logically • Topic explored & explained • Clear purpose	• Some ideas fit • Predictable plot • Details off topic	• Ideas underdeveloped • Thoughts lack focus • Unclear
Organiza-tion	• Compelling lead • Intriguing plot • Powerful ending • Smooth transitions	• Interesting lead • Detailed plot easy to follow • Connected ending • Clear transitions	• Some organization • Underdeveloped middle • Skeletal structure • Few transitions	• Lacks organization • Lacks coherence • Unclear sequence
Sentence Structure	• Varied length & structure • Structure enhances meaning	• Mostly correct sentences • Varied sentence length & structure • Varied beginnings	• Lacks sentence control • Repetitive patterns • Lists ideas	• Fragments or run-ons • Choppy & rambling
Language	• Precise language • Memorable word choice • Vivid descriptions	• Strong use of language • Words suite subject • Some descriptions	• Overused words • Few descriptions	• No descriptions • Poor use of language
Voice	• Honesty & conviction • Expressive & engaging	• Sense of audience • Mostly engaging tone	• Inconsistent sense of writer behind words • Little sense of audience	• Flat & lifeless • No sense of audience
Conven-tions	• Grammar gives clarity • Conventions occur for stylistic purposes	• Some errors in grammar, capitals or punctuation • Spelling generally correct	• Many errors in grammar, capitals or punctuation • Spelling detracts	• Serious & consistent errors in grammar, punctuation or caps • Spelling impedes reading

Katelyn, I can tell you had a great time at your first swimming meet. Your title made me think we would learn what the pool looked like, what people said to you, what your were feeling. This story told about the whole weekend. I wonder how you could

State /National Writing Assessments

Many grade levels across the country experience state and national writing assessments. Whether or not we agree with the process, we must still deal with the reality: State/national testing is here to stay. There is a huge difference between the writing process of Writer's Workshop and that of state assessments. In the state assessment, students follow a standardized format and must perform within time constraints. Still, you can prepare students for these assessments in several ways:

- Teach and practice writing to a prompt as a genre, as Nancie Atwell suggested. Together, as a class, review the tasks and the rubrics.

- Several times throughout the year, have some "scrimmages," or practice sessions, following the given time constraints and format of the test. This lets students become familiar with what to expect on test days.
- After each session, review and analyze the writing for the entire class. Notice the areas in which students are strong and identify areas that need to be taught.
- Have students self-evaluate based on the rubric and identify areas they want to improve.
- Then, plan some general teaching strategies and mini-lessons on writing craft that will be most beneficial to the entire class. Continue to work individually on specific skills during Writer's Workshop.

Writing Fluency—Ease and Speed in Which Students Write

By middle elementary, students should be fluent writers, writing with ease for increasingly sustained periods of time. Tompkins (2002) described four components to writing fluency: ideas, speed, ease, and automaticity. If writers have difficulty in any of these areas, they should have instruction and practice.

Use the "Guidelines for Fluency Analysis" to determine each student's writing fluency. Record your assessment on the "Class Writing Fluency Chart" (at the end of this section). Assess writing fluency of the entire class several times a year.

Guidelines for Fluency Analysis

Components	Criteria	Introduction to Develop Fluency
ideas	• enough ideas to write about? • begins writing after an initial thinking and idea-gathering period?	• brainstorming • review writing idea journal
speed	• writes fast enough to write a reasonable amount of text in a given time period	• quickwrites (writes for a few minutes about a topic without stopping)
ease	• writes fluidly with little difficulty?	• assisted practice (teachers begin a story on the board and students come up to add their ideas, one student at a time)
automaticity	• extensive repertoire of words that are spelled automatically without assistance? • keeps writing without struggling with conventions that could cause student to lose track of story thoughts?	• word structure analysis • Word Wall development (keep adding words to the wall chart—high frequency words and exceptions—and participate in many activities around it)

Student	Ideas	Speed	Ease	Automaticity
Katelyn	√	-	√	-
Anthony	+	√	√	√

How Is Assessment Shared?

It's important to communicate to students and parents about the learning that has taken place. It's a time to share the achievements, and to identify areas that need attention and how you plan to teach the writer. We share assessment information through conferences, portfolios, and grades.

Conferences

With Students—Assessment conferences are held with each individual about the time of reporting periods or major projects. It is an overview of writing performance within each time period. This is an opportunity to have a conversation with students and learn how they view themselves as writers and what goals they have set. Teachers and students work together during an assessment conference to:

- Discuss their writing—acknowledging the strengths of the writer and comparing the writing to standards
- Examine the portfolio collection to determine writing performance over time.
- Engage the students to reflect about their writing with these guiding questions:
  - What is easy and hard about each stage, each trait, etc.?
  - Which strategies have been helpful to them as writers?
  - How do they learn best?
- Decide on writing goals to work toward.

With Parents—The time we spend with parents is valuable for communicating information about their child's writing performance. The purpose of the conference is to answer these questions:

- How well does my child write?
- How does my child's writing compare to other children in this grade?
- What will you do to help my child become a more proficient writer?

This is the process we follow:

- Begin with positive comments about the child's writing.
- Show them evidence of their child's writing performance on several writing samples. Guide the discussion by using a rubric to indicate specific writing strengths and areas that need to be developed.
- Compare their child's writing samples with grade-level benchmarks that have reached or exceeded the standard.
- Explain how you plan to help their writer.

Portfolio

Portfolios are organized compilations of students' work over an entire school year to show growth and development. They are made up of three parts: (1) the physical container, (2) the contents of student's work samples, and (3) evaluations made by both student and teacher.

The entire portfolios are not graded, but contain individual evaluations of specific writing pieces. At the end of the year, the portfolios showcase the writers they were and the writers they have become—and the journey along the way.

© Heather Ferraro

- • Physical Containers: We use 12-inch x 18-inch artists' accordion envelopes to store artifacts of student work, such as audio and videotapes, computer disks, and paper documents. Have the children decorate it, give it a jazzy title, and put their personal stamp on it so that it is theirs. Other container possibilities are three-ring binders, file folders, oversized tag board pockets, and electronic portfolios (videotapes, CDs, and DVDs).

- • Contents. Table of contents, student work, and reflection sheets from the teacher and the student.

  - – *Table of Contents.* A sheet in the front lists the title of the portfolio entries and the date each piece was submitted. It is mounted on colored paper to make it visible.

  - – *Student Work.* Students choose selected pieces of work to include in the portfolio throughout the year, usually one piece per month. Each writing sample shows the history of

NAME __Josh__ DATE __3/11/03__
Writing Stories - Scoring with a Rubric
Evaluated by __Mrs. Westkott__

Story's title __the rock story prompt__

I have given you a score of __4__.

Things that you have done well are:

Lead - beginning gets reader right to the rock.
Suspense - rock didn't turn/change right away.
Description of dragon + "all of the classes fell like dominoes", all those fainting teachers.
Nice, tightly structured; ideas flow; good voice.

Some things you need to do to make this a better story are:

• Hot spot - Describe the mess when Shelly came into school with you. Show us what that looked like, smelled + sounded like.
• Ending - Great idea how she gave you a ride home. What did people do when they saw you? Who did you say this to? "Now I don't have to go to school?" Explain more to make your ending even stronger.

the piece, from the idea webbing, to drafts, to final copy. Some educators like to have students write to the same, specific open-ended prompt two to three times a year so that the content remains constant and the development of writing is evident.

Reflections and Evaluations. Both the student and the teacher reflect and evaluate selected pieces. A reflection sheet and a rubric are attached to the top of each piece.

Report Cards

Report cards are one of the hard facts of life in schools. Nobody likes them, but we all have to use them. We are well aware that qualitative scores are difficult to assign in writing because there are no clearly defined right or wrong answers. However, we want to ensure that our measurements of students' writing are accurate, valid, and reliable. These are a few ways we determine grades for writing.

- Use standards and rubrics to indicate expectations. Assess pieces that have been conferred, revised, and self-evaluated. Assign a grade based on your evaluation of a body of work.
- Let students select several pieces for evaluation that are representative of their growth and development.
- Use a variety of tools to assess the three components of writing: process, products, and fluency.
- Not all writing elements are equal. Make a list of all the various ways you will grade. Then, use a percentage to distribute a weight to each. Example: 6-Traits Rubrics 50%, Anecdotal Records 10%, Writing Fluency 10%, Self-Evaluation 10%, Presentation 10%, Disposition 10%. Disposition includes taking risks, trying hard, persevering, working cooperatively, and accepting and acting on feedback. Presentation includes appearance, correctness, consistency—all qualities that show a sense of pride.

Individual Trait Guides
for Students
(in Child Language)

Ideas

- Entertaining
- Close-up details
- Makes the reader think
- Makes sense

Organization

- Lead gets your attention
- Smooth transitions
- One thing leads to another
- Connected endings

Sentence Structure

- Varied sentence beginnings
- No extra words in sentences
- Varied sentence length and form
- Easy to follow

Language

- Precise words to <u>show</u>
- Vivid descriptions
- Uses five senses
- Unusual and fun-to-write words

Voice

- I like this writing!
- Sounds like me
- Readers will feel like I do
- Shows lots of energy!

Conventions

- Most things are correct
- Spelling would make Webster proud
- Clean, edited, and polished
- Ready to publish!

Narrative Writing Rubric

Based on Spandel's 6 Traits

Student: _____   Title: _____   Date: _____

Circle the bullets that best describe the writing.

	Outstanding — Exceeded Standard	Proficient — Achieved Standard	Developing — Approaching Standard	Needs Assistance — Below Standard
Ideas	• Fully developed ideas • Well suited to audience • Connections & insights	• Ideas fit logically • Topic explored & explained • Clear purpose	• Some ideas fit • Predictable plot • Details off topic	• Ideas underdeveloped • Thoughts lack focus • Unclear
Organization	• Compelling lead • Intriguing plot • Powerful ending • Smooth transitions	• Interesting lead • Detailed plot easy to follow • Connected ending • Clear transitions	• Some organization • Underdeveloped middle • Skeletal structure • Few transitions	• Lacks organization • Lacks coherence • Unclear sequence
Sentence Structure	• Varied length & structure • Structure enhances meaning	• Mostly correct sentences • Varied sentence length & structure • Varied beginnings	• Lacks sentence control • Repetitive patterns • Lists ideas	• Fragments or run-ons • Choppy & rambling
Language	• Precise language • Memorable word choice • Vivid descriptions	• Strong use of language • Words suite subject • Some descriptions	• Overused words • Few descriptions	• No descriptions • Poor use of language
Voice	• Honesty & conviction • Expressive & engaging	• Sense of audience • Mostly engaging tone	• Inconsistent sense of writer behind words • Little sense of audience	• Flat & lifeless • No sense of audience
Conventions	• Grammar gives clarity • Conventions occur for stylistic purposes	• Some errors in grammar, capitals or punctuation • Spelling generally correct	• Many errors in grammar, capitals or punctuation • Spelling detracts	• Serious & consistent errors in grammar, punctuation or caps • Spelling impedes reading

Expository Writing Rubric

Score—4 Points
- Text is well developed with more than enough information to inform the reader about the topic.
- Plenty of specific details fully explain the topic.
- Information is well organized and clearly presented.
- Language maintains a style or tone.
- Intended audience is clear.

Score—3 Points
- Text is fairly well developed with enough information to inform the reader.
- Some details adequately explain the topic.
- Organization is consistent and sticks to the topic
- Language may establish a style or tone.
- Awareness of the audience.

Score—2 Points
- Text shows some development with a minimal amount of information presented.
- Some details are inaccurate or don't explain the topic.
- Organization is inconsistent, and some ideas stray from the topic.
- Language simply informs without voice or style.
- Little awareness of the intended audience.

Score—1 Point
- Text has little development and is brief, confusing, or inaccurate.
- Few details fail to explain the topic.
- Organization is unclear, and the ideas stray from the topic.
- Language used does not contribute to style or tone.
- Intended audience not addressed.

Class Writing Fluency Chart

Teacher: _____   Date: _____

Mark: + (Advanced)   √ (Average)   − (Struggling)

- <u>Ideas</u>—Has enough ideas? Gets right to work after a brief thinking period?
- <u>Speed</u>—Writes fast enough to accomplish a reasonable amount of writing?
- <u>Ease</u>—Comfortable with and capable of sustained writing?
- <u>Automaticity</u>—Extensive repertoire of words spelled automatically without help?

Student	Ideas	Speed	Ease	Automaticity

8: Teaching Children to Write:

A Conceptual Framework for Instructional Decision Making

by Paul de Mesquita

Writing has emerged as an area of increasing national educational importance and is being recognized as a critical measure of student achievement and an indicator of a school's effectiveness. This increased emphasis on writing is beginning to produce small but positive results in the classroom. The most recent report of nationally administered writing assessment shows a small but statistically significant increase in the percentage of students in grades four and eight demonstrating writing skills in the basic or proficient skill ranges (U.S. Department of Education, 2003). Although overall this is good news, still only about 3 in 10 students nationally are considered to be proficient writers. When other demographic variables are considered, many of the remaining children do not reach basic writing skill levels. Children in certain states, urban areas, or minority communities show little or no improvement, and in some cases skills have declined.

With writing samples included as a component of most state performance assessments, and even college and graduate school entrance examinations, writing has returned to its rightful position as one of the important three "Rs" of schooling. This return to prominence has only increased the pressures on teachers to emphasize the acquisition of writing skills as a part of overall early literacy development. Unfortunately, as the field of writing instruction rapidly develops, many teachers are too busy to stay abreast of current research on the most effective methods for teaching writing. Because of either insufficient knowledge or a lack of confidence, many teachers may not respond to these demands and fail to meet the instructional writing needs of their students. In a recent national survey, 42% of the primary teachers who responded reported attempting few, if any, instructional adaptations to assist children described as struggling writers (Graham, Harris, Fink-Chorzempa, and MacArthur, 2003). Additionally, research reports are not always easily translated into classroom applications. When forced to make an uninformed decision on the best methods to teach writing skills, teachers may reluctantly turn to the same kinds of ineffective drill and skill practice activities they experienced as children.

Conceptual Framework

The purpose of this chapter is twofold: 1) to identify and describe several of the more important types of variables from the theoretical and research literature relevant to children's writing, and 2) to propose a conceptual framework to guide teachers when making instructional decisions about the teaching and learning of writing. Like a good recipe, theory and research on children's writing help to identify the essential ingredients and their proportional combinations that lead to effective instruction and a feast of writing outcomes.

Theory and research can guide the daily decision making process of teachers during a hectic and busy schedule. Knowledge from the fields of education, psychology, and child development provide a rich source of information to assist teachers in making their best decisions under the realities of the elementary classroom. Even so, teachers often find themselves in a dilemma, as they try to respond to the individual needs of their students, keep up with the latest instructional trends, and meet the growing expectations of school reforms. Given educational reform trends and state imposed curriculum standards that require competence in writing effectiveness, classroom application of research on children's writing is more important than ever. In addition, mandated performance assessments, public expectations for academic progress, and the mounting pressures of school accountability combine to place increasing burdens on teachers related to writing instruction (Strickland et al, 2001).

Contemporary views of writing have expanded greatly over the past several decades as evidenced by the increased number of publications in professional journals related to the development of children's writing skills (for extensive reviews see Danielson, 2000; Dyson & Freedman, 1990; Freedman, Flower, Hull, Hayes, 1995; Gersten & Baker, 2001; Pajares, 2003; and Sperling & Warshauer-Freedman, 2001). Of the numerous variables examined in the research on writing, five areas or domains appear most relevant and can be organized into a conceptual framework to inform and guide teachers' instructional decision making (see Figure 8-1). These domains consist of teacher-student relationships, cognitive development, the writing process, motivational factors, and teaching practices. When students experience difficulty reaching their writing potential, these five domains provide teachers with a mental heuristic to both evaluate the source of the difficulty and to decide on the best instructional practices to facilitate proficient writing skills.

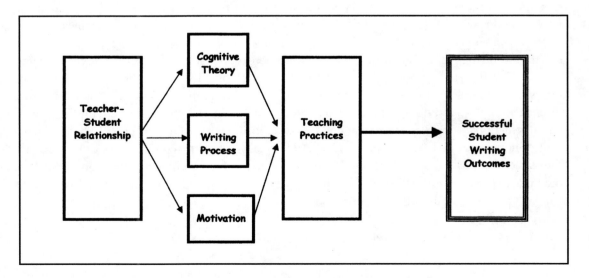

Figure 8.1: Conceptual Framework of Important Variables Influencing Teacher Decisions About Writing Instruction.

A discussion of each domain of the framework will follow. We begin by examining the teacher-student relationship. This is the foundational component that plays a fundamental role in good teaching.

Teacher-Student Relationship and Writing

In writing, students literally put themselves "on the line." In this sense, perhaps no other academic subject can be as personally revealing as writing. For example, when learning to read we decode the letters and words of others, we comprehend the ideas of others presented to us neatly and orderly and in interesting ways. In contrast, when learning to write, children must produce their own letters, generate their own ideas, and organize the order of their thoughts into an interesting style of their own for the benefit of an unknown reader. Children must create a product that represents what they know, think, and feel.

The demands of learning to express oneself in so many new and various ways require classroom conditions that are accepting and trustful, that encourage risk taking, and that are free from discouragement and penalty. More than any other ingredient, the nature of these conditions depends to a large degree on the nature of the teacher-student relationship. What do we know about this relationship generally and how might it contribute to the development of competent young writers?

Research evidence confirms the importance of teacher-student relationships in a number of school-related behaviors (Pianta, 1999). Relationships in the classroom can be characterized in various ways, depending on the nature, frequency, and quality of interactions between teacher and students. Research examining teachers' perceptions of their relationships with their students has identified types of relationships based on various levels of warmth, communication style, conflict, dependency, and involvement. For example, is the relationship warm and caring or cold and indifferent? Are the interactions frequent or infrequent, positive or negative, encouraging or critical? Different relationship types represent patterns of teacher-student interactions that are associated with a variety of successful social and academic performances in the classroom.

In terms of how the teacher-student relationship influences instruction and writing outcomes, the primary mode of interaction occurs within the context of communication. How teachers approach and talk with children is one of the basic mechanisms for promoting not only their social and emotional growth but also their motivation and cognitive development. Observational feedback and interchange about writing provide opportunities for establishing an authentic, caring, and supportive relationship that recognizes children's learning challenges, risk-taking, and vulnerability, especially during writing. In the proposed framework, the teacher-student relationship is the foundational component, the solid groundwork upon which all other components are built. Attending to other areas of writing instruction before analyzing the nature and integrity of the teacher-student relationship can hinder the successful implementation of instructional efforts. Assuming the teacher-student relationship is positive, supportive, and nurturing, in general, as well as within the context of writing instruction, teachers can focus their attention on the next three important variable domains of the framework. Next, we examine the component of the framework focusing on cognitive development as related to writing.

Cognitive Development and Writing

Understanding how children's thinking develops can inform and guide the teacher during instruction and help the teacher to become more responsive and adaptive to the individual learning needs of each child. This is especially the case when teaching writing, since writing is recognized as primarily a cognitive activity. In the elementary grades instructional writing assignments that are not matched to the cognitive development of children can pose a set of complex and unattainable demands that may discourage children with persistent feelings of frustration as writers.

Most teachers agree that good writing is a result of good thinking. We also recognize that as cognitive abilities of children change developmentally as they shift from early to middle childhood, so do their writing skills in a corresponding fashion. Understanding the importance of this link is one of the components for effective instructional decision making that leads to successful student writing outcomes. With this in mind, effective writing instruction requires a theoretical understanding of the associated cognitive development of students in the classroom.

The perspectives of two cognitive theorists Piaget and Vygotsky have shaped how we think about children's cognitive development and their views have direct implications for the teaching and learning of writing. Educators have long recognized the instructional usefulness and classroom applicability of Piaget's theory of cognitive development (1952). Piaget's observations and experiments involving children led him to conclude that by the time most children reach middle childhood or the mid to upper elementary grades, their once simple thinking and reasoning abilities become more sophisticated. They are capable of what Piaget described as *concrete operational thinking*; that is, they can carry out mental operations involving the manipulation or transformation of the various properties and characteristics of the objects in the physical world around them. For example, these mental operations include being able to solve problems that concern the weight, mass, height, and width of objects. Children at this stage can reason logically, can classify on multiple dimensions, and can mentally reverse physical actions when necessary to solve problems in various situations. They also are able to solve situational problems in the real world by using this ability to reason logically. Piaget also described children entering this stage as becoming less *egocentric*, and more able to recognize that not everyone shares their point of view. As a result, they are better able to consider the perspectives and feelings of others.

These cognitive developmental accomplishments under construction at this stage are prerequisite for the acquisition of effective writing skills. For example, logical thinking leads the child to better planning and organization of ideas. The ability to mentally handle multiple dimensions simultaneously allows young writers to manage the multiple tasks of creating ideas, drafting, and revising. A critical challenge for the developing writer is learning "to pursue multiple goals simultaneously and to automatize lower-level activities so that processing resources can be focused on a higher-level" (Siegler 1991, p. 322). Reversibility of thought might provide the mental flexibility necessary to devise or reorganize a narrative story. As egocentric thinking lessens, students can be more open to the feedback of others about their writing and accept suggestions for revisions. This also allows the developing writer to begin to consider the audience while drafting and revising.

Related to Piaget's focus on how children develop cognitively, the theoretical views of Lev Vygotsky also offer a number of possible applications to the classroom relevant to the teaching of writing. Piaget's focus on the developing mind of the individual child emphasized the way the child understood and adapted to the environment based on an active construction of knowledge. In contrast, Vygotsky proposed that children's thinking developed as a result of the influence of their social interactions under various sociocultural contexts (1978). Both Piaget and Vygotsky shared a constructivist view. However, it was Vygotsky who believed that the ever-increasing complexity of children's cognitive processes is primarily the result of their interactions with, and supportive assistance from knowledgeable adults. These interactions support children as they progress toward more independent thinking. Vygotsky described this shift from dependence to independence as occurring within a *zone of proximal development (ZPD)*. It is within this *ZPD* that children rely on teachers to support their development. This is provided through the adults' conversational interactions that guide, encourage, prompt, and offer problem solving feedback. Such guidance is customized to the individual needs of the child and offers the specific kinds of cognitive tutoring later referred to by Bruner and colleagues as *scaffolding* (Bruner, 1996; Wood, Bruner, & Ross, 1976).

With *scaffolding* in mind, the implications of Vygotsky's ideas for teaching are quite clear (Blanck, 1990), especially as they play a central role in the instruction of writing. For example, in the application of the writers workshop (e.g., Calkins, 1994), conferencing with students about their writing can be viewed as taking place within the *ZPD*. Scaffolding strategies (Palincsar, 1986) can be employed, for instance, during conversations about planning, drafting, and revising. During this dynamic interactive *process*, teachers support the child to move from a dependent position to a mostly independent level of writing.

Thus far we have reviewed the importance of the teacher-student relationship and the value of the teacher's understanding of cognitive development relative to children's writing in the middle to upper elementary grades. Next, we address writing as a process and its influence on writing instruction.

Writing As Process

Writing as a process is the third component of our framework for instruction. Six of the major processes of writing—prewriting, drafting, conferring, revising, editing and publishing—have been explored in detail in Chapter 3. However, consistent with the purpose of this chapter, relevant research knowledge will be reviewed and summarized as it lends support to the instructional practices and as it contributes to the proposed framework.

Educators have witnessed a refocusing in the research on writing over the last two decades from studies focused on the products, or the "what" of writing to investigations into the processes or the "how to" of writing. This trend resulted in new models of writing that help us better understand the psychological and information processing view of writing. (e.g., Bereiter & Scardamalia, 1982, 1987; Flower & Hayes, 1981). These writing process perspectives suggest that teachers also need to shift their focus from traditional emphasis on writing mechanics and correction of writing products to a deeper understanding and appraisal of the processes of writing.

Next we examine several of these specific writing processes. Robert Seigler (1991) examines the role of thinking in the development of academic skills, such as writing, and organizes the literature on the various aspects of writing into two major processes: initial drafting and revision.

Initial Drafting. The drafting phase of the writing process is particularly challenging for many students because of the multiple demands presented by most writing assignments. During drafting, students face different types of demands as described—responding to unfamiliar topics, managing the multiple goals of writing, and meeting the mechanical requirements of the task (Bereiter & Scardamalia, 1982; Seigler 1991).

When we instruct students to respond to various writing prompts, these prompts often involve topics that are not voluntarily selected. In these situations, children must allocate a large portion of their cognitive activity to retrieving information from long-term memory. As a result, their writing appears to be a simple listing of information, often randomly ordered as recalled, with few logical connections. Allowing children to use familiar or self selected topics minimizes these difficulties, since writing ideas may be more readily available.

To complete a writing assignment, children must consider numerous goals and keep several competing issues in mind. What is the purpose of my writing? What do I know about the topic? What is the format? Who is the audience of readers? What do I include and what do I leave out? How should I begin? How much time do I have? Earlier research on the teaching of written composition suggested that children deal with these multi-goal situations by resorting to a *knowledge-telling strategy* (Scardamalia & Bereiter, 1984). With this approach children simplify the various goals into a single strategy, that of telling what they know. Frequently this happens in a random order as ideas come to mind with little or no attempt to organize, sequence, or establish a structure of related ideas. Some studies suggest that as writers mature or gain expertise, they develop more of a *knowledge-transforming strategy* that reflects a distinctly different mental process associated with the formulation of problems and devising of solutions. Such problem solving involves a continuously interactive process of generating ideas and producing text.

A third and final set of challenges for students during the initial drafting phase of writing involves attending to all of the mechanical details of the writing task. This includes the actual physical production of text, transcription, handwriting, spelling, punctuation, capitalization, grammar, etc. Simultaneously balancing one's attention to the mechanical details while managing the various goals and generating sufficient topical content can overload and slow the writing process, even for the young writer with above average skills. Helping students postpone attention to mechanical details and prioritize the tasks of drafting can avoid such overloads, overcome writing blocks, and improve efficiency.

Revision. The second major aspect of the writing process is revision. The previous section on drafting underscores the importance of building a revision process into instruction to help young writers evaluate the form and function of the information they have generated. What does the research tell us about children and their process?

As reported by Fitzgerald (1987) in a research study investigating revision, many elementary children seldom review their writing and rarely revise their drafts. When they do, their revisions do not always translate into writing improvements and better papers. Clearly teachers need to plan this important element of the writing process into instructional time and explicitly model and encourage revising skills as an essential part of the writing process.

Revision has two component subprocesses. The first is the identification of errors and areas of weakness. Second are the corrections and improvements made as a result (Baker and Brown, 1984). Given the on-going nature of their cognitive development, how capable are elementary students at recognizing their writing errors? Siegler believed that children's "egocentrism exacerbates the difficulty of detecting weaknesses" in their writing (1991, p. 327). Research on the development of text revision skills presented essays filled with obvious errors to fourth and sixth graders and found that 4th graders failed to identify three-fourths of the errors. Sixth graders were slightly better in identifying about 60% of the problems (Beal, 1990). As discussed previously, this could be due to a Piagetian egocentric view of accepting and understanding the perspectives of others as children mature into the later grades. Such changes in egocentric thinking influence the child's ability to revise. Studies showed that students were better able to revise their classmates' writing than their own. Siegler concluded that it seems important in successful revising that one recognizes the difference between his or her perspective and the perspective of the reader (1991, p.328).

Are revisions better when prompted by a teacher, a peer, or students themselves? The source of corrective feedback has been studied to determine whether or not children were able to successfully complete revisions when they self-identified writing errors, compared to writing errors identified by another student or adult (Beal, 1990). Findings indicated that self-corrected revisions led to better quality for fourth and sixth grade children as compared to the revisions of errors identified by adults when initially missed by the children. However, when revising adult identified corrections, the older children were able to make corrections with less difficulty than the younger children, probably due to greater flexibility in receiving and accepting feedback from different points of view. These results again highlight the developmental differentiation among children from one grade to the next. Relatedly, a study of text revision from 3rd to 5th graders reported on an experiment focusing on the revision process. Outcomes showed that the 3rd graders produced shorter texts but engaged in more revising than 4th and 5th graders (Chanquoy, 2001).

Besides understanding writing as a process, teacher beliefs about writing shape their teaching in the classroom and influence their decisions when choosing instructional methods and strategies. Lipson, Mosenthal, Daniels, and Woodside-Jiron (2000) studied process writing in the classrooms of eleven fifth grade teachers. They reported that these teachers, with different orientations to teaching and learning writing, employed different teaching practices. For example, when teachers using a procedural approach were compared to teachers using a writer's workshop approach, the procedurally oriented teachers focused almost exclusively on mechanics. Research has also found that external policies and pressures can override teachers' instructional beliefs. When studying the relationship between fourth grade teachers' perspectives on the teaching of writing, and their instructional practices, Brindley and Schneider (2002) found that regardless of differing perspectives about how writing skills develop, state curriculum and writing tests appeared to exert the strongest influence on the teachers' instructional practices.

Motivation to Write

What motivates students to write and write well? What causes some students to engage in writing assignments while others elect to disengage and avoid such tasks. Why is it that for some students the task of writing an essay is a dreaded experience provoking anxiety or procrastination, and for others it becomes an enjoyable and creative form of expression approached with eagerness and enthusiasm? The answers to these and other related questions are addressed in the fourth domain of the proposed framework, the motivational factors to consider. Although there are numerous motivational variables in the educational and psychological literature from which to choose, (e.g., achievement motivation, intrinsic motivation, competence, mastery, etc.) several recent reviews of motivation relevant (Hidi & Harackiewicz, 2000; Pajares, 2003) to writing have focused on the concept of *self-efficacy* as the most salient of these.

Self-efficacy as a psychological construct originated from the work of Bandura (1989; 1997). Bandura proposed that *self-efficacy* consisted of our self-perceptions about our capabilities to perform certain actions or tasks, and that our beliefs and self-judgments actually influenced our performances. *Self-efficacy* beliefs are derived from four sources. Each of these is listed with a brief parenthetical example of how these sources are present in the context of writing: 1) interpretation of actual performance (self evaluation and positive self-talk about one's own written products); 2) vicarious experiences based on the performance of others (observing and learning from the writing processes of classmates); 3) positive persuasive messages that empower and encourage (positive teacher feedback during writing conferences), and 4) physiological states such as anxiety or stress (turning nervousness into enthusiasm). Clearly when one or more of these sources of information point in the direction of success and encourage our feelings of competence, we develop a greater sense of our own effectiveness. In turn, these enhanced beliefs of our own effectiveness lead us to higher levels of performance.

In an extensive review of the literature Parajes (2003) presents findings that show writing self-efficacy beliefs and writing performance are highly correlated. He continues to describe the many positive correlations between self-efficacy and mastery of proficient writing outcomes. Implications for instruction include the value of assessing student self-efficacy beliefs about writing and building a strong sense of confidence based on the accomplishment of challenging writing tasks.

Overall, teachers appreciate that self-efficacy beliefs about writing should be instilled from the earliest writing experiences. Describing writing as a dynamic problem solving process requiring continuous progress monitoring of task goals, Bruning and Horn (2000) propose four conditions for developing motivation to write: "1) nurturing functional beliefs about writing, 2) fostering engagement with authentic writing tasks, 3) providing a supportive context for writing, and 4) creating a positive emotional environment."

Finally, teachers might ask, "How do I motivate reluctant writers in my classroom?" "Should I use more rewards with unmotivated writers?" When reviewing the literature comparing extrinsic rewards and intrinsic motivation, one finds disagreement and controversial positions on either side of the issue. For several decades, research has shown that if used in certain ways under certain conditions extrinsic rewards can alter behavior but eventually undermine children's intrinsic motivation. During the 1990s two meta-analyses were reported, one that disputed the undermining effect and one that supported it. Deci, Koestner, and Ryan (2001) review the evidence on both sides of this controversy and conclude that tangible rewards in educational settings do undermine intrinsic motivation. Most teachers would agree that it is better to encourage intrinsic motivation than rely on tangible rewards and have to bother with complicated reinforcement systems in the classroom. Promoting intrinsic motivation with young writers can be accomplished by employing a number of simple strategies. For example, aligning instructional activities with student interests and using goal-setting strategies to promote intrinsic motivation are easily applied to lessons. Mastery of writing skills is often self-motivating and if strategies such as those proposed by Bruning and Horn (2000) are implemented consistently, students may develop into intrinsically motivated writers.

Teaching Practices

The final domain of our framework for writing instruction, Teaching Practices, involves consideration, selection, adaptation, and application of various teaching methods. It builds upon the previous components: integrity of the child-teacher relationship, understanding of cognitive development, writing as process, and motivational factors. The preceding chapters in this book focus entirely on presenting and explaining a wide range of recommended instructional best practices for the teaching of writing. These methods target specific skills and engage children in active learning experiences.

Before methods for teaching writing are chosen, a number of additional factors should be considered. Examples might include relevant academic standards, overall curriculum goals and objectives, specific skills to be mastered, the students' abilities and current skill levels, etc. The sound instructional decisions teachers make are based on these factors in relation to the needs of the writers. The challenge is not finding a particular method or affective lesson, but rather matching the instructional activity to the developmental level, abilities, and unique needs of each child.

The Framework in Action

Suppose eight-year old Ricky, one of the top students in your third grade classroom, excels in all subject areas except written expression. He frequently falters, even in his stronger academic areas, when he must complete any writing-based assignments. As Ricky's teacher you are seeking an instructional plan or teaching strategies that will improve his writing performance and help him prepare for the state writing assessment later in the year. The following six steps briefly outline how you might proceed according to the proposed framework.

1. **Teacher-Student Relationship.** In this situation, the teacher would take the initial step and reflect on the nature of the teacher-student relationship. Identify any areas of concern within this domain. Consider the frequency, duration, and nature of daily interactions with Ricky. Evaluate the quality of the relationship in terms of dimensions such as warmth, communication style, conflict, dependency, and involvement. Identify areas needing improvement and take steps to improve the general quality of your teacher-student relationship with Ricky. Remove any possible negative or judgmental features and make a concerted effort to renew a caring and supportive style of interaction with Ricky, especially around writing assignments. Then, begin to consider each of the next three domains.

2. **Cognitive Theory.** Through observation and informal interactions, determine the features of Ricky's stage of cognitive development, attending to which of the

characteristics of concrete operational thought he is able to display. Construct a mental picture of Ricky's *zone of proximal development* through deliberate conversational interactions. Provide the necessary *scaffolding* to assist and support his development, giving particular attention to those cognitive characteristics that are closely associated with a proficient level of writing.

3. **Writing Process.** The third step in using the framework would include an assessment of his writing abilities, noting strengths and weaknesses, and any specific skill deficits that would interfere with his writing performance. Use the two major writing processes of drafting and revising as a type of a mental checklist to note any difficulties. Target areas that need improvement, while acknowledging areas of strength. Offer supportive feedback. Avoid corrective or potentially discouraging criticism.

4. **Motivation.** The fourth step in applying the framework to this example would be to consider Ricky's level of motivation, both generally across all subjects and specifically as it applies to his reluctance to write. Review Ricky's self-efficacy beliefs regarding writing. Which of Bandura's four sources can be emphasized? Apply strategies proposed by Bruning and Horn.

5. **Teaching Practices.** Appropriate use of the framework would require that decisions about which teaching practices would work best to teach writing should follow deliberations of the four components discussed earlier: integrity of the child-teacher relationship, understanding of cognitive development, writing as a process, and motivational factors. The final step involves reviewing the various instructional methods and strategies for teaching writing described in the earlier chapters. A decision now can be made for selecting and applying the methods that best fit the instructional needs of Ricky, based on the various considerations outlined in the framework. Focus on activities that scaffold and match his individual developmental level.

6. **Evaluate Student Writing Outcomes.** Implement the strategies and methods selected. Observe and evaluate their effectiveness in terms of improvement in Ricky's approach to writing and his overall motivation. Invite Ricky to self-evaluate. Recycle back through the domains whenever necessary, shifting your focus, or emphasizing certain areas over others, depending on Ricky's responsiveness to the instructional changes.

This chapter reviewed instructional information drawn from the wealth of educational theory and research that is available to guide the teaching and learning of writing. A conceptual framework was proposed based on the social, developmental, motivational, and instructional factors that positively influence the writing abilities of children. Becoming more aware of what works, and why some methods are more effective than others, enables teachers to feel more confident when making science-based decisions as they help each child become a successful writer.

Dr. Paul B. de Mesquita is an associate professor in the psychology department at the University of Rhode Island. Through instructional and behavorial consultation with teachers, parents, and administrators for nearly 30 years, Dr. de Mesquita has helped translate the theory and research of psychology into daily classroom practices and school policy.

References

Bandura, A. (1989). Social cognitive theory. In R. Vasta (Ed.), *Annals of child development 6, 1–60.* Greenwich, CT: JAI Press.

Bandura, A. (1997). *Self-efficacy: The exercise in self-control.* New York: W. H. Freeman.

Beal, C. R. (1990). The development of text evaluation and revision skills. *Child Development, 61,* 247–258.

Bereiter, C., & Scardamalia, M. (1982). From conversation to composition: The role of instruction in a developmental process. In R. Glaser (Ed.), *Advances in instructional psychology.* Hillsdale, NJ: Erlbaum.

Bereiter, C., & Scardamalia, M. (1987). *The psychology of written composition.* Hillsdale, NJ: Erlbaum.

Blanck, G. (1990). The man and his cause. In L. C. Moll (Ed.). *Vygotsky and education: Instructional implications and applications of sociocultural psychology.* Cambridge, England: Cambridge University Press.

Brindley, R., & Schneider, J. J. (2002). Writing instruction or destruction: Lessons to be learned from fourth grade teachers' perspectives on teaching writing. *Journal of Teacher Education, 53,* 328–341.

Bruner, J. (1996). *The culture of education.* Cambridge, MA: Harvard University Press.

Bruning, R., & Horn, C. (2000). Developing motivation to write. *Educational Psychologist, 35,* 25–37.

Calkins, L. M. (1994). *The art of teaching writing.* Portsmouth, NH: Heinemann.

Chanquoy, L. (2001). How to make it easier for children to revise their writing: A study of text revision from 3rd to 5th grades. *British Journal of Educational Psychology, 71,* 15–41.

Danielson, L. M. (2000). The improvement of student writing: What research says. *Journal of School Improvement. 1,* 7–11.

Deci, E. L., Koestner, R., & Ryan, R. M. (2001). Extrinsic rewards and intrinsic motivation in education: Reconsidered once again. *Review of Educational Research, 71,* 1–27.

Dyson, A. H., Freedman, S. W. (1990). *On teaching writing: A Review of the literature.* Occasional Paper No. 20. Berkley, CA: Center for the Study of Writing.

Fitzgerald, J. (1987). Research on revision in writing. *Review of Educational Research, 57,* 481–506.

Flower, L., & Hayes, J. R. (1981). A cognitive process theory of writing. *College Composition and Communication, 32,* 365–387.

Freedman, S. W., Flower J., Hull, G., & Hayes, J. R. (1995). *Ten years of research: Achievements of the National Center for the Study of Writing and Literacy. Technical Report No. 1–C.* Berkeley, CA: National Center for Study of Writing and Literacy.

Gersten, R., & Baker, S. (2001). Teaching expressive writing to students with learning disabilities: A meta-analysis. *Elementary School Journal, 101,* 251–272.

Graham, S., & Harris, K. R. (2000). The role of self-regulation and transcription skills in writing and writing development. *Educational Psychologist, 35,* 3–12.

Hidi, S., & Harackiewicz, J. M. (2000). Motivating the academically unmotivated: A critical issue for the 21st century. *Review of Educational Research, 70,* 151–179.

Lipson, M Y., Mosenthal, J., Daniels, P., & Woodside-Jiron, H. (2000). Process writing in the classrooms of eleven 5th grade teachers with different orientations to teaching and learning. *Elementary School Journal, 101,* 209–231.

Pajares, F. (2003). *Self-efficacy beliefs, motivation, and achievement in writing: A review of the literature.*

Palincsar, A. S. (1986). The role of dialogue in providing scaffolded instruction. In J. Levin & M. Pressley (Eds.), *Advances in motivation and achievement* (Vol. 10, pp. 1–49). Greenwich, CT: JAI Press.

Piaget, J. (1952). *The origins of intelligence in the child.* (M. Cook, trans.). New York: International Universities Press.

Pianta, R. (1999). *Enhancing relationships between children and teachers.* Washington, DC: American Psychological Association.

Scardamalia, M., & Bereiter, C. (1984). Written composition. In M. Wittrock (Ed.), *Handbook of research on teaching* (3rd ed.). New York: Macmillan

Siegler, R. S. (1991). *Children's thinking* (2nd ed.). Englewood Cliffs, NJ: Prentice Hall.

Sperling, M., & Warshauer Freedman, S. (2001). Research on writing. In V. Richardson, (Ed.), *Handbook of research on teaching* (4th ed.). Washington, DC: American Educational Research Association.

Strickland, D., Bodino, A., Buchan, K., Jones, K., Nelson, A., & Rosen, M. (2001). Teaching writing in a time of reform. *Elementary School Journal, 101,* 385–397.

U.S. Department of Education, Institute of Education Sciences, National Center for Education Statistics. (2003). *The nation's report card: Writing 2002,* (NCES 2003–539). Washington, DC: U.S. Government Printing Office.

Vygotsky, L.S., (178). Mind in society: *The development of higher psychological processes.* Cambridge, MA: Harvard University Press.

Wood, D., Bruner, J., & Ross, S. (1976). The role of tutoring in problem solving. *British Journal of Psychology, 66,* 181–191.

Afterword: Celebrate!

There's a lot to celebrate throughout Writer's Workshop. We pause long enough to reflect on the entire writing experience and to celebrate the writers, not just the writing. We recall how:

James studied the synonym chart and wrote *remarkable* in place of *good*.

Nate's sense of humor found its way into every piece he wrote.

Gina and Vicky, with their heads together, searched for the lost "spider leg" revision strip that had been so thoughtfully added to Vicky's story.

Alex announced, "It's hard work writing dialogue when you have to indent *every* time someone different speaks!" But, she did it—and balanced it with action.

Nanase read and reread the book she had published during Sustained Silent Reading time.

Jadra carried herself away from the Author's Chair, straight and tall, beaming.

We remember how the children began the year stringing single words together to construct meaning and how gradually the stories inside flowed onto pages and pages of text. We notice how they don't just write stories; they write them well.

We celebrate our teaching of young writers. It affirms that the time spent with individual writers was significant as we honored their voices.

Writer's Workshop is not just a writing time—it is a teaching and learning time for students and teachers. We send children along to the next grade, aware of their great strides and of our contribution. We are proud that they are writing like writers.

> *Year's end is neither an end nor a beginning*
> *but a going on with all the wisdom*
> *that experience can instill in us.*
> —H. Borland

273

Glossary

alliteration—the use of several words beginning with the same letter or sounds to enhance the "sound" of language. It is especially effective in providing word pictures when writing.

antagonist—a character in the story who makes life difficult for the main character.

assessment—a balanced information-gathering process for providing a clear picture of each student as a writer. We assess writing in three ways: process, products, and fluency. Assessment tools help us determine what students know, how they apply what they've learned, and their progress over time. Equally important, we use this information to guide our instruction.

author's chair—a designated chair on which student writers sit to publicly read their writing to celebrate or to seek help.

autobiography—a story about a person's life written by that person.

benchmarks—the standards of work or level of outcome expected of students to achieve at a specific point in time.

biography—a written history about someone's life.

brainstorm—a collaborative strategy used to generate lots of ideas about a topic.

character—one of the story elements, a person or creature in a story or poem. Writers show us how a character looks, speaks, acts, and feels.

character map—a graphic organizer for webbing important information about a character. The map becomes a tool for planning how to develop characters in our stories.

conclusion—the end of the story in which the problems are solved.

conflict—the struggle, tension, or problem that exists between characters in well-developed stories.

chalk talk—a learning strategy for a whole group of learners to take silent turns writing down their own questions with chalk or marker. This strategy provides an opportunity to view student thinking, or to assess their understanding, or both.

contrast—how writers use antonyms for determining sharp differences that exist.

conventions—the correct usage of language, such as capitalization, punctuation, spelling, grammar, and paragraphing.

cooperative learning—a way of mixing students of all abilities and interests in small groups or as partners who work toward a common academic goal. Students are active learners in the process through positive social interaction, shared and individual responsibility for each other's learning, and peer coaching.

dialect—a regional language that has a distinctive vocabulary, pronunciation, spelling, and grammar.

dialogue—a conversation between two or more characters.

differentiated instruction—a teaching philosophy based on the premise that teachers should adapt instruction to match student differences by:
- <u>content</u> (what you teach and what students learn);
- <u>process</u> (how students think about or make sense of ideas and information);
- <u>interest</u> (what students choose to learn and research); and
- <u>product</u> (how students demonstrate what they know).

drafting—the stage in the writing process when a writer puts ideas down on paper.

editing—the stage in the writing process when writers reread to correct errors and ensure clarity.

editor's marks—a system of universal symbols used to signal where changes need to be made.

ending—the part of the story in which the writer not only solves the conflict that characters experience, but explains how they feel about the events. Endings commence at the high point of the story and continues until the final words

events—the situations a character experiences during the story.

error analysis—a technique of analyzing writing errors, similar to miscue analysis in reading. The information is listed and categorized to notice patterns of errors and plan instruction.

explicit theme—the way the author clearly states the underlying meaning of the story.

fiction—writing that is not necessarily based on facts.

figure of speech—a form of expression (such as simile, metaphor, hyperbole) used by writers to create visual images.

final copy—the final stage for a piece of writing prior to publication.

first person—the perspective when "I" tell the story.

fishbowl—a learning strategy in which modeling occurs within concentric circles of students/participants. Two people or a small group are engaged in a discussion in the center of the circle, while the remainder of the group observes from the outside circle. The teacher and/or students are in the center as models or facilitators.

fluency—Writing fluency is the smooth flowing rate and ease in which writers produce text. There are four components of writing fluency:

- <u>ideas</u>—has ideas to write about;
- <u>speed</u>—writes a reasonable amount of text in a given time period;
- <u>ease</u>—writes fluidly with little difficulty; and
- <u>automaticity</u>—spells words and uses conventions from memory and habit.

genre—a category of literature that has distinctive characteristics of form, style. or subject matter.

high-frequency words—words that occur most frequently in reading and writing. These are words that students should learn by patterns or memorization in order to increase their reading and writing fluency.

hyperbole—an extreme exaggeration such as, "He was so tall his head touched Jupiter." Found in tall tales.

implicit themes—the underlying meanings of the story that the author does not state directly, leaving the readers to draw their own inferences about what is valued by the writer.

lead—the beginning of a story. It is an opening sentence or paragraph that grabs the reader's interest, introduces the main character and setting, and sometimes introduces the problem that a character faces.

memoir—a form of writing in which the writers reflect upon pivotal moments in their lives, telling what happened and how they feel about it.

metaphor—a writing device to compare two ideas using word pictures, such as "The Earth is a big, blue-green marble."

mood—the feeling a reader gets from a piece of writing, such as happy, scared, and so forth.

multiple intelligences (MI)—a learning theory developed by Howard Gardner and associates at Harvard's Project for Human Potential. Gardner theorized the existence of nine intelligences in the cognitive profile of any learner: linguistic, musical, logical-mathematical, spatial, bodily-kinesthetic, inter- and intrapersonal, naturalistic, and existentialist. In teaching and learning, we use the MI to build upon the strengths of a student to develop teaching strategies and learning experiences that best suit the strongest intelligence(s) of each learner.

narrative—a story that tells a sequence of events in the order in which they happened.

narrator—the person or character telling the story.

nonfiction—writing that is based on actual experiences or factual information.

onomatopoeia—words that sound like what they mean, such as *snap, whoosh,* or *bang,* to intensify events or emotions. Their spellings can be actual or invented.

personification—a writing device in which human characteristics are given to nonhuman objects or to animals (e.g., "The Sun smiles down on me").

plot—a story element that shows the series of events that make up the action in a story.

poetry—writing that creates an emotional response from the reader through meaning, sound, and rhythm.

point of view—a story element; the perspective of who is telling the story: <u>first person</u> – the character is narrating; <u>third person</u> – someone outside the story is narrating.

portfolios—organized cumulative collections of student work that has been reflected upon; they may include student self-selected and/or teacher-selected entries. It shows student achievement and progress over time.

precise words—carefully chosen words of our language that show the reader the clearest sensory picture in their minds.

problem—the difficulty in a story that a character faces and must solve.

process assessment—the evaluation of the way children utilize strategies in their writing and their disposition toward writing (initiative, risk taking, perseverance).

process writing—the stages of writing through which writers proceed while working on a piece; planning, drafting, conferring, revising, editing, publishing.

product assessment—The evaluation of a piece of written work. It can be viewed as a whole piece (holistic assessment) or parts of the piece (trait assessment).

proofread—to check written work carefully for errors in order to make corrections.

protagonist—the main character in stories, the one for whom the reader roots.

publishing—the final stage of the writing process in which students prepare a final copy for an audience.

punctuation marks—the conventions writers use to clarify the meaning for the reader; standardized set of signs, such a period, question mark, and so forth.

Read Like a Writer—a learning strategy writers use when they study the literature, notice how authors write, name and discuss the craft used, and consider how they can emulate the writers.

repeated word or line—words or phrases used again and again and again for emphasis or rhythm.

revising—the stage of writing that writers use to "look again" at their work to make it better.

rubric—a tool used to interpret and evaluate students' writing performance. They are structured into three components: writing traits, levels of performance, and criteria that describe the performance. Information is used to guide instruction.

scaffolding—a strategy for supporting students as they learn new skills. We model, engage, guide, and teach so that students can be successful and independent writers.

senses—the way we gather information from seeing, hearing, touching, tasting, and smelling.

setting—a story element that tells the time of day or season, time period, place, and weather of a story.

Show, Don't Tell—a strategy writers use when they write to show what they think and feel. Writers can utilize precise or sensory words to give the reader those pictures.

simile—a device where writers compare two things using *like* or *as* (e.g., "She is as quick as a cheetah").

standards—a set of performance targets that provide a guide for teachers and students as accepted measures of comparison.

story elements—parts that make up a story structure: characters, plot, point of view, setting and theme.

strategy—a careful plan or method for teaching and learning.

tableau—a visually dramatic scene or situation that suddenly arises. Students depict a scene in a silent, motionless, statue-like representation.

text connections—three ways that readers connect to a piece of writing that enhances understanding:
- <u>text-to-self</u>—an author's words make us recall personal events or feelings;
- <u>text-to-text</u>—something we read or write that reminds us of another book, story, or text; and
- <u>text-to-world</u>—text that links the writing to something we know about the world.

theme—a story element that tells the underlying meaning of the story, such as, *family, courage, friendship,* and so forth.

think aloud—a strategy in which teachers talk out loud to give students a glimpse into what and how they are thinking.

think-pair-share—a three-part learning strategy based on the concept of "two heads are better than one." It helps to organize the writer's thinking and provide clarity for story development:
- <u>think</u>—children think about what they want to discuss about the piece;
- <u>pair</u>—get with a partner and exchange writing.
- <u>share</u>—talk about their individual stories.

titles—the name of a written piece that connects to the story and invites the reader in. Kinds of titles include names of characters, who a character is, place or setting, and ideas or words from the story.

trade books—any piece of literature that can be found at a library, at home, or purchased at a store.

trait—a particular characteristic that defines fine writing, such as ideas, organization, language, sentence structure, voice, and conventions.

transitional words—words or phrases to indicate change in a story from one point in time to another or from one place to another, such as "next day," "back at the ranch."

verb tense—the way a verb is used to express the different times at which action takes place. Present tense shows what is happening now, and past tense shows something that has already occurred.

visual imagery—the way an author's precise language shows a picture to the reader.

voice—the sound and tone of a piece of writing.

webbing—an organizational structure writers use to brainstorm and plan ideas.

word study—a careful examination of words and their origins to understand better the meaning of the word.

Word Wall words—a collection of words studied and displayed as a resource for high-frequency words and the exceptions, words that do not fit specific spelling rules.

writing craft—techniques that writers use as they compose to communicate clearly.

Writer's Workshop—a structured learning environment for students to work toward improving their writing. It is made up of mini-lessons, writing and conferring time, and sharing time.

Zoom—a learning strategy used by writers to make a focused examination of a place in writing. The writer can enlarge, expand, and describe a scene to its fullest; analogous to a camera's lens.

Bibliography of Children's Literature

Fiction:

Aardema, V. (1975). *Why mosquitoes buzz in people's ears*. New York: Dial.

_____. (1981). *Bringing the rain to Kapiti Plain*. New York: Dial.

Adler, D. A. (1999). *The Babe and I*. New York: Gulliver.

Agee, J. (1988). *The incredible painting of Felix Clousseau*. New York: Farrar Straus Giroux.

Ahlberg, J. (1986). *The jolly postman*. New York: Little, Brown.

Anno, M. (1977). *Anno's journey*. New York: Philomel.

Avi. (1995). *Poppy*. New York: Orchard.

_____. (2002). *Crispin: The cross of lead*. New York: Hyperion.

Babbitt, N. (1975). *Tuck everlasting*. Farrar Straus and Giroux.

Base, G. (1987). *Anamalia*. New York: Harry N. Abrams.

Baylor, B. (1992). *Guess who my favorite person is*. New York: Scribners.

Bedard, M. (1992). *Emily*. New York: Doubleday.

Bennett, J. (1985). *Teeny tiny woman*. New York: Putnam.

Bois, J. W. (1979). *A gathering of days*. New York: Simon and Schuster.

Brown, M.W. (1949). *The important book*. New York: HarperCollins.

Bunting, E. ((1990). *The wall*. New York: Clarion.

Byars, B. (1972). *House of wings*. New York: Viking.

Cannon, J. (1993). *Stellaluna*. New York: Harcourt.

Christelow, E. (1993). *The five-dog night*. New York: Houghton-Mifflin.

Cleary, B. (1950). *Henry Huggins*. New York: Avon.

_____. (1970). *Runaway Ralph*. New York: Dell.

_____. (1983). *Dear Mr. Henshaw*. New York: Morrow.

Clements, A. (1996). *Frindle*. New York: Simon and Schuster.

Clements, A. (2001). *The school story*. New York: Simon and Schuster.

Cole, J. (1987). *The magic school bus: Inside the Earth*. New York: Scholastic.

Coman, C. (1995). *What Jamie saw*. Arden, NC: Front Street.

Couloumbis, A. (1999). *Getting near to Baby*. New York: Scholastic.

Creech, S. (1994). *Walk two moons*. New York: HarperCollins.

_____. (2002). *Ruby Holler*. New York: HarperCollins.

Curtis, P. C. (1995). *The Watson's go to Birmingham—1963*. New York: Delacorte.

_____. (1999). *Bud, not Buddy*. New York: Delacorte.

Cushman, K. (1994). *Catherine called Birdy*. New York: HarperTrophy.

_____. (1995). *The midwife's apprentice*. New York: HarperTrophy.

Dadey, D., & Jones, M. T. (1990). *Vampires don't wear polka dots*. New York: Scholastic.

Danneberg, J. (2000). *First day jitters*. Watertown, MA: Charlesbridge.

Day, A. (1985). *Good dog, Carl*. New York: Scholastic.

dePaola, T. (1983). *The legend of the bluebonnet*. New York: Putnam.

DiCamillo, K. (2002). *Because of Winn-Dixie*. New York: Scholastic.

Edwards, P. D. (1997). *Barefoot*. New York: HarperCollins.

Erickson, R. E. (1974). *A toad for Tuesday*. New York: Beech Tree.

Fox, M. (1985). *Wilfrid Gordon MacDonald Partridge*. Brooklyn, New York: Kane/Miller.

Gantos, J. (2000). *Joey Pigza loses control*. New York: Harper Trophy.

Geisert, B., & Geisert, A. (1995). *Haystack*. Boston: Houghton-Mifflin.

Giff, P. R. (1997) *Lily's crossing*. New York: Dell.

_____. (2001) *All the way home*. New York: Delacorte.

_____. (2002). *Pictures of Hollis Woods*. New York: Wendy Lamb.

Gregorowski, C. (Retold). (2000). *Fly, eagle, fly: An African tale*. New York: Margaret K. McElderry.

Hall, D. (1979). *The ox-cart man*. New York: Viking.

Hamilton, V. (1974). *M.C. Higgins, the Great*. New York: Simon and Schuster.

_____. (2002). *Time pieces*. New York: The Blue Sky.

Hesse, K. (1992) *Letters from Rifka*. New York: Henry Holt.

_____. (1994). *Sable*. New York: Henry Holt.

_____. (1997). *Out of the dust*. New York: Scholastic.

Hopkinson, D. (2001). *Bluebird summer*. New York: Greenwillow.

Horvath, P. (1999). *The trolls*. New York: Farrar Straus Giroux.

_____. (2001). *Everything on a waffle*. New York: Scholastic.

Howe, D., & Howe, J. (1979). *Bunnicula*. New York: Athenium.

Howe, J. (2002). *Tales from the house of Bunnicula*. New York: Athenium.

Hutchins, P. (1986). *The doorbell rang*. New York: Greenwillow.

Jacques, B. (1996). *Outcast of Redwall*. New York: Philomel.

James, S. (1991). *Dear Mr. Blueberry*. New York: Margaret K. McElderry.

Johnson, P. B. (1993). *The cow who wouldn't come down*. New York: Orchard.

Johnson, P. B., & Lewis, C. (1996). *Lost*. New York: Orchard.

Jonas, A. (1992). *The thirteenth clue*. New York: Greenwillow.

Kellogg, S. (1997). *The three little pigs*. New York: Morrow.

L'Engle, M. (1962). *A wrinkle in time*. New York: Farrar, Straus and Giroux.

Lester, J. (1994). *John Henry*. New York: Dial.

Lowell, S, (1992). *The three little javelinas*. Flagstaff, AZ: Northland.

Lowry, L. (1989). *Number the stars*. New York: Bantam Doubleday.

Lyon, G. E. (1990). *Come a tide*. New York: Orchard.

MacLaughlin, P. (1985). *Sarah, plain and tall*. New York: HarperCollins.

Martin, B., & Archambault, J. (1966). *Knots on a counting rope*. Henry Holt.

McCully, E. A. (1992). *Mirette on the high wire*. New York: Putnam.

McDermott, G. (1994). *Coyote*. New York: Harcourt Brace.

McDonald, M. (1995). *Insects are my life*. New York: Orchard.

McLerran, A. (1991). *Roxaboxen*. New York: Scholastic.

Munsch, R. (1980). *The paper bag princess*. Toronto: Annick.

Naylor, P. (1991). *Shiloh*. New York: Dell.

Numeroff, L. (2002). *If you take a mouse to school*. New York: HarperCollins.

O'Brien, R. C. (1971). *Mrs. Frisby and the rats of NIMH*. New York: Aladdin.

Osborne, M. P. (2004). *The magic tree house* series. New York: Random.

Oughton, J. (1992). *How the stars fell into the sky: A Navajo legend*. Boston: Houghton-Mifflin.

Park, B. (1987). *The kid in the red jacket*. New York: Knopf.

Park, L. S. (2001). *A single shard*. New York: Scholastic.

Paterson, K. (1977). *Bridge to Terabithia*. New York: HarperTrophy.

Paulsen, G. (1987). *Hatchet*. New York: Simon and Schuster.

_____. (2003). *How Angel Peterson got his name.* New York: Wendy Lamb.

Peet, B. (1987). *Big bad Bruce.* Boston: Houghton-Mifflin.

Polacco, P. (1990). *Thunder cake.* New York: Philomel.

Rappaport, D., & Callan, L. (2000). *Dirt on their skirts.* New York: Dial.

Raschka, C. (1993). *Yo! yes?* New York: Orchard.

Rathmann, P. (1995). *Officer Buckle and Gloria.* New York: G. P. Putnam's Sons.

Ring, E. (1999). *Monarch butterfly of Aster Way.* Washington DC: Smithsonian.

Ringgold, F. (1991). *Tar Beach.* New York: Crown.

Robins, A. (1998). *The teeny tiny woman: A traditional tale.* Cambridge, MA: Candlewick.

Rowling, J. K. (1997). *Harry Potter and the sorcerer's stone.* New York: Scholastic.

_____. (2003). *Harry Potter and the order of the phoenix.* New York: Scholastic.

Rylant, C. (1985). *The relatives came.* New York: Macmillan.

_____. (1987–2003). *Henry and Mudge* series. New York: Simon and Schuster.

Sachar, L. (1998). *Holes.* New York: Farrar, Straus, and Giroux.

Schanzer, R. (2001). *Davy Crockett saves the world.* New York: HarperCollins.

Scieszka, J. (1989). *The true story of the three little pigs.* New York: Viking.

_____. (1995). *2009: The time warp trio.* New York: Penguin.

_____. (1995). *Math curse.* New York: Viking.

Selden, G. (1960). *The cricket in Times Square.* New York: Ferrar, Straus, and Giroux.

Sperry, A. (1940). *Call it courage.* New York: Collier Books.

Spinelli, E. (2001). *Sophie's masterpiece: A spider's tale.* New York: Simon and Schuster.

Spinelli, J. (1990). *Maniac McGee.* New York: HarperCollins.

Steig, W. (1982). *Doctor De Soto.* New York: Ferrar, Straus, and Giroux.

Stevens, J. (1995). *Tops and bottoms.* New York: Scholastic.

Stewart, S. (1997). *The gardener.* New York: Farrar, Strauss, and Giroux.

Taback, S. (1997). *There was an old lady who swallowed a fly.* New York: Scholastic.

Turkle, B. (1969). *Thy friend, Obadiah.* New York: Puffin.

Trivizas, E. (1993). *The three little wolves and the big bad pig.* New York: Margaret K. McElderry.

Van Allsburg, C. (1986). *The stranger.* Boston: Houghton-Mifflin.

_____. (1987). *The z was zapped.* Boston: Houghton-Mifflin.

_____. (1992). *The widow's broom.* New York: Scholastic.

Weil, L. (1984). *To sail a ship of treasures.* New York: Atheneum.

Wells, R. (1993). *Waiting for the evening star.* Dial.

White, E. B., (1952). *Charlotte's web.* New York: HarperCollins.

Wiesner, D. (1991). *Tuesday.* New York: Clarion.

_____. (2002). *The three pigs.* New York: Clarion.

Wilson, S. (1990). *The day Henry cleaned his room.* New York: Simon and Schuster.

Yolen, J. (1987). *Owl moon.* New York: Philomel.

_____. (1987). *Piggins.* New York: Harcourt Brace.

_____. (1993). *Honkers.* Boston: Little Brown.

_____. (1996). *Passager.* New York: Harcourt Brace.

_____. (1998). *Raising Yoder's barn.* Boston: Little, Brown.

_____. (1980–1999). *Commander Toad* series. New York: Coward-McCann.

Poetry and Word Play

Aylesworth, J. (1992). *Old black fly*. New York: Henry Holt.

Creech, S. (2001). *Love that dog*. New York: Scholastic.

Fleischman, P. (1988). *Joyful noise: Poems for two voices*. New York: HarperTrophy.

Florian, D. (1999). *Winter eyes*. New York: Greenwillow.

George, K. O. (1997). *The great frog race and other poems*. New York: Clarion.

Graham, J. B. (1999). *Flicker flash*. Boston: Houghton-Mifflin.

Greenfield, E. (1988). *Nathaniel talking*. New York: Black Butterfly

Grimes, N. (1994). *Meet Danitra Brown*. New York: Lothrop, Lee, and Shepard.

Janeczko, P. C. (1998). *That sweet diamond: Baseball poems*. New York: Atheneum.

Lewis, J. P. (1996). *Riddle-icious*. New York: Random House.

_____. (1998). *Doodle dandies: Poems that take shape*. New York: Atheneum.

Livingston, M. C. (1988). *Space songs*. New York: Scholastic.

Martin, B., Jr., & Archambault, J. (1988). *Listen to the rain*. New York: Henry Holt.

Myers, W. D. (1997). *Harlem*. New York: Scholastic.

Nelson, M. (2001). *Carver: A life in poems*. New York: Scholastic.

Nye, N. S. (1992). *This same sky*. New York: Four Winds.

O'Neill, M. (1989). *Hailstones and halibut bones*. New York: Doubleday.

Rogasky, B. (ed.). (1994). *Winter poems*. New York: Scholastic.

Rosen, M. (ed.). (1995). *Walking the bridge of your nose*. New York: Kingfisher.

Ryder, J. (1989). *Mockingbird morning*. New York: Macmillan.

Silverstein, S. (1974). *Where the sidewalk ends*. New York: Harper and Row.

Wells, R. (1994). *Night sounds, morning colors*. New York: Dial.

Willard, N. (1989). *Water walker*. New York: Knopf.

Yolen, J. (1990). *Bird watch*. New York: Philomel.

_____. (1996). *Welcome to the sea of sand*. New York: G. P. Putnam's Sons.

_____. (2000). *Color me a rhyme: Nature poems for young people*. Honesdale, PA: Boyds Mills.

Nonfiction

Aardema, V. (1992). *A bookworm who hatched: Meet the author series*. Katonah, New York: Richard C. Owen.

Adler, D. A. (1996). *Thomas Alva Edison*. New York: Holiday.

Barron's Educational Series. (1994). *Our planet: Earth*. Hauppauge, NY: Barron's.

Brunelle, L., & Otfinoski, S. (2002). *Mammals*. Milwaukee, WI: Gareth Stevens.

Crossingham, J. (2002). *Skateboarding in action*. New York: Crabtree.

dePaola, T. (1999). *26 Fairmount Avenue*. New York: G. P. Putnam's Sons.

_____. (2000). *Here we all are: A 26 Fairmount Avenue book*. New York: G. P. Putnam's Sons.

Dorling Kindersly. *Eye witness books*. (on varied Science and Social Studies topics). New York: DK Publishing, Inc.

Facklam, M. (1996). *Creepy crawly caterpillars*. New York: Little, Brown.

Fletcher, R. (2002, May 17). "Tips for Young Writers: Ideas for Revising Your Writing." *Ralph Fletcher*. Downloaded April 12, 2003 from http://www.ralphfletcher.com.

Fradin, D. B. (1992). *Hiawatha: Messenger of peace*. New York: Macmillan.

Freedman, R. (1987). *Lincoln: A photobiography*. New York: Clarion.

_____. *The Wright brothers: How they invented the airplane.* New York: Holiday.

_____. (1997). *Out of darkness: The story of Louis Braille.* New York: Houghton-Mifflin.

Gibbons, G. (1991). *From seed to plant.* New York: Holiday.

Hayden, K. (2000). *Astronaut: Living in space.* New York: DK Publishing.

Houston, G. (1992). *My great-aunt Arizona.* New York: HarperCollins.

Howe, J. (1994). *Playing with words: Meet the author.* Katonah, New York: Richard C. Owen.

Krensky, S. (2000). *Taking flight: The story of the Wright brothers.* New York: Simon and Schuster.

London, J. (1977). *Red wolf country.* New York: Scholastic.

Martin, J. B. (1998). *Snowflake Bentley.* Boston: Houghton-Mifflin.

Musgrove, M. (1976). *Ashanti to Zulu: African traditions.* New York: Dial.

Nicolson, C. (1998). *The planets.* Toronto: Kids Can.

Owen, R. C. (1992–present). *Meet the author* series. Katonah, NY: Publishers, Inc. (many children's authors' biographies and autobiographies)

Palazzo-Craig, J. (1999). *Manatees.* New York: Troll.

Peck, R. (1991). *Anonymously yours: A memoir.* Englewood Heights, NJ: Julian Messner.

Rylant, C. (1992). *Best wishes: Meet the author* series. Katona, New York: Richard C. Owen.

Shange, N. (2002). *Float like a butterfly.* New York: G.P. Putnam's Son.

Simon, S. (1988). *Galaxies.* New York: Mulberry.

_____. (1993). *Wolves.* New York: HarperCollins.

Sis, P. (1991). *Follow the dream: The story of Christopher Columbus.* New York: Knopf.

Sohi, M. E. (1993). *Look what I did with a leaf.* New York: Walker and Co.

Spinelli, J. (1998). *Knots in my yo-yo string: The autobiography of a kid.* New York: Knopf.

Stevenson, J. (1986). *When I was nine.* New York: Greenwillow.

_____. (1987). *Higher on the door.* New York: Greenwillow.

St. George, J. (2000). *So you want to be President.* New York: Scholastic.

VanCleve, J. (1993). *Janice VanCleve's animals.* New York: Wiley.

Winter, J. (1998). *Georgia: A portrait.* New York: Voyager Books.

Yolen, J. (1992). *A letter from Phoenix farm: Meet the author.* Katonah, NY: Richard C. Owen.

Bibliography of Teacher Resources

Anderson, C. (2001). *How's it going?* Portsmouth, NH: Heinemann.

Atwell, N. (Ed.). (1990). *Coming to know: Writing to learn in the intermediate grades.* Portsmouth, NH: Heinemann.

_____. (1998). *In the middle: New understandings about writing, reading, and learning.* Portsmouth, NH: Heinemann.

Barr, R., & Johnson, B. (1997). *Teaching reading and writing in elementary classrooms.* New York: Longman.

Bates, C. D., & Latempa, S. (2002). *Storybook travels.* New York: Three Rivers.

Beck, E. (Ed.). (1980). *Bartlett's familiar quotations.* New York: Little Brown.

Behn, R., & Twichell, C. (Ed.). (1992). *The practice of poetry.* New York: HarperPerennial.

Benet's reader's encyclopedia. (3rd ed.). (1987). New York: Harper and Row.

Bernays, A., & Painter, P. (1990). *What if? Writing exercises for fiction writers.* New York: Harpercollins.

Burns, M. (1991). *Math by all means, grade 3.* Sausalito, CA: The Math Solution Publications.

Calkins, L. M. (1994). *The art of teaching writing.* Portsmouth, NH: Heinemann.

_____ (2001). *The art of teaching reading.* New York: Addison Wesley Longman.

Chapman, G., & Robson, P. (1993). *Making books: A step-by-step guide to your own publishing.* Brookfield, CT: The Millbrook.

Cooper, D. J. (2000). *Literacy: Helping children construct meaning.* Boston, MA: Houghton-Mifflin.

Cunningham, P. M., & Hall, D. P. (1998). *Month-by-month phonics for third grade.* Greensboro, NC: Carson-Dellosa.

Cunningham, P. M., & Allington, R. L. (2003). *Classrooms that work: They can all read and write.* New York: Allyn and Bacon.

Dadey, D., & Jones, M. T., (2000). *Story sparkers: A creativity guide for children's writers.* Cincinnati, OH: Writer's Digest.

Diehn, G. (1998). *Making books that fly, fold, wrap, hide, pop up, twist, and turn.* New York: Lark.

Evans, J., & Moore, J. E. (1984). *How to make books with children, teacher resource cook.* Carmel, CA: Evan-Moor Corp.

Faber. A., & Mazlich, E. (1980). *How to talk so kids will listen and listen so kids will talk.* New York: Rawson, Wade.

Fletcher, R. (2002). *Poetry matters: Writing a poem from the inside out.* New York: HarperCollins.

Fletcher, R. (1993). *What a writer needs.* Portsmouth, NH: Heinemann.

Fletcher, R., & Portalupi, J. (1998). *Craft lessons: Teaching writing K–8.* York, ME: Stenhouse.

Fletcher, R., & Portalupi, J. (2001). *Writing workshop: The essential guide.*

Fountas, I. C., & Pinnell, G. S. (2001). *Guiding readers and writers.* Portsmouth, NH: Heinemann.

Fox, M. (1992). *Dear Mem Fox, I have read all your books even the pathetic ones: And other incidents in the life of a children's book author.* New York: Harcourt Brace Jovanovich.

Franko, B., & Damon, M. (2000). *The secret life of words: Poetry exercises and activities.* San Diego, CA: Teaching Resource Center.

Fraser, J., & Skolnick, D. (1994). *On their way: Celebrating second graders as they read and write.* Portsmouth, NH: Heinemann.

Ganske, K. (2000). *Word journeys: Assessment-guided phonics, spelling, and vocabulary instruction.* New York: Guildford.

Goldberg, N. (1986). *Writing down the bones: Freeing the writer within.* Boston, MA: Shambhala.

Graves, D. (1991). *Build a literate classroom: The reading/writing teacher's companion.* Portsmouth, NH: Heinemann.

Grolier multimedia encyclopedia 98. (1997). [computer software]. Grolier Interactive Inc.

Hancock, M. R. (2000). *A celebration of literature and response.* Upper Saddle River, NJ: Merrill.

Harvey, S. (1998). *Nonfiction matters: Reading, writing, and research in grades 3–8.* York, ME: Stenhouse.

Heard, G. (1989). *For the good of the Earth and sun: Teaching poetry.* Portsmouth, New York: Heinemann.

_____ (1999). *Awakening the heart: Exploring poetry in elementary and middle school.* Portsmouth, NH: Heinemann.

Johnsen, S. K., & Johnson, K. L. (1986). *Independent study program.* Waco, TX: Prufrock Press.

Johnson, K. L. (Ed.). (1998). *Writing with authors kids love.* Waco, TX: Prufrock Press.

Lamott, A. (1994). *Bird by bird: Some instructions on writing and life.* New York: Pantheon.

Lane, B. (1993). *After the end: Teaching and learning creative revision.* Portsmouth, NH: Heinemann.

Lindfors, J. W. (1999). *Children's inquiry: Using language to make sense of the world.* Amsterdam, New York: Teacher's College.

Lunsford, S. (1998). *Literature based mini lessons to teach writing.* New York: Scholastic.

Macrorie, K. (1985). *Telling writing.* Portsmouth, NH: Heinemann.

Mariconda, B. (1999). *The most wonderful writing lessons ever.* New York: Scholastic.

Murray, D.M. (1993). *Read to write.* Fort Worth, TX: Harcourt Brace.

Olmstead, R. (1997). *Elements of the writing craft.* Cincinnati, OH: Story.

Pike, K., & Mumper, J. (1998). *Books don't have to be flat!* New York: Scholastic.

Portalupi, J., & Fletcher, R. (2001). *Nonfiction craft lessons: Teaching information writing K–8.* Portland, ME: Stenhouse.

Ray, K. W. (1999). *Wondrous words: Writers and writing in the elementary classroom.* Urbana, IL: National Council of Teachers of English.

Reading and writing grade by grade. (1999). National Center on Education and the Economy and the University of Pittsburgh.

Routman, R. (2000). *Kid's poems: Teaching third and fourth graders to love writing poetry.* New York: Scholastic.

Salinger, T. S. (1996). *Literacy for young children.* Englewood Cliffs, NJ: Merrill.

Sebranek, P., Kemper, D., & Meyer, V. (1999). *Write source 2000: A guide to writing, thinking and learning.* Wilmington, MA: Houghton-Mifflin.

Spandel, V. (2001). *Creating writers through 6-trait writing assessment and instruction.* New York: Longman.

Stein, S. (1995). *Stein on writing.* New York: St. Martins.

Tomlinson, C. A. (1999). *The differentiated classroom: Responding to the needs of all learners.* Alexandria, VA: Association for Supervision and Curriculum Development.

Tompkins, G. (1990). *Teaching writing: Balancing process and product.* Upper Saddle River, NJ: Merrill/Prentice Hall.

_____. (2001). *Literacy for the 21st century.* Upper Saddle River, NJ: Merrill/Prentice Hall.

Walsh, N. (1994). *Making books across the curriculum.* New York: Scholastic.

Webster's II new Riverside University dictionary. (1984). Boston, MA: Houghton-Mifflin.

Wood, C. (1997). *Yardsticks: Children in the classroom ages 4-14, a resource for parents and teachers.* Greenfield, MA. Northeast Foundation for Children.

Worcester, T. (2003). *Fifty quick and easy computer activities for kids.* Eugene, OR: Vision Technology in Education.

Favorite Web Sites

www.narragansett.k12.ri.us/NES/NEShomepage.html—Pam's school site, Narragansett Elementary School, Rhode Island.

http://author-illustr-source.com—*Author Illustrator Source*. This is the place to find published authors or illustrators who make school visits or conduct professional development workshops and seminars. Authors and illustrators are listed alphabetically and by state with biographical information, published books, description of the presentations made, professional fee, and how to contact them.

www.carolhurst.com—*Carol Hurst's Children's Literature Site*. This is a collection of reviews of great books for kids, ideas of ways to use them in the classroom; and collections of books and activities about particular subjects, curricular areas, themes, and professional topics.

http://www.cbcbooks.org/index.html—*Children's Book Council*. A nonprofit trade organization dedicated to encouraging literacy and the use and enjoyment of children's books. It is the official sponsor of Young People's Poetry Week and Children's Book Week each year.

http://scils.rutgers.edu/%7Ekvander—*Kay E. Vandergrift's Special Interest Page*. This Web site is a means of sharing ideas and information with all those interested in literature for children and young adults.

http://nancykeane.com/rl—*ATN—All Together Now*. A selection of recommended reading lists created by members of the international school librarian's listserv.

http://www.nwrel.org/assessment/assessment.asp—*NW Regional Education Laboratory*. Their goal is to support teachers in using ongoing and continuous assessment. It includes a section on the 6+1 Trait Writing.

http://6traits.cyberspaces.net—*Six Traits*. This site provides ideas and lessons for teachers using Six Traits Writing Assessment in their classrooms.

http://www.ralphfletcher.com—*Ralph Fletcher*. He writes books for kids, as well as writing teachers. He has a special passion for nurturing young writers.

http://rwproject.tc.columbia.edu—The home page of Teachers College Writing Project directed by Lucy Calkins.

Children's Book Awards:

http://www.ala.org—*American Library Association Home Page*. It houses:
- *Newbery Medal Awards*—awarded to authors for the most distinguished American children's books of the year by the American Library Association.
- *Caldecott Medal Awards*—awarded to the artists for the most distinguished

American picture books for the year by the American Library Association; and

- *Coretta Scott King Awards*—awarded to authors and illustrators of African descent whose distinguished books promote an understanding and appreciation of the "American Dream."

http://www.hbook.com—*Boston Globe/Horn Book Awards.* Honors excellence in American literature for children and young adults.

http://www.scbwi.org/awards.htm—*Golden Kite Awards.* The only major children's book awards presented by authors' peers; therefore, it is one of the most respected honors.

Encourage Your Students to Think Outside the Box.

Subscribe to *Creative Kids*, "The National Voice for Kids."

Creative Kids is written for kids, by kids, and features original poetry, short stories, games, artwork, and much more. It's jam-packed with great ideas and fun commentary to inspire your students to think outside the box.

A favorite of teachers and kids for nearly 20 years, *Creative Kids* has recently undergone changes to reflect the tastes of the new millenium. While still appropriate for young readers, we're a bit edgier, funnier, and smarter … just like kids today. See why *Creative Kids* is the nation's largest magazine written for kids, by kids.

Let your students' voices be heard by submitting their very best work to *Creative Kids*. Anything that can be reproduced on a page can be considered for publication as long as it is suitable for readers ages 8–14.

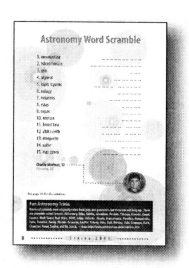

Check us out!

Your satisfaction is guaranteed. We're pretty confident that your students will like it, too.

One-Year Subscription: $19.95
Quarterly
Creative Kids
PO Box 8813
Waco, TX 76714-8813
(800) 998-2208

To download sample pages from *Creative Kids*, please visit http://www.prufrock.com and click on the "Journals & Magazines" link.

ACTIVITIES FOR ADVANCED LEARNING SERIES

Camp Fraction
Solving Exciting Word Problems Using Fractions
Set around a trip to summer camp, students work with fractions in a problem-solving form
while learning a little history, trivia, and fun facts about a number of different items.
Grades 4–6 $11.95

Creative Writing
Using Fairy Tales to Enrich Writing Skills
Use fairy tales to challenge and motivate your students. This activity book contains
reading and writing activities that pique students' interest in creative writing.
Grades 4–8 $11.95

Extra! Extra!
Advanced Reading and Writing Activities for Language Arts
The book includes standards-based independent language arts activities for students in gra
K–2 such as developing a newspaper and inventing new words.
Grades K-2 $11.95

Math Problem Solvers
Using Word Problems to Enhance Mathematical
Problem Solving Skills
The standards-based problem solving strategies addressed in this book include drawing
picture, looking for a pattern, guessing and checking, acting it out, making a table or list, a
working backwards.
Grades 2–3 $11.95

Puzzled by Math!
Using Puzzles to Teach Math Skills
Puzzled by Math! offers a collection of mathematical equations, knowledge, and skills in puz
form. Standards-based content addresses addition, subtraction, multiplication, divisi
fractions, decimals, and algebra. Thirty-five exciting and challenging puzzles are included
well as suggestions for using the material for a classroom learning center.
Grades 3–7 $11.95

Survival on the Reef
Exploring Amazing Animals and the Ways They Adapt
to Their Environment
This challenging activity book addresses many essential skills and knowledge contained in
National Science Teachers Association standards using activities focused on the excit
environment of a coral reef, its inhabitants, and the ways these inhabitants have adapted
their world.
Grades 2–3 $11.95

Writing Stretchers
15 Minute Activities to Enrich Writing Skills
Standards-based activities address the areas of reading, writing, vocabulary, content litera
creativity, and thinking skills, giving students a chance to enrich their writing skills.
Grades 4–8 $11.95

For a complete listing of titles in this series, please visit our website at

http://www.prufrock.com

PRUFROCK
PRESS INC.